BLACK BOSTONIANS AND THE POLITICS OF CULTURE, 1920–1940

BLACK BOSTONIANS AND THE POLITICS OF CULTURE, 1920–1940

Lorraine Elena Roses

UNIVERSITY OF MASSACHUSETTS PRESS
Amherst and Boston

Printed in the United States of America

ISBN 978-1-62534-242-3 (paper); 241-6 (cloth)

Designed by Sally Nichols
Set in Monotype Bell
Printed and bound by Sheridan Books, Inc.

Cover design by Sally Nichols
Cover art: Allan Rohan Crite, *Leon and Harriet*, 1941, courtesy of the Boston Athenæum.

Library of Congress Cataloging-in-Publication Data
A catalog record for this book is available from the Library of Congress.

British Library Cataloguing-in-Publication Data
A catalog record for this book is available from the British Library.

For Jonathan

CONTENTS

PREFACE

My interest in Boston's historic African American community was awakened on a bright February afternoon in 1985, when I attended a lecture by Dorothy West. The diminutive and vivacious seventy-eight-year-old West, billed as "the lone survivor of the Harlem Renaissance," captivated her audience when she vividly conjured up the heady years of a transformational era in American culture. The members of the audience, myself included, listened raptly to West's descriptions of her experiences with "Langston," with whom she traveled to Russia; "Wally"; "Zora"; "Countee"; and other literary luminaries she had met in Harlem. West wove her magical narrative thread around memories of riotous rent parties with writers, artists, and musicians struggling to make ends meet while nurturing their high-flying artistic hopes and dreams. In the mid-1980s, she had yet to be discovered by Jacqueline Kennedy Onassis, the Doubleday editor who would offer the still-vibrant and energetic writer a contract to complete an unfinished novel, *The Wedding*, but already West was making a dramatic return to the limelight.

As a New Yorker transplanted to Boston I was intrigued by the story of a Boston-born teenager who left the comfort of her family's middle-class home to taste success in Harlem. I began visiting Ms West at her island cottage on Martha's Vineyard; on each ferry trip back to Boston I felt the urge to learn more. As a literary scholar specializing in the contributions of black people to the cultures of the Spanish-speaking Caribbean, I wanted to cast my net wider, to explore the history of creative black people in the United States. Already in 1990 I had cowritten and published *Harlem Renaissance and Beyond: 100 Literary Profiles of Black Women Writers* and in 1996, an anthology of their work, *Harlem's Glory*.

When I began my project on black Bostonians I did not anticipate that it would occupy me for the next twenty years. Full of confidence, I set out to research the cultural history of contemporary black Boston. Surely I would find an abundance of bibliographic and archival resources at my fingertips. What I found instead was a haunting gap. The scholarly literature on the social, political, and cultural history of Boston was focused heavily on nineteenth-century Boston, the heroics of its Civil War combatants, and literary lions, with short shrift given to those protagonists who were black. Happily, many glaring omissions have since been rectified. Where the early decades of the twentieth century were concerned, however, the narrative of black Bostonian prowess seemed to have paled and faded out. Yet it was precisely at that time when a "New Negro" consciousness, emanating from Harlem, was resonating across the country. It was both frustrating and difficult to accept, for example, that over a decade's worth of back issues from the Boston *Guardian* and the *Boston Chronicle*, the city's two black newspapers, had mysteriously disappeared. But the many bibliographers and research librarians (including James Danky) whom I consulted confirmed my findings: I had entered a "twilight zone." This was dispiriting news, but it made me realize that here was an opportunity to explore *terra incognita*.

Digging in the rich archives and special collections of institutions ranging from the Boston Public Library, the Schomburg Research Center in Black Culture in New York, the Moorland-Spingarn Research Center in Washington, D.C., and the Camille Billops and James V. Hatch Archives in New York City proved fruitful but not sufficient. I needed to interview people who had participated in the black Bostonian cultural scene and witnessed its rise—as soon as possible and in the shortest time possible. These witnesses and participants were a quickly thinning group whose memories were the only living links remaining to the cultural pioneers and New Negro historical actors of Boston. They helped me fill in missing pieces of their story and helped me to see a continuum between their work and the artistic accomplishments of other performers, artists, and journalists. I owe a great deal to the many who welcomed me, no insider to black culture, into their homes. In some instances it was their children or grandchildren who entrusted me with photographs, correspondence, other unpublished writings, and, perhaps the most crucial component of all, audiotapes and videotapes. These materials reveal firsthand perceptions and illuminate the little known feats of culturally engaged African Americans during a poorly documented era of economic hardships and racial tensions. From these sources came my realization that the cultural leaders I profile here were no fans of black separatist movements. Instead, they were resolute integrationists who viewed their work—whether on the podium, on the stage, in concert halls, in exhibitions, on the pages of literary magazines, or in campaigns for social justice—as an integral part of the larger struggle for racial equality.

Ultimately my research yielded ample material with which to fashion a portrait of an illustrious black confraternity that experienced a cultural renascence—a veritable revival—not in the shadow of Harlem, but of their own making. Both male and female, often in equal numbers, they were active writers, journalists, visual artists, actors, theatre workers, and musicians who transcended the limitations imposed on them as people of color and thrived on self-created opportunity. Black Bostonians, doubly conscious of their Yankee heritage and their racial legacy, imbedded their cultural productions in the very fabric of a great iconic but racially divided American city.

I wish to express my gratitude first and foremost to the many Bostonians who agreed to be interviewed, met me in Boston cafés, welcomed me into their homes and offices, and generously shared their professional expertise and firsthand knowledge of African American cultural life. My understanding of the black cultural scene has been shaped in large part by elders of Boston's black community. Among those who contributed an especially generous quota of their time were Ruth Batson, Gretchen Coleman-Thomas, Eleanor O'Banyoun Collins, Allan R. Crite, Jackie Cox-Crite, Leona Coleman Flu, James Guilford, Jr., Ulysses S. Gore, Keitha Hassell, Joseph Harris III, C. Vincent Haynes, Reverend Michael Haynes, Clara Hicks, Lucy Mitchell Holland, Gretchen Jackson, Maude Jenkins, Elma Lewis, Georgia Reese London, Myra McAdoo, Sylvia McDowell, Aba Cecile McHardy, Marie Margetson, Rupert Margetson, Melvin Miller, Marcus Mitchell, Evangeline Montgomery, Elizabeth Rawlins, Joseph Savoy, Kenneth Silvera, Charles Walker, Betty LeSueur Warnum, Dorothy West, Esther LeSueur Williams, and Thelma Thornton Wynn. Thanks to Kay Bourne, longtime arts editor and writer for the *Boston [Bay State] Banner*, for generously sharing her expertise and items from her personal archives. To Jocelyn Coleman Walton and Gretchen Coleman-Thomas, I wish to express my gratitude for sharing photographs from their family archives and recollections of their grandfather Ralf Meshack Coleman.

Among the scholars whom I consulted to great effect were Doris Abramson, Ira Berlin, Henry Louis Gates, Jr., Gerald Gill, Jared Hardesty, Kathy A. Perkins, Mark A. Peterson, Marilyn Richardson, and James Spruill. Of the many research librarians who have assisted me, first mention goes to Laura Reiner, reference librarian extraordinaire at Clapp Library, Wellesley College, who by delving into ancestry and genealogy came up with answers to my frequent questions about the more obscure writers. Angie Batson and Susan Goodman of Inter-Library Loan worked swiftly, importing books and digital articles as fast as I requested them, and I thank them from the heart. Other librarians who have been both responsive and helpful are Douglas Black, reference librarian, Amherst College; Karen Jefferson, archivist, Robert W. Woodruff Library, Atlanta University; Danielle Kovacs, Du Bois Library, University of Massachusetts Amherst; Charles Niles, Gottlieb Research Center, Mugar Library, Boston University; Maryalice Perrin-Mohr, Spaulding Library, New England Conservatory; and Carol Wood, archivist, Galveston and Texas History Center. Francie Latour and Vanessa Jones, feature writers for the *Boston Globe,* took great interest in this project and interpreted its cultural and historical importance. My colleagues in the Spanish Department never flagged in their support, and Wellesley students Oni Lusk-Stover and Karlen Powell deserve thanks for their enthusiastic research assistance and for being excellent company in the search for black Bostonians who performed and persisted in their art and activism.

The National Endowment for the Humanities and the American Council of Learned Societies each provided fellowships that enabled me to spend extended time away from teaching to write this book. Two Harvard University institutions, the W. E. B. Du Bois Institute at the Hutchins Center for African and African American Research, directed by Henry Louis Gates, Jr., and the Bunting Institute (now the Radcliffe Institute for Advanced Study), directed by Rita Nakashima Brock, provided me with golden opportunities to be in the company of truly great scholars. I wish to express my deep appreciation to these Harvard institutes for greatly facilitating my research during the semesters I spent in residence. The earliest phases of this project, which were focused on African American women writers, were supported by the Wellesley Center for Research on Women, where Peggy McIntosh was both a shining example and a mentor.

Finally, the Faculty Awards Committee of Wellesley College furnished the support that sustained my work and for which I am truly grateful.

Many colleagues, family members, and friends, too numerous to list here, have helped bring this book to fruition over its two decades of gestation. Two University of Massachusetts faculty members, Jules Chametzky and Doris Abramson, encouraged me when this book was just a proposal and generously shared their expertise. Among the excellent readers of the manuscript in its early stages were Aviva Ben-Ur, Donald Burroughs, Crystal Marie Fleming, Lois Horton, Wim Klooster, Louis Marbre-Cargill, Sandra F. Tropp, and the anonymous readers for the University of Massachusetts Press. Finally, I thank Lisa Simmons, a member of a well-known black Bostonian theatre family and my collaborator on our joint website, "After Abolition: The New Century."

At the University of Massachusetts Press I was fortunate to fall into the capable hands of Brian Halley, the responsive and astute senior editor who shepherded my manuscript on its way to becoming a book and whose good judgment I learned to trust implicitly. I am also deeply grateful to managing editor Carol Betsch for her guidance and for assigning two superb editors to my book: Mary Bellino and Margaret Hogan. To Mary, a skilled manuscript doctor, I owe thanks for her dedication and precision. To Margaret, the consummate scholarly editor, I owe special thanks for her swift responses to my queries, her patience with my occasional puzzlement, and the engaging e-mail messages that helped me during the editing process.

For personal support, companionship, and fun I have always relied on family members, especially Miriam, Aviva, and Gabriel, as well as Aiden, Evan, Liam, Avi, Noah, and Ethan—may you always be as precious, affectionate, and bright as you are now. One extraordinary person, Jonathan Leigh Roses, has been my mainstay and fount of unwavering support—reader, editor, commentator, proofreader, and beloved husband who has enthusiastically accompanied me, camera in hand, on forays into the South End and Roxbury neighborhoods, photographing the people, the landmarks, and the public art whose images grace this book.

Portions of chapter 3 appeared in Crystal M. Fleming and Lorraine Elena Roses, "Black Cultural Capitalists: African-American Elites and the Organization of the Arts in Early Twentieth-Century Boston," *Poetics* 35, no. 6 (December 2007): 368–87.

BLACK BOSTONIANS AND THE POLITICS OF CULTURE, 1920–1940

INTRODUCTION
A Veiled History

This book examines the development of a vibrant arts scene that flourished in Boston during the New Negro Renaissance, thus bringing to light a cultural movement that I term the "Boston renascence" so as to differentiate it from New York City's Harlem Renaissance. This propulsive but understudied movement in the heart of the Athens of America yielded an impressive body of self-expression that extended across a wide range of creative writing, dramatics, sculpture, painting, journalism, music, photography, and independent scholarship. Within that spectrum, theatre stands out as the most expansive genre. To identify and closely examine the traces of this creative phenomenon is to reveal the complex inter- and intra-racial dynamics of a city that would become one of the nation's most ethno-racially diverse in less than a century, with an African American population of 24.4 percent as of 2010.[1]

In 1920, Boston's black population comprised only 2.2 percent of the city's total; by 1940 it had grown by only 1.1 percent. Yet the accomplishments of its creative cohorts were disproportionately greater than these statistics might suggest. Boston's "New Negroes"—young, talented, and black—like the "New Negro" generation described by Alain Locke, created "something beyond the watch and guard of statistics." Vastly different from the New York phenomenon, born of what historian George Hutchinson has described as a complex and fruitful convergence of black and white intellectual and institutional networks, Boston generated its own modest but significant body of work in response to the times. It was shaped at once by the cultural traditions of the city known as "the cradle of liberty" and its Black Yankee roots, as explored by historian William D. Piersen.[2] The cultural leaders of black Boston led the way with a distinctive merger of social activism with art, a commingling of ethics with aesthetics. These leading members of black society worked assiduously to challenge both the concept and the reality of racial segregation, using their influence to stimulate concurrent creative activities. Since the story of the Bostonian New Negroes has gone unexplored, the primary goal of this study is to dispel their invisibility and to enhance our understanding of their productive dynamics.

During the early twentieth century African Americans faced exclusion from most fields of economic endeavor and professional opportunity. Even as they militated against lynching and other forms of violence against blacks, they identified cultural production as an avenue to integration. It was in fact an equalization strategy, often a successful one, aimed at influencing the gatekeepers of mainstream art in elevating the status of Negro spirituals, literature, and historiography. But admission to theatres, concert halls, institutions of higher learning, and academies of art and music remained tightly restricted. In her 1938 essay "Angry Saxons and Negro Education," Anna Julia Cooper (1868–1964), the prominent author and activist, exposed the insidious workings of exclusion: "Due honor and high praise are loudly acclaimed for Negro spirituals, Negro literature, Negro history, [and] Negro 'attempts' at art," she wrote, "but don't try to crash the gates on a play of Shakespeare or to listen in on a Wagnerian opera, or to study the marbles of Phidias and Praxiteles."[3]

A Hole in the Fabric of History

Scholars dealing with Boston's black history have long focused on the mid-nineteenth century as a high point frozen in time, when black heroism came to the fore in the distinctive contributions of black Bostonians to the antislavery movement and on the battlefields of the Civil War. It is widely acknowledged that no city played a more prominent role in the antislavery movement than Boston, with its coalitions of white and black abolitionists. The body of scholarship on such nineteenth-century historical actors continues to grow, but the record falls silent at the crossroads of the twentieth century. The dimensions of black contributions to twentieth-century cultural production have barely been probed. A scarcity of source material—including the disappearance of many key documents—has conspired with the ephemeral nature of musical and dramatic performances to obscure a vital dimension of city life. Yet another motive behind the slim narrative about interwar black Boston is the fact that a hardening color line, the decline of interracial collaborations, the entrenchment of de facto segregation, and the bleakness of this panorama undermine the textbook notion of a "Progressive Era." To explore a period in which civil rights activism made little headway would further tarnish the image of a Boston that has fallen short of its high-minded ideals and claims to fame. Its reputation as "freedom city" has not fully recovered from the interracial strife over court-ordered busing in the 1970s. Little wonder, then, that few scholars have chosen to pursue the subject field of twentieth-century black Boston.

To compensate for the numerous gaps in the historical narrative this book presents evidence that black Bostonians accumulated abundant cultural (as distinct from monetary) capital, enough to spark their own creative renascence. Through this currency—defined by sociologist Pierre Bourdieu as the product of breeding, knowledge, sophistication, and familiarity with high culture—community leaders deployed culture as a vehicle that could cross over the racial divide.[4] Their goal was to penetrate and participate fully in the broader sphere of the dominant culture, beyond the boundaries of their insular community. In this sense, *Black Bostonians and the Politics of Culture* is a case study of an urban minority group whose leaders turned their cultural practices to advantage in the war against racial inequality.

This study does not offer a comprehensive narrative of African American cultural production across the centuries, although one is sorely lacking. Instead, it highlights the cultural dynamics of the 1920s and 1930s, when the black population, not large enough to wield influence through electoral politics, forged alternative strategies to bridge racial and socioeconomic divides. An analysis of their strategies highlights the interplay of constraint and agency, and the drive to assert a black presence by all means possible.

Afro-Bostonian cultural leaders were idealists, but they were also pragmatists who set out to counter demeaning stereotypes.[5] If these leaders were to represent Americans of African descent as a people of culture, they needed to build a platform for the activities in which men and women engaged to make their lives more meaningful—in a word, art. To display their advances and achievements in this realm was to pose a permanent challenge to notions of white superiority. Allan Rohan Crite's celebrated oil painting *Leon and Harriet*, seen on the cover of this book, exemplifies that principle. Art historian Edmund Barry Gaither describes the couple depicted crossing Shawmut Avenue, "going about their business, without regard for our gaze. By their indifference, they demonstrate the hegemony that they hold over themselves, setting their own agendas and pursuing their own ends. They do not care to entertain us. They do not require our aggrandizement."[6] Crite renders these symbolic figures in all their dignity and self-possession.

Any discussion of cultural vibrancy among African Americans in the 1920s and 1930s invites comparison to New York's Harlem Renaissance, whose literary output may be described as the first full-throated and sophisticated voice of a free people. Although black people in both cities had common concerns and a shared history of channeling contestations of the color line into art, the two urban centers differed dramatically in demographics, material resources, and achievements. Yet the timeline of the Boston renascence parallels the chronology of the Harlem Renaissance. Many cultural historians accept 1917 and 1935 as the beginning and end points of the era: 1917 marks the opening on Broadway of three iconic black plays. The Harlem Riot of 1935 is associated with the fading of the Harlem Renaissance, but in Boston the Federal Theatre Project (FTP) and its Negro Unit, which flourished from 1935 until 1939, prolonged the cultural renascence.

Chapter 1, "Where Is Black Boston? Geographies of Experience in the Cradle of Liberty, 1638–1900," seeks to pinpoint geographically and historically the propulsive drive of Afro-Bostonians to accomplish their sociopolitical goals. The city's ethno-racial geography and its shifting boundaries, a factor that has been largely overlooked in studies of Boston's cultural heritage, offers a useful lens for examining black cultural life. An awareness of the close linkage of race, space, and place helps to contextualize the first fruits of cultural production.

To trace this Boston phenomenon to the rich literary and rhetorical panorama of earlier centuries is a precondition for rendering its legacy visible and inserting it into previous narratives marred by gaps and silences. The chapter includes a synthetic narrative of black artistry as it developed during the colonial era; through the nineteenth century, when David Walker (1796–1830), Maria Stewart (1803–30), William Wells Brown (1814–84), and Edmonia Lewis (c. 1840–1907) made landmark contributions; and on into the twentieth century.

By 1920 the black community on Boston's Beacon Hill had shifted to

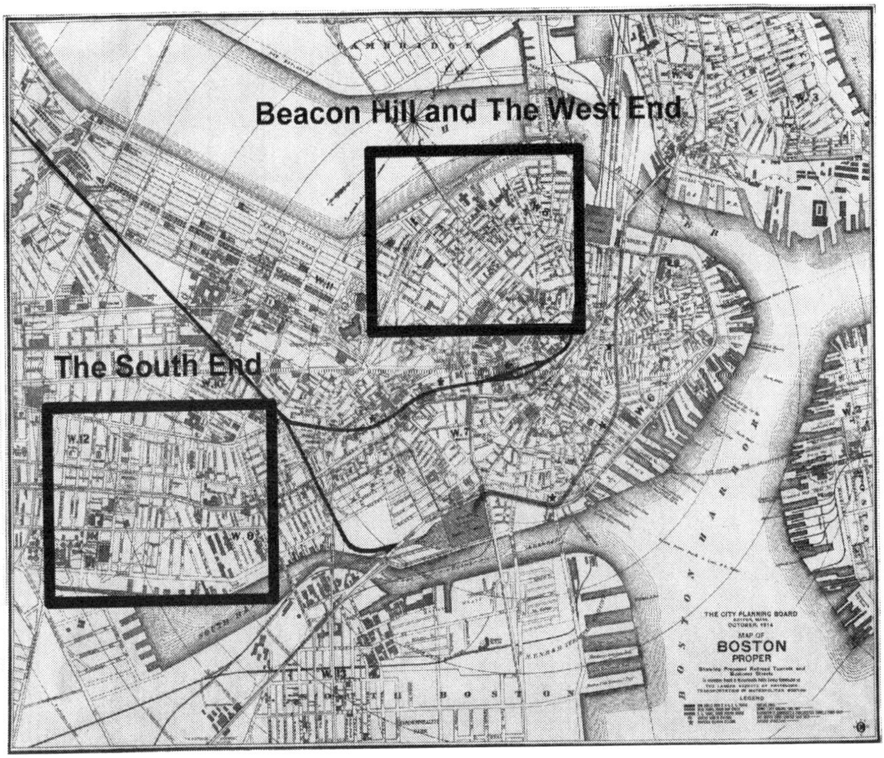

Boston's Beacon Hill and South End. Courtesy Norman B. Leventhal Map Center, Boston Public Library.

Lower Roxbury and the South End, the new hub of public life and cultural production. Black Bostonians established private institutions that opened their doors to intellectual, journalistic, literary, and other cultural pursuits. These artistic endeavors became part of their sociopolitical agenda to effect nonviolent reform.

The discussion of race, place, and space as they relate to black culture continues in chapter 2, "The Black Bostonian Elites: Color, Class, Culture, and Family, 1880–1920." The analysis centers on an exploration of black society and its social hierarchies in historical perspective, with a focus on a set of sophisticated black families as a major source of leadership. This discussion of the social pyramid serves to convey a concrete picture of the distinguished families who played a crucial role in fortifying the linkage of art to racial advancement and successfully perpetuated this agenda during the early twentieth century.

An analysis of gender dynamics informs chapter 3, "Gender and Culture: Black Women as Arts Organizers, 1917–1930," on the crucial part played by women in shaping aesthetic tastes and controlling the presentation of black artistry. While a cohort of elite males established an extensive array of fraternal, benevolent, and business associations, their female counterparts founded associations to promote the well-being of the community. An inquiry into one female-founded club in particular emphasizes the conditions required to encourage a social phenomenon like the early stirrings of a renascence. The League of Women in Community Service (LWCS) grew out of a program to aid black soldiers stationed near Boston. The fact that the organization evolved and developed to encourage the initiatives of local writers, educators, and artists, however, has been largely unknown. How Boston's black female cohorts, with modest resources, created an infrastructure for African American artistry is a central question. The answer relates to how the female participants borrowed from both dominant white and non-dominant black cultural repertoires to advance the appreciation of black culture in mainstream society.

The next three chapters are devoted to the rise of black theatre. Chapter 4, "Black Faces on the White Stage: Space and Race, 1925–1930," brings to light Boston's "Little Theatre" movement, similar to the one spearheaded by W. E. B. Du Bois in New York. Once again, race and space reassert themselves as powerful factors in the rise of dramatic and musical performance. The leader of the movement was Maud Cuney Hare, once the fiancée of Du Bois and a conservatory-trained musician, who founded the first noncommercial or "little theatre" group of aspiring black Bostonians. At the Allied Arts Centre, established in the "cultural district" of Huntington Avenue, Hare encouraged talented Afro-Bostonians to work in productive synergy. In an inclusive spirit, the Allied Arts Players drew black and white spectators to theatres where African American performers had not previously been seen on stage. Blending classical with black themes, Hare's productions attracted the attention of mainstream reviewers but also proved controversial.

Chapter 5, "Writing While Black: The *Saturday Evening Quill*, 1925–1930," explores a parallel between the beginnings of a thriving creative writing venture and a theatre scene. Eugene Gordon (1891–1974), a black journalist at the mainstream *Boston Post*, organized the Saturday Evening Quill Club for aspiring black writers, among them Dorothy West and Helene Johnson. Gordon edited and published the *Saturday Evening*

Quill, an annual collection meant to disseminate the work of his talented group, with black men and women writers appearing in equal numbers. A close examination of the magazine probes the divisions among the writers as they grappled with their complex situation as educated blacks in the North: whether to focus on black themes or produce "race-neutral" work was a matter of debate, as was the choice to embrace the New Negro themes of Harlem literature. In the end they revealed themselves as distinctively Bostonian. The Boston renascence writers ceased to publish around the same time as their Harlem counterparts, but one *Quill* member, Dorothy West, set out to revive flagging spirits with her self-financed magazine *Challenge* and its sequel, *New Challenge.* West navigated the turbulent waters of emerging black radicalism and its antagonism toward "bourgeois" writing to the point of open confrontation.

Chapter 6, "The Boston Players: Broadway Bound, 1930–1935," returns to the subject of the distinctive black theatre that developed in Boston. This chapter focuses on the leadership of Ralf Meshack Coleman, who was not part of the traditional elite but of the emergent middle class. Coleman broke away from the tutelage of Maud Cuney Hare to redirect the course of the Little Theatre movement. The versatile and persevering Coleman founded the Boston Players, designed to attract a more broadly based audience, and applied the lessons he learned from Hare. Coleman produced black-themed plays at mainstream venues that had previously been desegregated by Hare. Like his mentor, Coleman alerted white spectators to the talent of black Bostonians in their midst, lacing his repertoire with levity and shows from the Broadway stage. At the same time he promoted change by introducing black casts, going against the all too common practice of blackening up white actors with grease paint.

Chapter 7, "The New Deal for Boston's Black Theatre: Four Golden Years, 1935–1939," ventures farther afield into the unmapped territory of 1930s black theatre. In 1935, with the nation in the grip of the Great Depression, the future seemed bleak until the Roosevelt administration passed New Deal legislation that included a program to rescue unemployed theatre workers. When Hallie Flanagan, a professor of theatre at Vassar College, became the national director of the FTP, she chose Boston as one of only six pilot cities. Ralf Coleman was appointed to head the Negro Unit—the only African American to direct a Negro Unit from inception to finish. But the program's days were numbered almost from the start: the FTP was the most controversial of the federal arts programs and its adversaries in Congress were legion. Nonetheless, for its participants, the FTP era was golden. Productions by black Bostonians were staged at major downtown theatres in a departure from W. E. B. Du Bois's prescription for a "real" black theatre, one that in his mind should be entirely black, "about us, by us, for us, and near us."[7]

Coleman modified this call for a clear-cut racial separation. The numerous shows produced, directed, acted, and technically managed by black people were staged at venues around the commonwealth for audiences who came from a variety of socioeconomic and racial backgrounds. The alliance between activism and aesthetics was nowhere more striking than in the FTP social experiment, but it ultimately went up in flames amid a "Red Scare" and the cancellation of federal funding.

It is high time to demonstrate that in Boston African Americans invested their seemingly boundless energies and substantial cultural capital in contesting the color line through art. Black Bostonians harnessed the power of the word, the image, the paintbrush, and the instrumentality of music to advance the struggle for racial justice in their divided city.

1

Where Is Black Boston?

Geographies of Experience in the Cradle of Liberty, 1638–1900

> One of the things you have to remember is that the black community in Boston back in the '30s was relatively small. It was almost like a village, everybody knew everybody, and everybody knew everybody's business.
>
> —Allan Rohan Crite

In a corner park in Boston's tree-lined South End stands a bronze sculpture of two imposing figures, a man and a woman. They step forward unafraid onto the unknown road that lies before them. Some passers-by pausing to admire the commanding ensemble would be hard pressed to identify *Emancipation* by Meta Warrick Fuller (1877–1968) were it not for the engraved stone plaque; but others, more informed, would recognize the hand of the distinguished African American sculptor, a participant in the vibrant black arts scene that flourished in Boston between the two World Wars.[1] In their era Fuller and her fellow artists were widely admired for exhibiting their art, writing and performing plays, and concertizing.[2] Fuller's work links her to a century-old legacy of Afro-Bostonian accomplishments in the twin arenas of political activism and art.[3] Identifying as both Negro and Bostonian, Fuller and her peers created a significant body of visual art, books, play scripts, and musical scores reflective of their political concerns. To fathom the significance of their legacy requires a historically grounded discussion of race, place, and space. This chapter and the next focus on black Boston's social geography and its literary, artistic, and performance cultures.

Emancipation, by Meta Warrick Fuller. Courtesy Jonathan Leigh Roses.

Meta Warrick Fuller, sculptor. Courtesy Moorland-Spingarn Research in Black Culture, Howard University, Washington, D.C.

The Convergence of Race, Place, and Space

According to legal scholar David Delaney geography may be understood as "the shifting arrangement of social space, the creation and transformation of real places, and the differing experiential geographies of real people." His dynamic definition underscores "the significance of conflicts over space and the historical politics of race relations between blacks and whites," and is particularly useful for understanding the entity called "Black Boston."[4] I contend that this alliterative phrase can serve to reference both the physical presence and the lived reality of African Americans who have long occupied a distinctive place in Boston's and, by extension, New England's cultural history. Geography as an element of social reality is particularly relevant in a city of ethno-racial enclaves, considered by some to be the most segregated of all American cities. A mapping of the shifting spatial coordinates of the black presence will better enable us to trace the evolution of black cultural production across the centuries. My three-fold goal is to identify the principal neighborhoods associated with Afro-Bostonians, to highlight the dynamics of a cohesive and accomplished community, and to explore the cultural continuum that gave rise to a Boston renascence, a term I use in contradistinction to the celebrated and controversial New Negro or Harlem Renaissance of New York. But in discussing this phenomenon from a historical perspective one cannot ignore the existence of slavery, which persisted in Massachusetts from 1638 to 1780 and haunts us still. In recent decades racial conflict has prompted scholars to bring "the peculiar institution" out of the shadows and to expand the body of knowledge upon which I draw in the following synthetic narrative.

Origins: Africans on New England Soil

In February 1638, just eight years after the founding of the town of Boston, the first contingent of black people arrived—in chains—on the ship *Desire,* licensed to the Salem privateer William Pierce. Governor John Winthrop had originally contracted with Pierce to transport "Indians" to Bermuda, but "he, missing it, carried them to Providence Isle," the "other Puritan colony."[5] The Massachusetts Bay Colony's first governor recorded in his journal that Pierce traded seventeen Indian captives for an unspecified number of Africans with whom the *Desire* sailed to Boston. The ship's exact landing point in Boston Harbor, long unknown, is now thought to be the Town Cove, in what would become Dock Square.[6] The landing site is buried underneath today's Faneuil Hall, the bustling marketplace known for its dining, entertainment, and other commercial establishments. Winthrop makes no mention of the names, genders, or ages of the Africans or of their languages, appearance, or deportment. He lists "negroes" after specifying the commodities cotton and tobacco—ample evidence that dehumanization was the first principle of slavery. The voyage of the *Desire,* a tragic event for the captive Africans, nonetheless inaugurated the black history that is celebrated in contemporary Boston.

Winthrop's vision of a godly polity of Christian worship could not be realized without a plentiful labor supply. In a letter of 1645, his brother-in-law made the point that "a stock of slaves" was necessary for the colony's survival. African slaves would be far less costly than servants from England, for "to maintain 20 moors" would be "cheaper than one English servant."[7] So it was that slaves' unpaid labor made it possible for England to maintain her colonies. Three years after the landing of the *Desire,* the

Massachusetts Bay Colony became the first to legalize slavery. By the same token, a century and a half later, the first state to enshrine the abolition of slavery into its constitution was the commonwealth of Massachusetts.[8]

The Puritan colony qualifies as a "society with slaves," unlike the thorough-going "slave societies" of the American South.[9] For nearly two centuries the enslaved tilled the land; tended to the children of Puritans; managed their homes, farms, and livestock; and worked as apprentices to craftsmen—coopers, potters, printers, and weavers. They were part of a workforce that included enslaved Native Americans as well as white indentured servants, all constituents in a society that was far more diverse than is often imagined.[10] The regime of slavery in Massachusetts has sometimes been described as an attenuated version of the peculiar institution of the South, based on the fact that slaves enjoyed full legal status, contracted legal marriages, could appear in court as litigants and witnesses, and retained access to the courts throughout the colonial era. However valid these assertions, scholars have rejected the notion that New England slavery was somehow a milder form of enforced labor. Sociologist Adelaide M. Cromwell notes that the mere fact "that slavery in any form could have coexisted with the ethical principles on which this country was founded was and continues to be an embarrassment."[11] Historian William D. Piersen too, while allowing that family slavery in New England fostered "close and relatively humane relationships that approached a fictional kinship between masters and slaves," was clear that such relationships were rife with bitter internal inconsistencies and disempowerment inflicted by the slaveholder.[12]

Through slavery wealthy ship owners, property holders, and merchants could purchase luxury goods, travel, and enjoy time at leisure, while for the enslaved there was no such thing as luxury, leisure, or even travel without permission. Their incorporation into New England households did not amount to true assimilation, which was never allowed: instead, the enslaved and the indentured were subject to rigid work regimes, violence, and, for the enslaved, the possibility of sale at the whim of their owners. While it is obvious that African men, women, and children contributed to the viability of the economy, it is less often recognized that they also planted the seeds for the emergence of a distinguished community of free black Bostonians with its own cultural practices and pursuit of self-expression.

Indeed, even under the shadow of slavery, strong and courageous African men and women mounted resistance to oppression. In New England slavery was largely domestic, as the rocky soil precluded the establishment of plantations—unlike in the South, where Africans and their American-born descendants lived in close quarters—and New England colonists with sufficient income to purchase slaves held only a few or even just one. Under circumstances of constant surveillance the chances that the African-born could retain their oral traditions and craftsmanship were slimmer than in the South, and it is not surprising that northern societies with slaves developed no rich treasure trove of oral culture and traditional crafts comparable to those of the South.

The closest New England analogue to a southern plantation may be found at Ten Hill Farm, on the southern bank of the Mystic River in today's Medford, some six miles north of Boston. Its owner, Isaac Royall, from one of New England's richest families, owed his wealth to his family's plantations in Antigua. (Royall's estate endowed a professorship at Harvard Law School).[13]

Meanwhile, the slave quarters at Ten Hill Farm represent the last such structure standing in the northern United States. Visitors to the site learn about one house slave who had no bed but slept on the floor outside her mistress's door, at her beck and call at all hours.[14] Over the course of more than half a century sixty-three servants labored on the six hundred acre property until Royall, being a Tory, fled to Canada at the outbreak of the American Revolution. The servants' names have been lost, with the exception of the African-born Belinda, who from 1765 to 1783 initiated some eighteen freedom suits against the Royalls in Massachusetts courts.[15] In 1783, she petitioned the legislature for her freedom and sued for reparations. The sixty-three-year-old's suit was successful: she won her freedom, and the Royall estate was ordered to pay compensation for her years of servitude.[16]

One of the darkest outcomes of emancipation was that the freed men, women, and children were left to fend for themselves. A study by historian Elise Lemire reveals that in wealthy Concord, Massachusetts, some twenty-five miles west of Boston, freed slaves were abandoned by their owners and exposed to brutal winters. Prevented from settling in other towns with "warning out laws" designed to avoid the burden of supporting indigents, countless numbers of black men, women, and children endured desperate conditions with remarkable bravery and resourcefulness.[17]

In Boston proper, deeply prejudiced white people treated manumitted slaves inhumanely, denying them employment and maligning them, to the point that Beacon Hill resident Prince Hall (1745–1807), the son of a biracial mother and an English father, declared in a 1797 speech: "Were we not possessed of a great measure of [patience], you could not bear up under the daily insults you meet with in the streets of Boston; much more on public days of recreation. *How are you shamefully abused, and that at such a degree, that you may truly be said to carry your lives in our hands, and the arrows of death are flying about our heads.*"[18]

With respect to the beginnings of black self-expression and cultural production during the colonial era and beyond, the black population was widely distributed and denied the right to free assembly, minimizing the opportunity to collaborate creatively. There were no proprietary black spaces and no "neighborhoods" to speak of. Any concerted effort at formal cultural association or intellectual exchange would have prompted suppression and varying degrees of punishment. Unlike free blacks, the enslaved could scarcely form affinity groups like those that would emerge after 1780. Even so, enslaved men and women mingled in church and at public events, markets, and festivals. Some also handled business matters on their masters' behalf and were entrusted to travel, thus potentially establishing communication networks far more often than we can know due to lack of documentation.

The Nature of Incipient Cultural Production, 1773–1780

For all the limitations imposed by slavery, colonial-era African Americans—whether enslaved, free, emancipated, or fugitive—left considerable evidence of their engagement in creative activities. William Piersen painstakingly documents the perpetuation of such seventeenth- and eighteenth-century activities as festivals and ceremonies derived from ancestral practices. Historians of oral traditions note that even as they were slowly displaced by mainstream modes of communication through writing and printing, such traditions did not entirely disappear. The case of Lucy Bijah Terry Prince (1730–1821) of Deerfield Village in western Massachusetts illustrates the resilience of the oral tradition and its perpetuation in the form of versifying and speech-making. This African-born woman embodied the art of appropriating white discourse to great advantage in her struggle for justice, as in the many court appearances she and her sons made to defend the family's right to their land.[19] Terry was also a people's poet and storyteller to whose home young black people flocked. "Bars Fight," Terry's only surviving work, is a ballad memorializing white neighbors, some of whom perished and others taken captive in a 1746 Abenaki Indian ambush. "Bars Fight" was not published in Terry's lifetime. It appeared in print seventy-four years later, in 1895.[20] The fate of Terry's work suggests that other black men and women of whom we have no record may well have manifested literary talent. In fact, the black literary field took root in poetry when Phillis Wheatley famously published a volume of her selected works.[21]

Recent scholarship has corroborated the hypothesis that blacks who commingled and formed relationships in other towns and with other marginalized people engaged in music making, verbal play, dancing, and games, all of which were reflections of both ancestral and European American practices. Music making was of vital importance to African Americans, as seen in documents that afford glimpses of the leisure activities of New Englanders. Black people excelled in music. Horn pipers and fiddlers provided accompaniment for step dancing and jigs, which were widely popular across lines of color and class. American founding father John Adams once attended a "frolic" with dancing and music and greatly appreciated the musical accompaniment of black fiddlers. In 1760, Adams visited a tavern where "every Room, kitchen, Chamber was crowded with People. Negroes with a fiddle [and] Young fellows and Girls dancing in the Chamber as if they would kick the floor thro."[22] If direct evidence of these activities does not abound for Boston and Massachusetts, one can extrapolate from documents from other New England locations.

Newport Gardner (1746–1826), born in Africa as Occramar Marycoo, became accomplished in European American musical traditions. Captured by slavers and sold into bondage, Marycoo was purchased by Caleb Gardner of Newport, Rhode Island, and renamed for that city. He so impressed Gardner's wife with his affinity for music that she arranged for him to have lessons—in the same way that Susanna Wheatley tutored seven-year old Phillis in literature and classical languages.[23] It became apparent that Gardner was multitalented: he could "cipher, write passable poetry, and speak French." In 1791, Gardner's fortunes changed: he won the lottery, purchased his freedom with part of the proceeds, and with the rest established his own singing school. Among the pupils enrolled were both blacks and whites, including his former mistress. Gardner had long supported the colonization movement, believing that the Negro race "c[ould] never be elevated here." He was fluent in three languages, which helped him to converse with new arrivals from Africa and especially qualified him to receive a mission to Africa.[24] On January 4, 1826, Gardner joined a group of missionaries and set sail from Boston for Africa, fulfilling his dream to return to his homeland but dying in Liberia only a few months after his arrival.

In Portsmouth, New Hampshire, some fifty-five miles north of Boston, black musicians were ubiquitous, and we can extrapolate that similar activities existed in the Boston area. Music was both a livelihood and a common pastime for African New Englanders who perfected their musicianship after work hours. The portability of their instruments "enabled ready combinations with other employment." Cuffee, or Cuff, Whipple played music at a 1783 festive ball held for George Washington in Portsmouth five years after his owner freed him. An eyewitness described Whipple as playing from the musicians' gallery "to the elite of the town on the floor below, as he labored with his violin to keep up with the mazy dance!"[25] There is no reason to believe that Boston and its environs did not have its own cohorts of black musicians.

The Primacy of Print Culture

Afro-Bostonians participated enthusiastically in the print culture, and Boston holds the distinction of generating some of the earliest black-authored texts. Black authors "do not easily fit into a coherent group united by any organizing principle other than their African heritage," writes literary scholar Vincent Carretta; instead, their work "reflects the various geographical, social, and temporal settings" in which African-American, like Afro-British authors, produced their writings."[26]

The written tradition first took root among blacks in legal petitions and lawsuits, as seen in the case of Belinda Royall. In 1773, a contemporary of Belinda's known only as "Felix" submitted an eloquent petition to the Massachusetts legislature, one that laid bare the truth about the so-called benevolent regime of northern slavery: "How many of [our] Number have there been and now are in this Province, who have had every

Day of their Lives embittered with this most intolerable Reflection, That, let their Behaviour be what it will, neither they, nor their Children to all Generations, shall ever be able to do, or to possess and enjoy any Thing, no, not even Life itself, but in a Manner as the Beasts that perish."[27] These passionate words have lost none of their power since the day they were written. From 1765 to 1783, slaves like "Felix" and Belinda continued to file freedom suits in the Massachusetts courts.[28] Literary scholars have argued persuasively that the self-expression of African Americans in such documents invite textual interpretation and allow for the appreciation of black aesthetic values. Prince Hall may have ghostwritten the petition of Felix, and Belinda's white attorney may have written hers, but the words represent the sentiments communicated to the attorneys by the petitioners themselves.

The iconic example of highly refined literary self-expressions is Phillis Wheatley (c. 1753–84), the African-born slave whose voice continues to reverberate across the centuries through her rich and stirring classic work, *Poems on Various Subjects, Religious and Moral. By Phillis Wheatley, Negro Servant to Mr. John Wheatley.* Unlike Lucy Terry Prince, who worked in the oral tradition, Wheatley enshrined her writing in print. Mastering Anglo-American literary forms, Wheatley accomplished what poet June Jordan has called "the difficult miracle" of black poetry in America.[29] Her standing as the first published black poet, or the first published black woman poet and the first black poet to gain international notice in British America, has been debated, but surely she was among the earliest in all three categories.[30] In this respect, Wheatley may be considered a counterpart of Anne Bradstreet (1612–72), a white woman of status who lived over a century before her, as both were among the earliest American women writers.[31] In Wheatley's poetry, as in Bradstreet's, the reader does not encounter folk themes, colloquialisms, dialect, or detailed self-descriptions—these were not characteristic of New England culture. In her isolation and eloquence, Wheatley emerges as a kind of Emily Dickinson figure—a solitary literary genius—among black poets.[32]

In rare moments of self-revelation Wheatley evoked her childhood in Africa, but for the most part her personal story was shrouded in metaphor and protective silence. The precocious Phillis fully embraced Anglo-American high-culture, deftly incorporating the neoclassic syntax, diction, and meter of the poets she read, including Alexander Pope and John Milton.

The influence of classical Greco-Roman literature also echoes in her work, which rose to a level of sophistication far above that of the women of her time.[33] Her detractors initially refused but were ultimately forced to admit that the African-born poet had mastered the most venerable of the cultural traditions of their era. In privileging the classical tradition over the vernacular, Wheatley foreshadowed the decided predilection for high culture that would prevail among the black Bostonians who would bring about a cultural revival during the New Negro Renaissance of the twentieth century.

But Wheatley did more than emulate: she subverted convention by infusing Eurocentric forms with messages that planted the seeds for the protest writing of the future: "Some view our sable race with scornful eye," she wrote, making the case that African peoplc had every right to "join the heavenly train" as co-equals with whites.[34] Wheatley was also outspoken on the subject of northern racism, anticipating not only Afro-Bostonian orators and authors of the nineteenth century such as Maria Stewart, David Walker, and William Wells Brown, but many a twentieth-century writer who, consciously or not, was her spiritual heir.

In another triumph of black creativity over oppression, Scipio Moorhead, a friend of Phillis Wheatley, executed a famous engraving of her image for the frontispiece of her first volume of poetry.[35] To express her admiration for Moorhead Wheatley dedicated a poignant sonnet "To S. M. a young African Painter, on seeing his Works." The poem vividly conveys her delight at his artistry: "When first thy pencil did those beauties give, / And breathing figures learnt from thee to live," she wrote, "How did those prospects give my soul delight, / A new creation rushing on my sight!" Wheatley's touching sonnets envision art as a portal to heaven where all constraints will be transcended and give way to sublime delight. The beauty and extent of Wheatley's poems make it all the more regrettable that she died at the age of thirty-one.[36]

In the field of artisanry, as many colonial documents suggest, apprenticeships provided an outlet for artistic talent. Evidence of black artistic talent is furnished in an advertisement placed by a watchmaker by the name of McLean. Published in the *Boston News-Letter* on January 7, 1773, the notice made known the availability of "a Negro man whose extraordinary genius has been assisted by one of the best masters in London: He takes faces at the lowest rates."[37] This "genius" was most likely Pompey Fleet, a slave of Thomas Fleet. Sometime between 1742 and 1754, Thomas Fleet, who owned Peter, published "The Prodigal Daughter," a pamphlet illustrated by an impressive pen and ink drawing. The drawing shows a girl on the verge of death seen rising from her sickbed to the astonishment of her parents. Shown above the girl is an angel who lifts her up to heaven. The initials "P. F." that appear below, according to historian Jared Hardesty, may well be those of the talented Pompey Fleet.[38]

Historian William Piersen cites archaeological evidence of black artisanry, including pottery, that points to "retentions of an African aesthetic, even given their overlay of Anglo-American materials and style, [which bespeak] the continuity of African values."[39] Master craftsmen capitalized on the fact that unlike white apprentices, enslaved artisans had little chance of becoming competitors. Also striking is that in Boston archaeologists excavating on Beacon Hill have found pottery shards with what appear to be African-inspired designs, suggesting that blacks moved through the ranks of middle-class artisans and attained mastery of the technologies of their time. The stories of Pompey Fleet, Newport Gardner, Phillis Wheatley, Scipio Moorhead, and other artists and artisans, both famous and obscure, demonstrate that black creativity was an integral part of New England cultural life in the colonial era. These examples help to flesh out William Piersen's concept of the "Black Yankee," which he applied to the men and women who merged African and New England cultures: "A combination of choice, circumstance, oppression, and exploitation," writes Piersen, "led . . . African immigrants to become Black Yankees—a very special breed of Afro-American New Englanders." Piersen bases his concept of the "Black Yankee" on W. E. B. Du Bois's famous understanding of black identity as a duality. Piersen extends this idea to the African-descended people in New England who participated in the creation of "a black American hybrid flowering against the odds, in the chill Yankee air."[40] Historians James O. Horton and Lois E. Horton conceive of these early infusions of African customs, rituals, and, above all, music, into everyday life as "symbolic of the multiracial society" that was emerging in the United States.[41] However, the countervailing force of pressure to conform to their masters' culture suppressed the efforts of the enslaved at overt forms of expression. The individual contributions of both enslaved and free, as well as broader issues of musical and artistic genius, remain to be explored in further depth.

The complex process of acculturation and adaptation of Africans to the linguistic, religious, and cultural practices of the dominant white group, while fraught with the trauma of loss, had an enormously fruitful outcome. Wheatley, Moorhead, Fleet, and Gardner, as well as countless others who remain anonymous, demonstrated mastery of Anglo-American literary and pictorial forms. These artists and artisans, by applying their talents to creative projects in ways both small and large, nourished the budding tree of New England culture. Their contributions take on a deeper meaning when viewed from a geography-based perspective that focuses on the specific zones of the city where Afro-Bostonians have clustered.

The Earliest Black Neighborhoods

By 1790, the year of the first U.S. Census, black people had become part of the thriving commercial life of Boston's North End, whose shops and alehouses reminded one British traveler of those he knew in London.[42] In this area surrounded by water on three sides, free black men residing in the section known as "Nigger Hill," or sometimes "New Guinea," names which to our ears carry unmistakably negative connotations, found work at the waterfront, building the wharves, selling merchandise in the bustling marketplaces near the docks and on ships, and otherwise boosting the nascent economy.[43] For their part, sisters and wives provided stability at home and earned income selling items in produce markets, running households, raising children, transmitting core values, and engaging in many other activities that have gone largely unrecorded. The hundreds of black residents, including the eminent Prince Hall, interred on the Snowhill Street side of Copp's Hill Burying Ground bear witness to the black people who trod the streets of the North End.[44] But ultimately the North End did not become a "black neighborhood" with a centralized or enduring economic and cultural community life. That description, however, fits the community that grew up on Beacon Hill near the banks of the Charles River and close to the central markets of the city.

The Celebrated Black Bostonians of Beacon Hill, c. 1830–1900

Of Boston's black neighborhoods none boasts a history as rich in accomplishment as Beacon Hill.[45] Today's visitors to its cobbled streets and brick houses may find few black people residing there, but the historic presence of African Americans dates back to the 1750s, when servants of wealthy and powerful Boston Brahmins settled in courtyards and alleys adjacent to their mansions. By 1830 one third of the city's almost 1,900 blacks lived on the lower north slope of Beacon Hill, where the highly regarded community acted like a magnet to attract those departing from the South. Newcomers from the West Indies and Canada further increased the diversity of the antebellum community.[46] The "softer drawl of southern-born blacks" mingled with the tones of northerners and "a sprinkling of foreign accents" by midcentury. By 1864 Beacon Hill accounted for nearly two thirds of the city's black population. The Hortons conjure up "the clipped tones of British and Canadian English and the musical strains of West Indian speech" in addition to the lilting tones of Irish-born blacks and the accents of Spanish, French, and African dialects. All "lent a cosmopolitan flavor to Boston's black community."[47] The infusion of southern blacks irritated longtime residents who saw them as outsiders and who wished to associate only with those of a similar social status.

In many workplaces, however, blacks intermingled with whites of similar class backgrounds and black men gained a foothold as craftsmen, artisans, and small business owners. That stronghold was put at risk by stiff competition from impoverished Irish immigrants who settled along the waterfront district in cellars and shacks, and displaced blacks "scrap[ing] up temporary jobs as day laborers—sweeping streets, rending horses, cleaning stables, unloading ships, and cutting fish."[48] Even so, in the emergent hierarchy of the free black community, a rising class of black professionals and business entrepreneurs did well enough to live in comfortable homes along the streets of Beacon Hill and the adjacent West End.[49]

The iconic African Meeting House, built in 1806 with black capital and labor, still stands on its original site, its interior having been renovated and dedicated to educational purposes. At its inception the meetinghouse was a beehive of religious, political, and social activities and a prime venue for inspired lectures. From its podium the powerful voices of gifted orators, both black and white, rang out, even persuading many who were proslavery and reluctant to join the antislavery cause. Historian Benjamin Quarles, a born and bred black Bostonian, describes black abolitionists who brilliantly persuaded some of their adversaries "to reflect seriously upon the impropriety of holding men in bondage," because "the feeling that slavery was inconsistent with the ideals of the war cropped up in many quarters, becoming manifest in the formation of abolitionist societies."[50] Among the most prominent orators was David Walker (1796–1830), a free black man from North Carolina who made Boston the headquarters of his unparalleled militant campaign.[51] From the relatively safe haven of Beacon Hill Walker delivered inflammatory speeches attacking slaveholders.

The art of oratory, long cultivated and honored among blacks, thrived when the voice of the eloquent Walker rang out. No less eloquent—and provocative—was his widely disseminated *Appeal in Four Articles, Together with a Preamble, to the Coloured Citizens of the World, but in Particular and Very Expressly, to Those of the United States of America.* In this arresting, ninety-page pamphlet of 1829, Walker referenced the extensive travels that had brought him to the "full and unshaken conviction" that "we (coloured people of these United States) are the most degraded, wretched, and abject set of beings that ever lived since the world began." Walker boldly denounced the hypocrisy of any who called themselves Christians but oppressed their fellow human beings. Most terrifying to slaveholders was his bold prophesy, addressed to "Americans": "Your DESTRUCTION *is at hand, and will be speedily consummates, unless you REPENT.*[52] Walker's *Appeal* called for insurrection against slaveholders, as the publication traveled from North to South through a clandestine network of railroad porters. On August 21, 1831—two years after Walker's *Appeal* went into circulation—Nat Turner led a slave rebellion in Virginia that culminated in the tragic massacre of some sixty whites and, in the aftermath, nearly two hundred blacks. Walker was exceptional, however, among black leaders, few of whom advocated violence. Instead, they promoted nonviolent social change through existing political channels—a position that would continue to predominate well into the twentieth century.

The influence wielded by Walker was so great, according to the Boston *Transcript*, that the city's black population "glorie[d] in its principles, as if it were a star in the East, guiding them to freedom and emancipation."[53] Byron Rushing, a twentieth- and twenty-first-century state legislator and lecturer on Boston's history, describes Walker as representing "the radical ideas about liberation and participation in society" that originated in the black community.[54] This powerhouse of a man threatened white supremacists, and some modern historians speculate that the cause of Walker's death at age thirty-four was poisoning (others argue that this notion is part of "a great body of lore" and "embellishment").[55] It is no exaggeration to see a reincarnation of Walker's radicalism in the person of William Monroe Trotter (1872–1934), the aristocratic black Bostonian who from 1901 to 1934 would edit the crusading Boston *Guardian*.[56]

Another outstanding orator directly inspired by David Walker was Maria Miller Stewart (1803–79), who did not allow her gender to interfere with her career as a public speaker. Stewart's place in history is secured by her extraordinary lectures, which were first published by William Lloyd Garrison. Linking her cause to that of her friends and allies, Stewart declared that "God hath raised you up a Walker and a Garrison. Though Walker sleeps, yet he lives, and his name shall be had in everlasting remembrance."[57] Stewart ventured to deliver her iconoclastic speeches amid widespread disapproval at a time when women were not expected to be part of the public sphere. Stewart was the first American woman of any race to give a political speech before a "promiscuous audience" (one made up of both men and women) and to have those speeches published. It was pure nerve that drove her to address audiences including both men and women. On September 21, 1832, Stewart delivered a lecture that seemed to echo Phillis Wheatley by countering the widely held belief that northern blacks enjoyed "freedom." Turning her fire on northern racists, Stewart unmasked the supposed liberalism of Boston that was actually a camouflage for the reality of racial discrimination: "Tell us no more of southern slavery; for with few exceptions . . . I consider our condition but little better than that."[58] This was a daring allegation to make in public when other black people hotly disagreed. Another illustrious black Bostonian female, Pauline Elizabeth Hopkins, would take up the cudgel for this counter-position at the turn of the twentieth century, defending New England against charges of racism. Hopkins would go so far as to liken Boston to Jerusalem when she proclaimed in biblical terms, "May my tongue cleave to the roof of my mouth and my right hand forget its cunning when I forget the Benefits bestowed upon my persecuted race by noble-hearted New England."[59]

Returning to Maria Stewart, this daring woman brilliantly linked the phenomenon of discrimination to the denial of advanced education for blacks. Freedom itself "can be an enemy where education is denied," she wrote, "[for] there are no chains so galling as the chains of ignorance—no fetters so binding as those that bind the soul, and exclude it from the vast field of useful and scientific knowledge. O, had I received the advantages of early education, my ideas would, ere now, have expanded far and wide." Stewart continued to increase her range to speak, in proto-feminist terms, of gender issues: "O, horrible idea, indeed! to possess noble souls aspiring after high and honorable acquirements, yet confined by the chains of ignorance and poverty to lives of continual drudgery and toil. Neither do I know of any who have enriched themselves by spending their lives as house-domestics, washing windows, shaking carpets, brushing boots, or tending upon gentlemen's tables. I can but die for expressing my sentiments; and I am as willing to die by the sword as the pestilence."[60]

This foremother of black feminism demanded to know, "How long shall the fair daughters of Africa be compelled to bury their minds and talents beneath a load of iron pots and kettles?" Stewart did not hesitate to call out black men: "I would implore our men, and especially our rising youth, to flee from the gambling board and the dance-hall." Their affinity for "frivolous amusement . . . has been carried on among us to such an unbecoming extent, that it has become absolutely disgusting." But Stewart was not letting women go blameless either. She dared to challenge black women: "O, ye daughters of Africa! what have ye done to immortalize your names beyond the grave?" With pronouncements such as these Stewart antagonized her audience to the point that she was either forced to leave the city or made the decision to leave of her own accord. Perhaps both were true, as her parting words lay bare the internal dissent that she generated: "For I find it is no use for me as an individual to try to make myself useful among my color in this city. . . . Wherefore, my respected friends, let us no longer talk of prejudice, till prejudice becomes extinct at home."[61] For her militancy Stewart paid the price of self-exile: On September 21, 1833, she announced that she was giving up her work in Boston and moving to New York. Still, through the publication of her speeches in the *Liberator*, her words have become an indelible part of print culture.

William Wells Brown (c. 1814–84), the towering figure of nineteenth-century black cultural accomplishment, ranks highest among Afro-Bostonians who combined oratory and publication. It is most remarkable that even as this man who escaped slavery militated tirelessly in the anti-slavery struggle, he assiduously cultivated the craft of writing. In recognizing this art for its intrinsic value he expanded the range of African American literature into virgin territory.[62] Without the precedent set by Brown, whose literary career is ensconced as one of the most extraordinary in nineteenth-century black literature, the aspiring black Bostonians of the following century might not have mustered the courage to venture into an unknown realm. Brown's story exemplifies and reinforces the concept of a two-pronged black movement, one that focused simultaneously on political action and on *belles lettres*, the fruit of solitude and contemplation—in metaphorical terms, the sword and the pen.

Brown published in virtually all the literary genres but is perhaps best known for his 1853 novel *Clotel; or, The President's Daughter: A Narrative of Slave Life in the United States*, widely considered the first novel ever published by an African American.[63] Written in the florid style characteristic of the period and by turns elegantly sentimental and passionate, *Clotel* has been called a literary compromise between conflicting agendas, one literary and the other propagandistic.[64] I contend, however, that Brown in fact merged two strains of literature: one that served as advocacy and the other as aesthetic creation. Harriet Beecher Stowe advocated for abolition in her masterpiece *Uncle Tom's Cabin*, but Brown's trenchant descriptions flowed from lived experience. As a slave he had observed the behaviors of his white masters when they were uninhibited and dropped all pretense, oblivious to his watchful gaze. In his *Narrative of William Wells Brown, a Fugitive Slave*, the author recalled in an aside that his owners would wash down pitchers of mint julep before breakfast, prior to holding their morning worship services.[65] Like Wheatley, Walker, and Stewart before him, Brown reserved his most intense attacks for the glaring contradictions in the behavior of self-described Christians, one of whom "tied up a woman of his, by the name of Delphia, and whipped her nearly to death; yet he was a deacon in the Baptist church, in good and regular standing."[66]

In *Clotel*, too, the motif of Christian hypocrisy is laced with flights of irony: "The writer of this is able to put th[e] whole congregation [of the Rowe Street Baptist Church, Boston], minister and all, to flight, by merely putting his coloured face in that church."[67] As a counterpoint to his story line, Brown inserted bold denunciations of the racism he encountered in the North, a recurrent theme among black intellectuals from Phillis Wheatley to Maria Stewart and beyond: "Even the slave who escapes from the Southern plantations is surprised when he reaches the North, at the amount and withering influence of prejudice."[68] This comment supplements his declaration that "after all . . . liberty in the so-called Free States was more a name than a reality: that prejudice followed the coloured man into every place that he might enter."[69] Brown's remarkable and distinguished works, written in a distinctive voice, showcase his unparalleled eloquence and fury, leavened with flights of irony.

William Wells Brown's Precedent-Setting Dramas

An important accomplishment of Brown's is his authorship of the first published black play in America, *The Escape; or, A Leap for Freedom: A Drama in Five Acts.*[70] Consciously or not, the black Bostonians of the 1920s and 1930s New Negro Renaissance era would privilege this specific genre and establish its primacy at the core of their cultural production. Brown, however, had no access to dedicated rehearsal and performance spaces. Instead, he gave numerous dramatic readings of his play to benefit the American Anti-Slavery Society. *The Escape* was not produced during Brown's lifetime, but in early 1968, Boston director James Spruill read a scholarly article that described *The Escape* as excessively melodramatic and "unproducible." Spruill, who had worked with Amiri Baraka in New York before going to Boston, rose to the challenge and obtained a copy of the original manuscript from the Boston Athenæum. He then produced and directed it with singular success in 1971 at Boston's Emerson College and again in 1977. Theatre critics Erroll Hill and James V. Hatch, citing reviews of the production, make the comment that "a completely satisfying experience is likely to be the judgment of anyone fortunate enough to have seen either of two modern productions."[71] Brown's plays and performances enhanced a career that reflected the close linkage between activism and art. The oratorical and literary accomplishments of William Wells Brown, like those of David Walker and Maria Stewart, manifest a remarkable alignment of political and aesthetic goals in the Beacon Hill period. The voices of these and other artists, like the distinguished historian William Cooper Nell (1816–74), are an integral part of what may (and should) be recognized as an established black Bostonian literary canon.[72]

Some groups founded by African Americans for intellectual exchange are well known to cultural historians, and their work is considered to have reinforced the initiation of literary projects. The Afric-American Female Intelligence Society, established in 1832, hosted lecture series and study groups for women only; for their part, black men had the Young Men's Literary Debating Society. The Boston Philomathean Society, however, opened its doors to both genders, further widening opportunities for Afro-Bostonians.[73] Daily life, filled with unrelenting hardship, was also enriched by literary salons and drama clubs, many meeting at private homes or churches. The *Liberator* (1831–65), Garrison's antislavery newspaper, identifies a broad range of cultural practices that were a vital part of the cohesive black community. Even when material needs were great, Afro-Bostonians found ways to engage in many branches of cultural activities—particularly those related to an appreciation of high culture in the European American tradition.

Pictorial and Plastic Art

Amid the flurry of oratorical and literary activity reviewed here, visual art made a brilliant showing in the work of two artists, Edward Mitchell Bannister (1828–1901) and Mary Edmonia Lewis (c. 1840–1907).[74] These black Bostonians stand out for the way in which they navigated uncharted territory made rough by societal obstacles. Bannister while still in his thirties was included by William Wells Brown in his historically oriented work *The Black Man: His Antecedents, His Genius, and His Achievements.*[75] Born in the seaport town of New Brunswick, Canada, Bannister arrived in Boston during the 1850s with the goal of studying art at the Lowell Institute. While doing so he earned his livelihood as a barber and photographer. He married Christiana Carteaux, a wealthy black businesswoman who owned hair salons in Boston and Providence. The marriage greatly furthered Bannister's career, placing him in the company of other culturally engaged Bostonians and giving him considerable social and geographical mobility. During the 1860s, while the Bannisters lived on Beacon Hill at 70 Southac (now Phillips) Street, Christiana organized participatory musical and theatrical events for the enjoyment of her prominent circle of friends. William Wells Brown, who was an occasional participant, dramatized his play scripts before this audience, distributing roles among those who attended.[76]

In much of his work Bannister divorced art from racial politics, in which he took an active part as a member of abolitionist groups. A frequent participant in mainstream (white) as well as black artistic circles, he refrained from treating black themes overtly or including black figures in his paintings. Instead, he executed portraits of leading black citizens, tinted daguerreotypes, and painted seascapes with ships. According to art historian Juanita Marie Holland, the image of a ship leaving harbor during the days of slavery evoked "the horrors of the transatlantic slave trade" but also the bold escapes to England of fugitive slaves and the black community's rescue missions of those fleeing to the North.[77] In 1870, the Bannisters moved to Providence, Rhode Island, where William developed a reputation as a fine landscape painter. He painted shorelines and drew on biblical themes for his subject matter, thus evading the general expectation that African Americans would gear their art to depictions of the African American struggle. The couple's move to Providence likely gave Bannister an opportunity to free himself from expectations and to cultivate formal values according to his own aesthetic criteria. In the sense that Bannister avoided explicitly black themes in his work but worked in more subtle ways to dismantle stereotypes and underscore black excellence, he anticipated William Stanley Braithwaite (1878–1962), the early twentieth-century Bostonian poet who also chose not to reflect his identity in his art and in whose work black themes were conspicuously absent.

The second distinguished visual artist of this period was Mary Edmonia Lewis, who arrived in Boston in 1863 with a degree from Oberlin College and a letter of introduction to William Lloyd Garrison in hand.[78] Garrison's endorsement helped her obtain lucrative commissions from white abolitionists. Lewis worked in the "Old Studio Building," a site now occupied by Suffolk University School of Law at the corner of Bromfield and Tremont Streets and strategically located a short walk from Beacon Hill. One of Lewis's sculptures, commissioned for the 1864 Colored Soldiers' Fair in Boston, was a full-length figure of Sergeant William H. Carney, a black Bostonian who was awarded the Congressional Medal of Honor, the military's highest award. Another of her best-known works is a marble bust of Colonel Robert Gould Shaw, the white commander of the illustrious black 54th Massachusetts Regiment, who died in battle at Fort Wagner with seventy of his black soldiers.

Lewis emphatically refused to define herself solely by the African strand of her heritage. Instead, she highlighted the complexity of her ethno-racial identity. *Old Arrow Maker* exemplifies her pride in her Native American (Ojibwe and Mississauga) heritage. From Lewis's sojourn in Boston there remains only *Hygeia*, an imposing monument situated in Mount Auburn Cemetery in nearby Cambridge at the gravesite of the prominent white medical doctor Harriot K. Hunt (1805–75), a noted feminist and one of the first female physicians to practice in the United States. All Lewis's sculptures bespeak her eclectic orientation and her belief that African American artists should not be bound by the expectation that they focus on racial identity. The scholarship on Lewis indicates that in 1865 the artist moved to Rome, the world capital of sculpture. There she joined a community of expatriate artists and completed several famous works as well as others that have been lost to history.

Independent Scholarship

If the invisibility of Afro-Bostonian accomplishments is to be dispelled, the term "writer" must be broadened to encompass independent scholarship. In 1881, sixteen years after seeing combat with the black 55th Massachusetts Regiment in the Civil War, James M. Trotter (1842–92) became a published scholar. In his *Music and Some Highly Musical People* Trotter documented and provided valuable details of African American musical accomplishments.[79] Few white people knew or even took an interest in these musicians. Thus, Trotter's writing was doubly important, serving art not only for its own sake but also to further the sacred cause of racial equality.

Proclaiming the unique powers of music and its transcendence over everyday concerns, Trotter affirmed the centrality of high culture—art and literature—in black society. Trotter's book celebrated the refinement of and taste for classical music among elite Bostonians like himself. At the same time, the author deliberately excluded all mention of performers who could not read music. The strong class bias exhibited in this decision is one common to upper-class works, whether black or white. Trotter's efforts paved the way for the landmark study of Maud Cuney Hare, *Negro Musicians and Their Music,* published in 1936.[80] Above all, however, Trotter ensured that the outstanding black musicians of his times would not be forgotten.

Similarly, in 1883, Dr. Rebecca Crumpler, the first black female gynecologist to practice in Boston, published *The Book of Medical Discourses.* Crumpler's book is a compendium of medical advice based on her extensive experience traveling across the American South and in England. The writings of this extraordinary woman, about whose life little is known, are suffused with determination to expose the misguided treatment provided to black children "by mothers, nurses and all those who may desire to mitigate the affliction of the human race" but who lack access to health care.[81] Crumpler's two greatest achievements were to disseminate practical knowledge and to advance the cause of racial progress through the promotion of physical and mental health. Her contributions, far removed from the realm of high culture, were nevertheless cultural to the extent that they refined the art of applied medicine. Her prominence and achievements as both black and female presage the strong showing of twentieth-century black women, including those who accomplished their work in the interwar era of 1920–40.

Artists of the Nadir Era of the Black Experience

Black writing, with its characteristic themes of liberation and elevation through the arts, enjoyed considerable popularity among nineteenth-century white readers. Once slavery was abolished by the Constitution, however, racial progress largely dropped off the progressive agenda.[82] The end of the nineteenth century marked a low point for aspiring black writers, and they found little enthusiasm for their manuscripts among publishers. William Wells Brown's final book, *My Southern Home*, published in 1882, was also one of the last known black contributions in Boston before the onset of a stretch of silence.[83] Former activists were lulled into complacency, and Afro-Bostonians were left to reassess the very terms of their self-expression.

This silence was short-lived. The first year of the twentieth century saw the founding of the *Colored American* magazine, with Pauline Elizabeth Hopkins (1859–1930) at its editorial helm. Hopkins, born in Portland, Maine, and raised in Cambridge, Massachusetts, began her career as a stage performer with the Hopkins Family Troubadours when she was twenty years old. By 1900 she had changed careers, blossoming into a respected editor and writer of essays and fiction.[84] Hopkins sparked a new era of cultural ferment that would include her own widely read novels, published in serial form by the *Colored American.*

The Boston-born and -bred William Stanley Braithwaite, nineteen years younger than Hopkins, began his remarkably successful career at the turn of the twentieth century with two volumes of lyric poetry and a stream of influential literary reviews in the Boston *Transcript*, the city's venerable newspaper. Braithwaite would rise to prominence decades later during the early phases of the Harlem Renaissance.

The Emergence of a New Hub of Black Cultural Activity.

Beacon Hill's long reign as the heart of black Boston effectively ended soon after the publication of William Wells Brown's last book. At that point a population shift had begun from Beacon Hill to Boston's South End. Writer Florida Ruffin Ridley (1861–1943) noted this "general movement of colored people from the West End [co-extensive with Beacon Hill], which had always been their home, to the South End."[85] The exodus from Beacon Hill came about as longtime residents of the West End—white, black, and ethnic Americans alike—were displaced by new waves of European immigrants. Byron Rushing, citing these events, cautions against the notion that black people "were pushed out of the Beacon Hill area," adding that it was also "a matter of class."[86] The more well-to-do blacks led the way to the South End. It was close to the city center and convenient for the employees at fine hotels like the Parker House. Pullman porters and workers at the Boston and Albany railyards also could be in close proximity, as boardinghouses operated by blacks met their needs for affordable lodging while compensating for the effects of racial discrimination. The transfer of religious, benevolent, business, and cultural institutions from the old Beacon Hill district to the newer South End facilitated community engagement as well as the continuity of cultural production.

The arts were not first on the agenda of community activists, but no black community had ever considered itself complete without them. Art was a source of solace, spiritual uplift, enrichment, and pure enjoyment. Additionally, this type of creativity was seen to furnish unassailable proof that blacks were intellectually as capable and talented as whites. An abundance of musical activities in these communities validates the assertion of historians James Horton and Lois Horton that "it would be hard to imagine a black community in whose daily life music did not play a trenchant role."[87] Through the arts the community could continue to press for racial equality and civil rights.

The concept of geography as a dynamic element of social reality draws our attention to the fact that black Bostonians built up vibrant neighborhoods in ways that transcend static notions of geography. Through communal and individual acts of agency a broad spectrum of cultural activities emerged. As the new century began, a temporary lull would give way to a renewal of invigorated momentum. The "New Negroes" would distinguish themselves by continuing to participate and excel in literature, art (including photography), and music. Mapping the spatial coordinates of black settlement reveals a more extensive panorama of black cultural production than has previously been acknowledged. Like Meta Fuller's *Emancipation*, the imposing monument that presides over the Harriet Tubman Park in the South End, the accomplishments of Afro-Bostonians are a tangible reminder of their presence throughout Boston's history. Fuller, like other Boston artists who were her contemporaries, shared in the spirit of the exhilaration and hope that spread during the New Negro Renaissance.

2

The Black Bostonian Elites

Color, Class, Culture, and Family, 1880–1920

> At the peak of our prominence and during my childhood we had a French governess, white servants in the home and our white coachman, Bernard. . . . Our friends were all part of a tightly knit small and extremely restricted Negro social circle to which barbers, railroad men and other service people were not admitted. There weren't any . . . dark people.
>
> —Anonymous

While the experience of growing up with a French governess and a white coachman was hardly the norm in Boston's *fin de siècle* black society, the testimony of this individual about her experiences is useful for understanding the racial politics and the paradoxes of the era. Black Bostonians, long ensconced in the city, were subject to de facto segregation, which their leadership contested by every means available, including cultural initiatives. These highly influential programs have been little explored. Through a careful examination of the evidence it becomes clear that black Bostonian leaders, primarily females, were instrumental in driving the emergence of a Boston renascence, which, in turn, was an integral part of the New Negro era.

It should come as no surprise that the interwar cultural renascence was inflected by class, since the Harlem Renaissance itself, according to David Levering Lewis, began "as a cultural nationalism of the parlor" managed to some extent by civil rights leaders in New York to improve race relations "in a time of extreme national reaction to, and annulment of economic gains won by African Americans during the First World War."[1] The

New Negro group included outspoken statesmen like the distinguished James Weldon Johnson and other advocates who refused to accept Jim Crow segregation or the dissemination of demeaning stereotypes of African Americans. The generation that reached maturity during the 1920s were in a position to engage an expanded spectrum of themes because of the accomplishments of their elders. The relationship between the two generations—the "Old Negroes" and the "New Negro"—was not oppositional but deeply symbiotic: both conceived of art as one of many means of civic engagement. This was a conscious choice but also an imperative at a time when the political paths to advancement available to ambitious Irish, Italian, and other ethnic Americans were not equally open to black people. To fully appreciate the cultural life of Boston's New Negroes we must take into account the involvement of black society's upper class in the process of accumulating political and cultural capital and consolidating high-culture practices in the early twentieth century.[2]

The issue of social class necessarily arises because, according to the great sociologist E. Franklin Frazier (1894–1962), "the institutions and other forms of associated life and various phases of culture in the Negro community can be understood *only when studied in relation to its class structure*."[3] As it happens, both the activist and the artistic impulses of the Afro-Bostonian community may be traced to the initiatives of a steadfast cohort of upper- and some middle-class families who were uniquely positioned at the intersection of black and white societies. Obviously, these blacks had a personal investment in the struggle against white supremacy. Less obviously, they created symbolic boundaries and aesthetic distinctions that defined status within the community and represented that community to the outside world. Their collaborative dynamic was instrumental in bringing about the cultural renascence of the 1920s and 1930s.

To speak of upper-class black society is to acknowledge the historic chasm between the well-to-do and the majority of black Bostonians. Conversely, to ignore intra-racial divisions and tensions would only contribute to the perpetuation of the myth that black society is homogeneous. As in mainstream society, these social divisions were mirrored at the neighborhood level. The elegant Rutland Square home of the Butler R. Wilson family, located in the South End, stood in stark contrast to the black-operated boardinghouses bordering the railroad tracks of Albany Street on the fringes of that district. Far less is known about the leading black

Bostonians of the early twentieth century and their cultural practices than is known of those of the antebellum era.[4]

Historian Willard Gatewood places Boston's black elite, as it was constituted from 1880 to 1920, in the company of those that existed in many other American cities. This "black aristocracy," self-described as "the black Four Hundred" or "Upper Tens," could be found in Washington, D.C., Charleston, New Orleans, Little Rock, Nashville, Atlanta, Chicago, Cleveland, Detroit, Seattle, and Denver, as well as Boston. The typical black aristocrat, writes Gatewood, has been described as an imprecise combination of "respectability, moral rectitude, social grace, education, sometimes ancestry, and skin tone," but much less often actual wealth. Turning his attention to specific families in Boston, Gatewood identifies the Duprees, Haydens, Baldwins, Allstons, Wilsons, Latimores, Lewises, Grimkés, and Ruffins.[5] It is striking that among the prominent few who gained wealth were those who poured it all into the defense of the race, as was the case with George Ruffin and William Monroe Trotter, both of whom are discussed later in this chapter. Historians and sociologists agree that the numbers of the elite families diminished markedly around the turn of the twentieth century—lack of progeny and the tendency of their offspring to leave Boston contributed to the erosion, but their exclusivity surely played a part as well, making them easily as vulnerable to attrition as their white counterparts.

Historically the black community, poor in money but rich in tradition, prized self-expression as a political tool and as cultural capital. Historians James O. Horton and Lois E. Horton have identified early examples of the high regard in which the black community held both oral tradition and print culture. In the eighteenth century, for instance, Dean Cyrus Foster was honored for his knowledge and ability to entertain with "stories that were transcribed and included in the first black-authored regional history." This revered individual was "well known and appreciated for his tales of New England blacks during the Revolution and early period of American nationhood."[6] Although print culture became the coin of the realm, oral traditions persisted in speechmaking and in the elaborate toasts that were a feature of Afro-Bostonian communal life.[7]

Literary societies were a major part of every free black community—a high rate of literacy, which was prevalent in both men and women, provided ideal conditions for the establishment of literary associations. But music reigned supreme, as black Bostonians formed orchestras, bands, choirs, and small vocal groups, and "consciously cultivat[ed] a taste for the European music commonly associated with 'high culture.'"[8] The New Negroes of the interwar era inherited the refined tastes cultivated by the older generation. Both cohorts, Old and New, forged their identities in the crucible of double consciousness, the term coined by W. E. B. Du Bois, which may be usefully applied to the distinctive upper classes of black Boston. The cultural work they accomplished eased the transition from a society steeped in Victorian customs to one that partook of twentieth-century modernity.[9]

Ray Stannard Baker, a prominent white journalist and author, visited Boston at the dawn of the twentieth century. He took great interest in the social hierarchies of black Boston, interviewing many "intelligent, educated, ambitious members of the race," some of whom were "so white that they c[ould] not be told from white people, yet they are classed as Negroes."[10] Baker's book *Following the Color Line* is a revealing study of race and class in Boston that underscores the inherent contradiction of the color line and of the black-white binary itself, calling attention, as do other writers, to the sensitive subject of intra-racial colorism, or the determination of social status according to one's skin tone.

But the contours of a social pyramid as it existed in the years directly preceding the New Negro Renaissance are most successfully explored in the sole comprehensive study we possess on twentieth-century black Boston, published by social worker and researcher John Daniels on the eve of World War I. In his in-depth study *In Freedom's Birthplace*, Daniels explored the "real" Negro upper class, which constituted some 2 percent of the black population. This group included lawyers, physicians, salaried employees, business proprietors, and others whom Daniels differentiated from those who "had all the earmarks of the idle rich." A unique feature of Daniels's study is his careful attention to the issue of taste as a defining element of culture. By contrast, neither Willard Gatewood nor Adelaide Cromwell (in her classic study *The Other Brahmins: Boston's Black Upper Class, 1750–1950*) is sensitive to the arts.[11] Daniels observed the refined tastes and fine aesthetic sensibilities of those whom he knew: "The attractive homes of this high status group bear witness to their genuine good taste." Daniels marveled at their "superior education and refinement," and noted specifically that they cultivated literature and the arts, founding associations with "a serious purpose." Daniels's book also reports that some fifty men and women, "most of whom had little time to spare from their day's work," sang grand opera, including *Aida, Faust, Cavalleria Rusticana,* and *Carmen,* under the direction of Theodore Drury (c. 1867–1945), a black director from New York.[12]

Daniels provided no first names for orchestra conductors Wolff, Matthews, and Portuondo, and they remain obscure, but Ransom's Choral Union of fifty vocalists is easily identified with the distinguished minister, civil rights activist, and orator Reverend Reverdy Ransom (1861–1959). Further on in his discussion of musical pursuits, Daniels noted appreciatively that "when a large group of [Negroes] sing in unison, the rhythmical and emotional vehemence of their singing is compelling." These words of praise, however, are followed by blunt criticism: "Finished musical performances are rare among them, and wretched ones are common." To his credit Daniels acknowledged that "comparatively few have the material means to acquire a solid musical education," but he would have done well to note that even blacks with sufficient disposable income were systematically rejected based solely on race. This oversight is a reminder that even sympathetic and enlightened whites like Daniels were subject to some of the same prejudices that ran rampant in the dominant culture. Nevertheless, Daniels reported that "many people believe that as the Negroes advance they are going to contribute to the composite life of the nation much of distinct value in music and various fields of art."[13] Only eleven years after the publication of Daniels's book, musician and outstanding cultural organizer Maud Cuney Hare would validate his prediction by founding the Musical Arts Studio, the predecessor of her Allied Arts Centre, which would become a crossroads of black artistic activity.[14]

Daniels conducted many personal interviews and obtained a number of written statements from outstanding black Bostonians, including some men of culture—alas, no women. But otherwise, his study is decidedly gender inclusive, unlike Cromwell's, which she limited to women of the upper class. Daniels included every social class. Among the statements he collected was one from William Stanley Braithwaite (1878–1962), who, building on his early success as poetry critic for the Boston *Transcript,* went on to publish seventeen volumes of his well-respected *Anthology of Magazine Verse and Yearbook of American Poetry.* These annual volumes, compiled and edited by Braithwaite and issued from 1913 through 1929, began publication in the pre–Harlem Renaissance years and continued on into the last phase of the movement.[15] The widely respected Braithwaite, born in Boston, the city he loved and revered, is little studied today, perhaps because his landmark anthologies of poetry include very few blacks and his aesthetics were more Victorian than modern. The consummate aesthete, Braithwaite found supreme meaning in art: "At fifteen," he told John Daniels in 1914, "like a revelation, there broke out in me a great passion for poetry." His description of his "yearning for that ideal life which fosters the creation of things that come out of dreams and visions and symbols" is an eloquent definition of literature itself.[16] Braithwaite's work was well known in white intellectual circles—many of his readers were not aware that he was black. They "knew" him only from his writing in the *Transcript* and by way of his anthologies.

Balancing Art and Activism: The Outcomes as Seen in Two Elite Families

The significance of the upper-class family has not previously been a category of analysis in discussions of black Boston's cultural heritage, but its characteristics are demonstrably relevant to creative outcomes. As it happens, the activist and artistic impulses of the community may be traced to the initiatives of leading families who acted as a centering force in the cultural community. The Ruffins and Trotters, well-known elite families who operated at the intersection of two races, were prominent in the work of improving race relations, but their intense involvement with cultural life has been largely overlooked. An examination of these families in historical perspective reveals how they helped build an infrastructure that would both nurture and sustain cultural life. On another level they were instrumental in creating symbolic boundaries and aesthetic distinctions that determined status in their social circles.

Placed in the context of the classical studies on black Boston by authors such as Cromwell, Gatewood, and Daniels, family histories take on expanded meaning, emphasizing the collaborative dynamic that sustained the cultural renascence of the 1920s and 1930s. Even as such families worked to instill and perpetuate their cultural values and traditions, they appropriated the arts and letters for political ends. While the elite families constituted only a sliver of the black population, their small numbers belie the breadth of their contributions.[17] These African-descended, dyed-in-the-wool Bostonians shaped the distinctive patterns of cultural life, both solidifying the bonds of black identity and engaging in the cultural politics of racial art.

The Ruffins

A commemorative plaque affixed to a pale yellow brick building at 103 Charles Street on Beacon Hill marks the one-time home of George and Josephine Ruffin, a couple viewed by both whites and blacks as members of the "colored" upper class.[18] Josephine St. Pierre Ruffin's (1842–1924) reputation as a civil rights leader, feminist, and journalist who remained active into the 1920s is legendary, but in the present context, of greater significance is the role she and her only daughter, Florida Ruffin (Ridley) (1861–1943), played in fortifying print culture in the service of their ideals. Their role as leaders in developing an infrastructure for the performance arts in the interwar years also merits extended consideration.[19] Josephine is famous for having founded *New Era* magazine, a black feminist publication started in 1895, but less known is her influence on the cultural flowering that would occur in the 1920s. She had unusually deep roots in New England and was adamant in claiming all three strands of her personal identity—African, white, and Native American. An event recorded by W. E. B. Du Bois highlights his admiration of Josephine, whose mother was from England and father was from Martinique, for boldly asserting her tripartite racial heritage. When a white clubwoman told the elegant Bostonian that she admired "her race," Josephine retorted, "What race?"[20] The notion that one could have a multiracial identity, though admissible in other parts of the world, was unheard of in the United States. The "one drop" rule left little room for nuance, as it still continues to do, and it has prevented many multiracial Americans from officially declaring a multiple identity.

Testimony to the impression Josephine made on those who met her are the words of memoirist Walter J. Stevens (1880–?). As a child he lived near the Ruffin home and would watch the distinguished Josephine in awe as she walked through his neighborhood: "[When] Mrs. Ruffin passed me on the street, I would look up at her with timidity and shy wonder as though I were in the presence of a deity. A woman of cosmopolitan ways, she was strikingly beautiful, brilliant, charitable, [and] progressive."[21] At the lively gatherings at their Charles Street home, Josephine and her daughter,

Florida Ruffin Ridley, c. 1910.
Courtesy Maude T. Jenkins.

Florida, two eminently sophisticated women, welcomed the members of what historian David Levering Lewis describes as the "high and mighty freeborn families—Grimkés, Pindells, Trotters, and others." Du Bois and William Monroe Trotter were among the guests at this "intellectual meeting house for the local black intelligentsia."[22]

Although the resolute Josephine is known for her inspired oratory, deployed at conferences and public gatherings, the printed word was her weapon of choice. With George W. Forbes, Louis E. Baldwin, and Butler R. Wilson, all prominent members of the black elite, Ruffin cofounded the *Boston Courant*.[23] This black weekly newspaper gave Du Bois his first opportunity to write for a large audience. "In this [newspaper]," he stated, "I published many of my Harvard daily themes."[24] Ruffin also founded the magazine *Women's Era*, which promoted the writing of black women and provided rich material for book clubs.[25] By showcasing excellent writing in her magazine, Ruffin amplified the voices of African American women and implicitly demonstrated the intellectual parity of blacks and whites.

Emulating the values instilled in the Ruffin home, their children developed their own artistic gifts and encouraged those of other blacks. Florida

Ruffin, later Ruffin Ridley, joined the Saturday Evening Quill Club, and from 1928 to 1930 published her writing in its annual magazine, the *Saturday Evening Quill.* Florida's brother George L. Ruffin, Jr. (1867–1952), sang in the Theodore Drury Opera Company's production of Handel's *Messiah*, presented in December 1911. In 1947, George was still performing as a violinist with the Trinity Church Choir.[26] Another family member with artistic talent who contributed to the cultural scene in a spectacular way was Ella Nahar, a niece of Josephine, who made her public debut as a professional harpist in 1886. Adopting the stage name of Ednora Narr, she was "an overnight sensation," an elocutionist at a time when literary recitals were in vogue and African Americans could perpetuate their fondness for the oral tradition. Nahar appeared more than sixty times in Boston between 1886 and 1892, performing on two occasions for an audience of five thousand at the Boston Theatre. By 1892 Nahar had performed more than eight hundred times in thirty cities in thirty-one states and in Canada. Like her cousins Florida and George, the versatile Nahar carried the family legacy forward into the twentieth century.[27]

But in 1927, Florida R. Ridley expressed some skepticism that artistically talented blacks would remain in Boston:

> There are indications of good work being done by the young colored people of Boston in the arts. How far their efforts will be encouraged remains to be seen . . . whether these will be able to get the financial encouragement without which even art must die, is a question. The probable answer is that this promising material which might and should enrich Boston life will find its maturing in some more favorable environment than that of Boston, whose characteristic attitude is that of giving to Negroes opportunities along every line except that of making money.[28]

The Trotters

A discussion of the Trotter family further illustrates the dynamics of black family networks, but the differences among such families also provide an instructive contrast regarding their legacies. While some families were activists who made strategic use of print culture to wage the civil rights struggle and left a literary legacy as well, William Monroe Trotter made journalism, but also public protest, his sole channels of influence. From 1901 to 1934, Trotter edited the Boston *Guardian*, a weekly newspaper circulated nationally, provoking endless debate and controversy.[29] Under any circumstance the relationship between politics and art is a fraught one and difficult to maintain in the face of pressures and competing demands, but the equilibrium between the two callings was especially tenuous in Trotter's case, and ultimately the cause was lost.

Trotter, known to his intimates as "Monroe" or "Mon," was the son of James Monroe Trotter, a Civil War combatant who became a recorder of deeds in Washington, D.C., and was successful as a realtor and author of a classic study of outstanding "colored" musicians. The brilliant Monroe was destined to excel in any field of his choice, or so it seemed while he was a student at Harvard University. He arrived at Harvard with the finest attributes of his dual heritage, Bostonian and black.

Harvard Was Heaven

When the self-confident Trotter began his freshman year at Harvard in 1891, he crossed paths with W. E. B. Du Bois, the aloof native of Great Barrington, Massachusetts, who would famously describe himself as being "in Harvard but not of it." Du Bois stood in awe of Trotter, who enjoyed good relations with his white peers. Graduating magna cum laude in 1895, Trotter made history as the institution's first black Phi Beta Kappa, to which, as an added distinction, he was elected during his junior year. Harvard was heaven for Trotter, very unlike the cold world he would later encounter as a "colored" man. He began a master's degree at Harvard in 1895, the same year that Du Bois received his Ph.D.[30] Surprisingly, given that Trotter would dedicate his professional life to journalism, "his worst marks at Harvard were a C and a C+ in English composition courses."[31]

While at Harvard, Trotter courted Geraldine ("Deenie") Louise Pindell (1872–1918), whom he had known since childhood. Her family line included a great-uncle who had participated in the 1840s and 1850s battles to integrate the Boston public schools.[32] Du Bois also took an interest in Pindell, whom he described as "a fine forthright woman, blonde, blue-eyed and fragile" (although a photograph of her in the family's papers at Boston University shows a thin woman with dark eyes and dark hair—not blue eyes and blonde hair).[33] "In the end," wrote Du Bois, "I had no chance to choose her . . . because she preferred Trotter."[34] Trotter married

Deenie Pindell and with an inheritance from his father the couple bought a large home at 97 Sawyer Avenue on Savin Hill, a largely white part of the Dorchester neighborhood of Boston.[35]

At First Equilibrium

Early on in his career Trotter divided his attentions between editing his newspaper and playing a key role in the Boston Literary and Historical Society, one of two leading groups of sophisticated and politically engaged black Bostonians. His sister Maude was president of the other prestigious black cultural group, the St. Mark Musical and Literary Union.[36] However, Trotter's commitments to the *Guardian* and his zeal for public protest appear to have sidelined the more reflective and culturally enriching pastimes that might have tempered his passionate nature. Consciously or not, in neglecting the cultivation of the arts and literature Trotter broke with a proud "Black Yankee" tradition.[37] Why this occurred and the significance of that broken link is a matter for debate.

Regardless of Trotter's own activities, the family were still affluent members of black society. When Maude married Dr. Charles Steward, the gifts that the couple received were indicative of their status: solid silver dishes, gold-lined coffee spoons, cut-glass accessories, and the like. Monroe Trotter, however, gave his sister a simple two-shelf bookcase to which she could "add sections as her library grew."[38] This was a clear statement from Trotter signaling early on that culture mattered to him more than material possessions, and that he intended it to be a large part of his life. Ultimately, however, this would not come to pass.

Emerging from Harvard in 1901, Trotter fully expected to find success in a professional field of his choice but experienced rejection in the job market solely because of his race. Not one for half measures, he changed course completely. In 1901, he joined forces with George W. Forbes—a friend, Amherst College graduate, and librarian at the Boston Public Library's West End branch—to found the now legendary Boston *Guardian*, which became the mouthpiece of the group called the Boston Radicals. Trotter provided the money and Forbes the technical expertise and writing talent that characterized the first few years of the newspaper's run. With the lofty mission of speaking to and for all blacks as well as to a wider audience, the *Guardian* achieved a circulation of 2,500 by its first birthday. The crusading newspaper soon would transcend black Boston and make its mark on the political landscape. At this early stage, from approximately 1901 to 1904, Trotter was dividing his attention between editing his newspaper and playing a leading role in the Boston Literary and Historical Society.[39] It appeared that he would continue to maintain a balance between his fondness for literature and his commitment to activism. Maude Trotter Steward, who had married the Harvard-educated Dr. Charles Gould Steward, a dentist from a distinguished old family, joined her brother as associate editor, supporting his work as he devoted his time increasingly to the paper. Geraldine Trotter also worked at the *Guardian* offices, assisting with the society column and keeping the books.[40] The crusading weekly may be described as an overnight success, although some black newspapers were bitingly critical. The *New York Age*, the most influential of them, issued a particularly nasty headline on January 6, 1905: "Editor Trotter of the Boston Skunk Makes Himself Smelt If Not Felt." According to local historian Robert C. Hayden, "Trotter's *Guardian* appeared on the news stand every Saturday, filled with local and national news concerning black affairs. Correspondents in New York, Chicago, and Washington attracted readership outside New England, and the *Guardian* sold for a nickel, or $1.50 for a yearly subscription."[41] Trotter's editorials, appearing on the paper's fourth page, vigorously attacked Booker T. Washington, the leading spokesman for the black race in America. An ardent and uncompromising advocate of social integration, Trotter abhorred Washington's philosophy of accommodation to the segregationist demands of whites.

The Boston Riot, a Turning Point

On July 30, 1903, Trotter and his allies were among the two thousand spectators present at the Columbus Avenue African Methodist Episcopal Zion Church for an address by Booker T. Washington. Trotter, like much of the black upper class from which he sprang, was relentlessly opposed to Washington because the latter advocated for agricultural and industrial training rather than college education for black people. No sooner had the event begun, Trotter's supporters began to hiss loudly at each mention of Washington's name, to which the event's convener retorted, "If there are any geese in the audience they are privileged to retire." Undeterred, Trotter fired off nine rapid-fire leading questions that he had drafted with the *Guardian* staff. Pandemonium broke out—Trotter, his sister Maude, and *Guardian* stalwart Granville Martin, a butler, were arrested, and Maude was charged with stabbing a policeman with a hatpin.[42] Trotter's opposition to Washington was fierce in the extreme and certainly impolitic. Historian Adelaide Cromwell once implied as much when she remarked off the cuff: "Up here there was a cesspool of anti-Bookerites, always dunning Booker T. But no one has exercised the control that Washington had over African Americans."[43] Trotter was tried and sentenced to jail for a month. Meanwhile, the press coined the name "Boston Riot," making high drama of the internecine conflict between pro- and anti-Washington forces in Boston. After the melee was over and Trotter had served a month in jail, coeditor Forbes "found he no longer had the stomach for combative politics" and opted for a quieter life in his position as a librarian.[44] Trotter made the opposite choice, leaving behind high-culture activities in favor of politics.

Unfortunately, as Trotter's biographer, Stephen Fox, notes, following Forbes's 1904 withdrawal, the *Guardian* "lacked literary polish and journalistic distinction."[45] Apart from the fiery Trotter's eloquent calls to action and petitions, his writing was unremarkable (recall his grades in English when he was at Harvard). Eugene Gordon, a black journalist with the mainstream *Boston Post* and the founder of the *Saturday Evening Quill* magazine, did not mince words in his assessment of Trotter's performance: "This nationally known agitator undoubtedly has done some splendid things for his people," Gordon wrote in 1926, "but if he lives to twice his present fifty-odd year he will never be a newspaper man."[46]

Trotter's involvement in culture appears to have declined considerably in inverse proportion to his increasing absorption in the Boston *Guardian*. As early as January 1903, Trotter rose at a meeting of the Boston Literary and Historical Society to comment on the "great books" of the Western tradition. "I never felt the need of reading books for amusement," he stated.[47] When Trotter made his wedding gift of a bookcase to his sister, he declared that he read books "only for the refinement they gave [him]," rather than for their intrinsic value.[48] The contrast with his father, who published a significant scholarly book on the achievements of black Americans in musical performance and composition, is patent.[49] As Fox notes, Trotter's "life-long quarrel with the English language remained at best a stalemate."[50]

Face to Face with Woodrow Wilson in the White House

Trotter became well known in London, Paris, and other capitals of the world for his leading role in two spectacular events: a 1914 face-to-face dispute with President Woodrow Wilson and his launching of a mass public protest against the screening of the film *Birth of a Nation.* Trotter arrived at the White House as a representative of the National Independent Political League and the *Guardian.* When he met with Wilson, Trotter challenged the president over the imposition of racial segregation of black and white government clerks, who for over fifty years had worked side by side in the nation's capital.[51] Wilson declared himself "offended" and had Trotter removed from the White House. The next morning it was on the front page of the *New York Times* and other papers across the country. The confrontation and Trotter's disrespect of the president of the United States projected an unfortunate image of the *Guardian* editor as a hothead extremist.[52]

Birth of a Nation, *1915*

One of Trotter's most controversial public acts was the famous 1915 confrontation involving the film *Birth of a Nation,* a film so odious to African Americans and others for its historical distortions and monstrous portrayals of black southerners that it had sparked wide public protests in other cities. When the film was booked for a Boston showing at the Tremont Theatre, Trotter and his allies decided to block the proto-racist film. The film was launched at the Tremont Theatre on April 10, with tickets selling weeks in advance due to widespread coverage in the press. Protests in other American cities had led to the film's banning in Chicago, St. Louis, all of Ohio, and elsewhere, including Massachusetts—outside of Boston. A similar success seemed likely in Boston. Trotter and his allies staged a mass protest, a prolonged battle involving public officials, the police, impressive demonstrations of thousands of black Bostonians, and a march to the State House on Beacon Street. But to the shock and disappointment of the protestors, the cause was lost. *Birth of a Nation* was a commercial success to boot, playing for six and a half months and 360 performances."[53]

Nevertheless, victory was won in the spring of 1921, when *Birth of a Nation* was booked for a run at the Shubert Theatre. This time Trotter mounted a broader and more successful campaign, joining forces with the Knights of Columbus, the Catholic association, which had reacted strongly to the glorification of the anti-Catholic Ku Klux Clan. The film never returned to Boston. Ironically, in terms of Trotter's relationship to cultural pursuits, his vocal criticism of the film's racist content was, as far as can be determined, one of his few direct engagements with a cultural event of great magnitude.[54]

The Near Demise of the Boston Guardian

Through the 1920s Trotter persevered, periodically traveling to Washington, D.C., to petition the president and to lobby Congress to pass civil rights laws. On the local scene Trotter took up the cudgel in the fight to block the formal establishment in 1907 by Dr. Cornelius Garland of a Negro hospital in Boston, even though it was already functioning.[55] The hospital operated on a semi-cooperative plan supported by black churches and other organizations, and was founded to provide opportunity for black physicians, excluded from city hospitals, to engage in clinical work and for women to train as nurses. But Trotter was an intransigent proponent of integration and saw only that the hospital was segregated. More constructively, Trotter fought to open up the public nursing programs to train colored nurses and interns.[56] Trotter epitomized the Boston "Radical," unconditionally committed to nonviolent social change. His brand of radicalism, however, lost favor, and Trotter's repeated clashes with other leaders and organizations, such as Du Bois and the National Association for the Advancement of Colored People (NAACP), did no favors to the progress of the civil rights struggle.

Trotter's cavalier dismissal of great literature and his failure to cultivate his writing, apart from the editorials he wrote for the *Guardian*, led to an imbalance in his legacy. While others honored culture through books, poems, and essays as well as political action, Trotter's tangible print legacy is slim.[57] The paper that once "belonged to everyone, from Haverhill to Harlem, and was read by an increasing number of whites" proved to be truly ephemeral.[58] It was a cruel fate for a man who "willingly sacrificed his inherited upper-class position" for his obsessive pursuit of protest and agitation through the *Guardian*.[59] He also sacrificed his chance for a place in the annals of black literary culture by not participating in any direct way in the Boston renascence. The Trotters, in addition to leaving no extensive collection of their personal papers, had no progeny to curate their documents or prolong their influence. Nonetheless, William Monroe Trotter was a force to be reckoned with during the Harlem Renaissance years. The *Guardian* exerted influence on its own, helping to shape a virtual community through the print media. This effect reinforced the perimeters of the black community and created solidarity among black Bostonians. That solidarity was manifested at the protest against *Birth of a Nation* in which thousands participated.

The tragedy of Trotter's premature death has been retold many times. On April 6, 1934, the night of his sixty-second birthday, Trotter fell from the roof of 41 Cunard Street, where his newspaper had its offices.[60] Did he lose his footing while pacing back and forth, as was his habit, or did he mean to end his life? The *New York Times* deemed him a suicide, but some in the black community believed that the death was accidental.[61]

The *Guardian* came close to extinction but was rescued by Trotter's sister Maude, who valiantly assumed the position of editor.[62] Her husband, Dr. Charles Steward, acted as her right hand in all matters at the *Guardian*. He continued to practice dentistry and gave most of the proceeds to keep the newspaper in print. The couple poured their wealth into the sustenance of the now-iconic *Guardian*, as had Trotter and his wife before them. Still, after Maude's death in 1957 it ceased publication. "But almost every day thereafter until his death [Steward] went to the office of the *Guardian* at 977 Tremont St. where he sat for awhile with his memories," wrote newspaper editor Melvin B. Miller.[63] The tensile strength of the extended Trotter family prolonged the life of the *Guardian*, in the same way that strong family bonds fortified the accomplishments of the Ruffin family. It was this strength that enabled the iconic publication to survive, far better known than the Boston *Chronicle*, a black weekly founded in 1915 that outstripped the *Guardian* in circulation. Neither the Trotters nor the Stewards had children: the newspaper was their child. The Boston *Guardian* absorbed all the family's time, as well as its financial and emotional resources.

But "Doc" Steward saw to it that the *Guardian* would not leave a void in its wake. One day he went to see Melvin Miller, at the time a recent Harvard graduate, saying: "You are the successor to the *Guardian*. If you don't carry it on, our lives will have been worth nothing." Miller was convinced, and in 1966 he established a new weekly, the *Boston (Bay State) Banner*.[64] At this writing the *Bay State Banner*, owned and edited by Miller, has recently added an online edition. It remains New England's only journalistic voice for people of color. The *Banner*'s pedigree—its descent from the *Guardian*—is a proud one, and its courageous advocacy continues to command a loyal audience.

The name William Monroe Trotter was largely forgotten but the reclamation of his legacy began in 1969, when the William Monroe Trotter School opened its doors on Humboldt Avenue in Roxbury. It was the city of Boston's first racially mixed school under the commonwealth's Racial Imbalance Law. In 1984, the University of Massachusetts–Boston established the Trotter Institute, with the permanent mission of "addressing the needs and concerns of the Black community and communities of color in Boston and Massachusetts." Its signature publication is the *Trotter Review*, a social science journal.[65]

Trotter, the most forceful of black leaders of his time, did not become a great man of letters, but his influence is legendary. He is credited with initiating the protest tradition, which in the 1950s and 1960s would play a major role during Boston's civil rights movement. He antecedes two political figures whose conscience was raised in Boston and were destined for worldwide renown. The first is Malcolm X (Malcolm Little, 1925–65), whose formative years were spent in a Boston jail, where he surely would have learned about the militant Trotter.[66] While serving his sentence Malcolm converted to Islam and became known as one of the most influential black orators of the twentieth century. Consciously or not, he was also following in the oratorical tradition of black Boston. The second major figure is Eugene Wolcott (b. 1933), who also converted to Islam while he was still in Boston and reinvented himself as a religious leader with political influence. As Louis X (later Louis Farrakhan), he rose to lead the Nation of Islam.[67] This musically gifted Bostonian followed in the footsteps of black Boston's devotees of music. Wolcott embraced an even more radical direction than Malcolm, who had encouraged him to join the Nation.

Neither Malcolm X nor Louis Farrakhan followed in the footsteps of Trotter, the crusading journalist and protest leader, and a Boston radical at a time when that term meant engaging in public agitation, protests, and confrontations. Malcolm X and Farrakhan, having witnessed the utter failure of gradualism, embraced racial separatism, a philosophy that Trotter strove to defeat all his life. But in their emphasis on nonviolent social change these two younger men may be considered part of the Trotter legacy.

3

Gender and Culture

Black Women as Arts Organizers, 1917–1930

> There were many women's organizations in the early days. The group at 464, and the one at 558, which tended to be more la-de-da. I was never interested in joining these organizations. I was more interested in the fight for freedom.
>
> —Ruth M. Batson

Anyone familiar with Boston's black community is aware of two women's clubs that over the course of the past century have generated myriad civic, social, and cultural events. The League of Women in Community Service (LWCS) at 558 Massachusetts Avenue and the Women's Service Center at 464 Massachusetts Avenue, known as "558" and "464" respectively, are distinctive and perhaps unique in their vision and the scope of their cultural accomplishments.[1] This chapter adds some nuance to the perception that the women's clubs of the day were "la de da," a turn of phrase used by civil rights leader Ruth M. Batson (1920–2003), a leading proponent of political activism for education reform.[2] My goal is to demonstrate that one of the two, the LWCS, went beyond carrying out social service projects for the benefit of their community to engage in a significant amount of cultural entrepreneurship.[3] This orientation was unusual for black women's clubs of the era. Most remarkably, these particular groups contributed significantly to the renascence of an artistic and literary scene in black Boston. At the time of their founding no one could have anticipated that the women's clubs would play such a distinctive role in spreading the spirit of the New Negro Renaissance in sedate and stolid Boston. In retrospect, it is likely that black Boston's renascence might never have taken shape without them.

The origins of the women's clubs can be traced back to early 1917, when at the height of World War I two groups of black women joined forces to explore how they might support black troops stationed in the Boston area. At a time when the U.S. armed forces were strictly segregated by race—and would remain so for another three decades—black soldiers training for combat faced discrimination and demoralization on a daily basis. Under such circumstances the support they received from the civilian community was vital. The organizers of the project—Maria Louise Baldwin (1856–1922), a distinguished educator, and Mary Patterson Evans Wilson (d. 1923), the wife of prominent attorney Butler R. Wilson—each headed a group of women with sufficient leisure to pursue activities outside their homes. Baldwin's group began modestly as a bridge club and Wilson's, equally modest, as a knitting class. Their origins hardly suggest that the women were as socially and politically aware as they indeed proved themselves to be. In the short space of a few months they organized and carried out their mission to support the servicemen, always intending to revert to their identities as two separate groups. The group headed by Maria Baldwin would evolve in such a way as to transform the cultural landscape of black Boston during the era of the New Negro.

Of Soldiers, Service, Culture, and Female Leadership

The women's work began with Baldwin's and Wilson's groups meeting for Sunday tea at each other's homes to discuss what they could do "for the boys."[4] They decided to establish a Soldiers' Comfort Unit (SCU) at the so-called Rest House, no more than a hut at the edge of a city playground in the South End that would later be named in memory of a black Bostonian fallen in combat.[5] The military base closest to Boston was Fort Devens in Ayer, Massachusetts, some thirty-five miles west of Boston. Early in 1917, members of the SCU began traveling there in small groups, bearing warm hats and scarves as protection against the fierce New England winters and handing out candy, playing cards, and cigarettes (considered harmless at the time).[6] It is noteworthy that one of the women who helped to make life more bearable for the soldiers was Geraldine Pindell Trotter, the wife of William Monroe Trotter and associate editor with him of the Boston

Guardian. Clearly, not all of the community's activist women worked through the women's clubs. Ruth Batson, for example, militated on behalf of civil rights through other organizational channels.

In 1918, the SCU split into two separate organizations, reverting to their original affiliations: the LWCS, to be led by Maria Baldwin, and the Women's Service Club (WSC), to be headed by Mary Wilson.[7] The reasons for the separation are unclear, and it would be difficult, notes sociologist Adelaide Cromwell, to explain it "without becoming enmeshed in personality conflicts of bygone days."[8] In the absence of other primary sources, the records of the LWCS are essential for identifying the substance and sequence of its evolution from its original mission of social service toward an agenda that included culture-oriented activities. The organization's original charge was to undertake civic, social, educational, and charitable work to benefit the community. But its website today also shows that in retrospect, current LWCS members take pride in having accomplished significant cultural work: "Throughout its existence, the League has fostered intellectual and artistic activity among Black Bostonians. Over the years '558,' as it is also known, has hosted numerous public art exhibits, concerts, literary study groups, and lectures. . . . The organization also provided space for Black cultural productions of music and drama." Club women clearly identified themselves as agents of culture who embarked on a twofold mission of service and intellectual enrichment.[9] Their concern with culture is reflected in the minutes of their meetings (which always began with a Christian prayer). A comparison of the LWCS, incorporated in 1920, with the WSC, incorporated at the end of 1919, would be illuminating, but the WSC records have disappeared. At some point in the 1980s, an unidentified club member moved to Ohio, took the record books with her, and has not been heard from since.[10] The history she hoped to write never materialized. As a result, this chapter focuses solely on the LWCS.

Baldwin, the LWCS's president from 1918 until her sudden death in 1922, was surrounded by four culturally engaged and artistic women who guided her in shaping the club's expansive agenda: Josephine Ruffin was the distinguished orator, editor, feminist, and civil rights advocate; her daughter, Florida Ruffin Ridley, had collaborated with Ruffin on the *Women's Era* magazine in the 1890s; and Maud Cuney Hare was a musicologist and a concert pianist trained at the New England Conservatory of Music.

Meta Warrick Fuller was the most distinguished of Baldwin's close collaborators. She had studied in Paris, and before she arrived in Boston had become renowned for her dioramas, commissioned for the 1907 Jamestown Tercentennial Exposition. From a historical viewpoint, she bears the distinction of being one of the first African American female sculptors of importance.[11] Without the active collaboration of Ruffin, Ridley, Hare, and Fuller, it is fairly certain that the LWCS could hardly have realized their ambitious goals.

During the earliest days of the SCU the women identified music as essential to troop morale. The group's first endeavor was a collaboration with an officer sent as an envoy from Fort Devens to form a black military band. One of the recent draftees was a saxophonist without an instrument, so the SCU resolved to purchase one for him. Maud Cuney Hare organized a series of "soirées musicales," or musical evenings, that yielded the sum of seventy-five dollars, a large amount of money at the time, to buy the saxophone. This decision to help the young musician play in the band underscores the seriousness with which the clubwomen regarded the cultural aspects of their projects. Going forward, concerts would become an integral component of their work.[12]

Just as Maud Cuney Hare led the drive to hold musical events, so Meta Fuller added a component of art appreciation. In October 1918, the LWCS sponsored an exhibition of Fuller's own sculptures. A Boston *Transcript* columnist, E. H. Clement, attended the exhibition. At the LWCS's December meeting Maria Baldwin read aloud from Clement's review, noting with satisfaction that the critic paid it "high tribute."[13] A review in the venerable *Transcript* was a critical component of the cultural model the women strove to emulate.[14] The efforts made by the women to obtain such publicity reflect their intention to showcase the work of black artists. At the instigation of its leading members and with the support of its membership, the LWCS worked to wrest their artistic efforts from critical inattention.

The High-Culture Model

Not surprisingly, the black clubwomen's tastes leaned toward a Eurocentric aesthetic, made manifest in a fondness for classical music. The city's black elites had long laid claim, and rightfully so, to the kind of music and art favored by white elites whom they regarded as their counterparts. With virtually no indigenous folk-inspired traditions to draw upon, black Bostonians enjoyed high-culture practices like attending concerts, actively organizing choral and instrumental music groups, singing opera, and promoting the construction of public monuments to black heroes. The interest in classical music among Afro-Bostonians was keen, as James Monroe Trotter, the father of William Monroe Trotter, made manifest in his landmark book *Music and Some Highly Musical People.* In his study on the foremost black musicians of his era, the eminent black Bostonian and Civil War combatant eloquently invoked "The Power, Beauty, and Uses of Music."[15] The LWCS honored high culture while also featuring middle-brow and popular music by African American performers.[16] The inclusion of more popular culture and homegrown models was as much to their liking as it was strategic, to appeal to an intended audience of servicemen and the general public. The older club members who remembered fondly the highly successful musical plays performed by the Hopkins Family Troubadours of the 1880s would have welcomed occasional alternatives to a high-culture diet.[17] The league's tastes were eclectic enough to sponsor a concert by the Sedalia Quartet of North Carolina, founded by Scott Joplin, "the king of ragtime music." The performance took place in early April 1919, five months after the armistice was signed on November 11, 1918.[18] Thereafter Camp Devens was converted to a "separation center" for over 150,000 troops returning from France.

There is no better example of the LWCS's wide-ranging tastes than the concert given by James Reese Europe and his 369th Regiment band on March 13, 1919. Lieutenant Europe and his band had just returned from France, where they saw combat and won acclaim for their distinctive syncopated music. In constant demand to perform across France, they played frequently for French president Raymond Poincaré and General John J. Pershing. Only a few weeks earlier, on February 17, 1919, Europe and his band had marched up Fifth Avenue to Harlem in a joyous victory parade at the beginning of the Harlem Renaissance. The LWCS-sponsored concert in Boston, taking place only a month after the Fifth Avenue parade, was a real coup for the women organizers and a resounding success, but the aftermath was tragic. On May 9, less than two months after the concert, Europe and his band came to Boston again. During this second performance the brilliant leader was stabbed to death by a drummer.[19]

With the addition of musicales organized by Maud Cuney Hare, such events became a fixture on the calendar. She performed a piano concert on May 11, 1919, after another she gave in March of that year at the Harriet Tubman Settlement House. The LWCS was intensifying its efforts to expose its membership and the general public to music by black performers. Some of the concerts were aimed at raising funds for their club's beneficent work. The league boosted its cultural programming as part of a dual agenda: to promote cultural awareness while raising money to support such social services to the community as lunches for schools with substantial numbers of black pupils. The club leaders linked social consciousness to art appreciation in the broadest sense for as long as their ambitious agenda could be sustained.

Race, Place, and the Cityscape

In 1920, the LWCS, whose early meetings had been held in rented space, purchased the brownstone at 558 Massachusetts Avenue in the South End that would serve as their permanent headquarters. The members who lived in the South End and neighboring Roxbury found the location quite convenient. Fittingly, the mansion was built by an abolitionist, a wealthy sea captain named John Farwell, and is thought to have been a station on the Underground Railroad.[20] According to the group's oral tradition, during the era when the Fugitive Slave Law held sway, the railroad's conductors moved fugitives through a secret passage on the third floor to the next attached brownstone on the street so as to foil federal officials arriving with arrest warrants. This was a history in which league members could take pride.

Among the impressive architectural and decorative features of the house were marble fireplaces, French gold leaf chandeliers, wrought iron work around the outside front windows, mahogany staircases and doors, elaborate plasterwork, Venetian mirrors along the walls, and elegant Victorian furniture. The mansion's beauty is still in evidence even in the midst of structural decay, and a campaign to finance a restoration is underway.

From 558 it was but a few minutes' walk to some of the city's major culture institutions: Symphony Hall, Horticultural Hall, the Christian Science Mother Church, and the Museum of Fine Arts, on Huntington Avenue (now "Huntington Avenue, the Avenue of the Arts"). Symphony Hall, the massive edifice that occupies the northwest corner of Huntington and

League of Women for Community Service building, 558 Massachusetts Avenue. Courtesy Jonathan Leigh Roses.

Massachusetts Avenues, holds special significance for African Americans. In 1917, on the cusp of the Harlem Renaissance, Symphony Hall became the venue for a concert given by Roland Hayes. The great black tenor had already received acclaim in Europe but the managers at Symphony Hall allowed him to perform only on the condition that he finance the concert himself. The concert he gave at the formidable citadel of music not only sold out but also broke the color line.[21] Another cultural landmark on Huntington Avenue was the New England Conservatory of Music, the alma mater of musicians Maud Cuney Hare and J. Rosamond Johnson, the prolific songwriter, librettist, and performer; poet Waring Cuney; and many other black artists.[22] People "of the darker races"—the term that appeared on the masthead of the *Crisis* magazine—were not warmly welcomed at these venues, but neither were they systematically excluded. As a result, many a black Bostonian with an appetite for high culture held season tickets to Symphony Hall, frequented the Museum of Fine Arts, and visited the nearby Isabella Stewart Gardner Museum. Annamae Crite, a South End resident, introduced her son Allan Rohan Crite, the painter, to both art museums at an early age. Crite recalls his mother having tea with Isabella Stewart Gardner herself.[23] Given the symbolic value of these venerable institutions and the intellectual and creative aspirations of sophisticated black people, locating the LWCS's headquarters at 558 appears to have been a wisely calculated choice. But the major consideration of the black female leadership was that the South End had become the heart of the black community after its demographic shift out of Beacon Hill.

The Collaborative Leadership Model

The success of the LWCS—a small, undercapitalized organization—in promoting culture and rendering social services to the community had much to do with its leadership cadre and the sharing of power among Maria Baldwin and her circle of sophisticated, arts-oriented associates. Josephine Ruffin, Maud Cuney Hare, Meta Warrick Fuller, and Florida Ruffin Ridley were prestigious Afro-Bostonians not only within the community but in mainstream circles. Maria ("Mollie") Louise Baldwin was the first of her race to occupy the position of headmaster in a New England school, the Agassiz, an almost entirely white public school at 20 Sacramento Street in Cambridge. The prominent educator left a strong impression on the children of the Agassiz School, as seen in the testimony of e. e. cummings, the eminent American poet known for twisting the rules on capitalization. Cummings described Miss Baldwin as a woman "blessed with a delicious voice, charming manners, and a deep understanding of children. Never did any demidivine dictator more gracefully and easily rule a more unruly and less graceful populace. Her very presence emanated an honour and a glory: the honour of spiritual freedom—not mere freedom from—and the glory of being, not (like most extant mortals) really undead but actually alive. From her I marvellingly learned that the truest power is gentleness."[24] Baldwin extended her educational work by creating a study group for black students at Harvard University, located only a few blocks from the Agassiz School. Her reputation as an orator who could speak on any subject raised her profile in the mainstream community.

Baldwin, who was single and without children, derived strong support from her family of origin. Her father, Peter Baldwin, was a mariner from Haiti employed as a letter carrier by the U.S. Post Office, a position that conferred job security and middle-class status in the black community at a time when most professional avenues were blocked. Baldwin's brother, Louis E. Baldwin (b. 1865) worked with Josephine Ruffin as an editor for a black newspaper, served as a member of the Cambridge Common Council from 1891 to 1893, and founded the firm of Baldwin and Dorsey Real Estate. Louis Baldwin was evidently held in high esteem, as he was invited by Booker T. Washington to deliver the keynote speech at the conference of the National Negro Business League, held in Boston in 1900.[25] Maria resided at her brother's home until 1906, when she moved to the Franklin Square House, a well-known residence for single working women in the South End. There Baldwin surely found kindred spirits and even sisterly support.[26] The close proximity of the Franklin House to 558 Massachusetts Avenue would prove advantageous for the league president.[27]

Josephine St. Pierre Ruffin was perhaps Baldwin's closest ally. In 1893, Ruffin and a group of some sixty prominent black women members had founded the Woman's Era Club in Boston. Baldwin edited and was a contributor to its influential magazine, *Women's Era*.[28] The club was one of two major pillars nationally of the black women's club movement.[29] Ruffin first came to wide public attention when on July 9, 1895, she addressed the historic First Conference of Colored Women in Boston. In her plenary speech Ruffin articulated the rationale for a national organization:

> All over America there is to be found a large and growing class of earnest, intelligent, progressive colored women, women who, if not leading full useful lives, are only waiting for the opportunity to do so, many of them warped and cramped for lack of opportunity, not only to do more but to be more. . . . But when skeptics ask for an estimate of the number of such colored women in America, the inevitable reply, glibly given is: "For the most past ignorant and immoral, some exceptions, of course, but these don't count."[30]

Ruffin urged African American women to take a stance against such defamation by demonstrating that black women were indeed "intelligent" and "progressive"—it was not any intrinsic limitation but only the denial of opportunity that held them back from cultivating the mind through education and the spirit through the arts. *Women's Era* magazine gave a prominent space to literature in its content. The second and third of Baldwin's strongest allies, after Ruffin's daughter Florida, were Maud Cuney Hare and Meta Warrick Fuller. Hare's professional standing as a musicologist and Fuller's national reputation added prestige to the expansion of the LWCS's efforts in the arts field as cultural philanthropists.[31]

Black Bostonian Women and Cultural Philanthropy

Although the black women's club movement has generated a vast bibliography, the phenomenon of arts organizing by these entities during the early twentieth century constitutes uncharted territory.[32] To reveal the specific connections between the black women's club movement in Boston and the promotion of high- and middlebrow cultural events in the community is to illuminate the distinctiveness of black Boston. While other black women's clubs across the country acted to shape the ideological contours of their communities, the Boston club exerted a particularly strong influence despite its exceedingly small numbers—female elites constituted perhaps 1 percent of the educated and professional group that itself made up only 2.2 percent of the city's total black population.

The 1920s were a crucial decade in the reshaping of American cultural life, and the New Negro, or Harlem, Renaissance undoubtedly played a central role in spreading updated aesthetic and ethical codes. The founding of the LWCS coincided with the early stirrings of the Renaissance, an overlap that suggests that Bostonians might have received a boost from an infusion of New York energy. Baldwin and her circle of associates were well acquainted with the writings of W. E. B. Du Bois and Alain Locke, particularly Locke's famous anthology *The New Negro*, and both men were welcomed as speakers at the league's headquarters. According to Locke the era of the New Negro was "a new dynamic phase, the buoyancy from within compensating for whatever pressure there may be of conditions from without."[33] His much-heralded anthology wrought a sea change in the consciousness of young intellectuals and artists, including blacks and some whites, and it included three born-and-bred black Bostonians—William Stanley Braithwaite, Angelina Weld Grimké, and Helene Johnson—as well as a portrait of Roland Hayes (who built his career in Boston) by Winold Reiss. Both the rise of the New York movement and the impulse to create a SCU were war-related. The Boston entity came into existence as a response to the Great War, which led to the mobilization of thousands of African Americans, and historians agree that the return of the black servicemen to America lit the spark of the first phase of the Renaissance.

The relationship of connections among the members of the LWCS to their cultural work to the Harlem Renaissance is important to consider in light of the league's efforts to privilege art as a means of demonstrating racial parity. In important ways black Bostonians followed the paths laid out by Du Bois, James Weldon Johnson, and others who identified art both as an inherently valuable endeavor and as a potent way to sway the opinions of whites who contested blacks' worth. In turn, Boston's black women strove to expand the meaning of legitimate culture to include the products and tastes associated with an African American sensibility. It was the goal of racial integration as much as the development and promotion of black arts per se that motivated LWCS members to press forward against many odds. Their persistent attention to the expressive arts was part and parcel of a strategy designed to use high-culture attainments (but without excluding more popular forms) as a tool for eradicating racism.[34] Working against the menacing tide of Jim Crow, the LWCS women, like the Harlem Renaissance intellectuals and artists, clung to the conviction that interracial bridges could be effectively built through the arts. Moreover, by locating their institutional headquarters on the edge of the cultural precincts of elite white Boston, the women positioned themselves to redraw symbolic boundaries of inclusion and exclusion.

Boston: A Cultural Mecca of the Northeast

The Afro-Bostonian women who adopted the cultural practices of the dominant race and their world of concert halls and galleries were well aware of Boston's status as a preeminent city of high culture. Its wealthy white Brahmins, patrons of the arts and letters, had endowed Boston with museums, concert halls, private libraries, and theatres rivaling those of Europe. Another component of Boston's distinctive profile was its prestigious colleges and universities, including Harvard University, the oldest American institution of higher learning, founded in 1636. It was this wealth of educational resources that had drawn so many aspiring African Americans to settle in Boston in the first place. Their encounters with what one might call an "ice ceiling," because of the city's arm's-length formality (and bone-chilling winters)—greatly limited black citizens' opportunities but did not deter them from chipping away and occasionally scoring breakthroughs.

The league's leaders' decision to purchase a South End mansion was, as noted earlier, a strategic choice that placed them in close proximity to the bastions of Anglo-Bostonian culture. Huntington Avenue, to whose name there would later be appended "avenue of the arts," functioned as an invisible demarcation between ethno-racial homogeneity and ethnic diversity in early twentieth century Boston. On the north side of the avenue there stood the imposing temples of secular and religious culture, while on the south side (the South End and Roxbury) lay a racially diversified district of lower property values. Spatial separation was imposed—it was not the free choice of the women nor of most Afro-Bostonians of the era. Racial segregation was forced on them, and they worked assiduously to weaken its grip. The LWCS's founders were integrationists who would have thrilled to the prophecy spoken some forty years later by Dr. Martin Luther King, Jr., of one day transforming "the jangling discords of our nation into a beautiful symphony of brotherhood."[35]

Obviously the black elites of Boston could never reach the levels of socioeconomic position and power of upper-middle-class Americans. But the refined tastes, family backgrounds, and decisive leadership of the black upper class qualified them as cultural elites. Sociologists have noted that privileged individuals are able to practice class exclusion through the arts because of their monetary capital and leisure time to serve on nonprofit boards and engage in philanthropy. This occurred in black circles as well, and in this sense, too, black women emulated the standards and norms of the dominant culture. They did not, however, relinquish their own traditions. Prior to World War I, notes sociologist Adelaide Cromwell, northern blacks took pride in *not* living in a segregated society, but in Boston they were a more "insular group, a black village, a world apart in a white city. Whites controlled their destinies but hardly knew them; blacks were physically visible but socially invisible." The majority of blacks "knew little beyond their psycho-social village boundaries and even less beyond their actual city limits."[36] Some of the elites, however, moved between social worlds.

Maria Baldwin crossed the color line through many of her affiliations, as a member, for example, of the Twentieth Century Club, the Boston Ethical Society, and the Teachers' Association, all of which were overwhelmingly white and not integrated except for token blacks like Baldwin. Josephine Ruffin belonged to the New England Press Club, another mainstream entity, and various national women's organizations. More generally, community leaders adapted to dominant norms while also conforming to a different set of tastes and cultural practices that conferred status among their peers. The league women believed that they could aim to target two audiences simultaneously, thus causing cultural worlds to overlap. Always working against social exclusion, the group endeavored to draw on several different cultural repertoires at the same time. This occurred when LWCS members explicitly tailored their performances and art exhibits for integrated audiences. The female artistic organizers associated with the LWCS were familiar with both African American and Eurocentric cultural capital, an advantage that allowed them to garner the attention and attendance of both black and white elites.[37]

Cultural Considerations: The "Right" Environment

How the LWCS leaders went about nurturing black talent is an essential point to investigate. For any amateur artistic group to succeed it needs a reasonably favorable environment, a receptive audience, and critics to evaluate its artwork. For a racial subgroup such as African Americans it was more difficult than for comparable white groups. Black groups were less likely to be granted access to organizational resources and less likely to garner critical attention from mainstream cultural gatekeepers. The most critical requirement was proper venues: for meetings, rehearsals, exhibitions, and, above all, performances. This is where the women's clubs played a crucial role: they freely loaned their premises to cultural groups, enabling aspiring artists to get their start through social networking and creative collaboration. For example, the LWCS provided Maud Cuney Hare with the space she needed to spearhead the little theatre movement, discussed further in chapter 4. When Hare's protégé Ralf Coleman launched his own theatre group, as he recalled, he turned to the Women's Service Center for the use of their premises.[38] Black Bostonians inhabited a far smaller territory than Harlem, but they worked with their own resources, on their own terms, and without white intervention to showcase black achievement.[39] New York was not particularly relevant to their practices or even their identity. For Florida Ridley Boston was "the home of Liberty, the breeding spot of liberal ideas and of abounding philanthropy." While she admitted that "Boston's attitude [was] one of pure color discrimination," she also made the point that "Negroes have been identified with the history of Boston almost from the earliest days of the town, and even as slaves made outstanding contributions."[40] Ridley's statements make it clear how much she valued her identity as a black Yankee.

Boston did not and could not compare itself to New York; after all, New York was the capital of black America and home to the major race organizations that fostered and facilitated artistic production, including the two most influential journals, *Crisis*, produced by the National Association for the Advancement of Colored People (NAACP), and *Opportunity* magazine, the organ of the National Urban League. By contrast, the Boston artistic cohorts relied on self-endorsement, family support, and local race institutions, which is why the women's clubs became so crucial. In a city of segregated spaces black cultural creators of the 1920s and 1930s deployed their ingenuity to dismantle or at least circumvent the hurdles in their path.

Even so, black Bostonians kept careful track of the cultural sea change occurring in Harlem. They were avid readers and frequently invited black luminaries like Du Bois, Locke, and James Weldon Johnson to lecture and mingle with them. In this manner Boston was touched by the emerging New Negro Renaissance. As early as October 1918, at around the same time that Johnson delivered a lecture in Boston, Du Bois gave a talk for league members.[41] Just as black artists demonstrated the distinctive value of their art, intellectuals sought to absorb and disseminate the ideas that animated the movement. Consciously or not, the LWCS blended their uniquely African American tastes with a Boston-flavored aesthetic. The organization's leaders were inspired by the same lofty, if ultimately unfulfilled hopes as Du Bois, Locke, Johnson, and other major literati and race leaders. The women of the league believed that their race would achieve social and economic justice and equality once a strong cohort distinguished itself in literature, art, and intellectual leadership. It was in this larger ideological context that Boston's black female elites carried out their agenda.

The LWCS continued to offer its space as a venue for cultural organizations as the Harlem Renaissance entered its second phase (between 1924 and 1926). The Aristo Club, founded in 1924 by Boston schoolteacher and league member Wilhelmina Crosson, was an intellectual forum that held its meetings at 558. This organization, through the 1970s, sponsored pageants, musicals, and a black history exhibit each February.[42] The remarkable fact that the LWCS could support an array of social, educational, and cultural activities shows their willingness to include cultural production, which was otherwise tangential to their philanthropic work. The members invested their unpaid labor as well as their cultural and monetary capital for the greater good of the community. Additionally, many LWCS husbands made regular donations whose importance cannot be overestimated. With such support, the league was able to sponsor numerous performances of black musical groups like the Malcolm Lang Quartette and the Carlo White Serenaders, who performed on April 17, 1924, and September 23, 1926, respectively.[43]

By framing the arts as important and valuable pursuits, the ladies of the league contributed to the construction of a cultural legacy for posterity. In addition to creating a space for music, the club served as a gallery for pictorial art. In the 1930s, repeating the success of earlier exhibitions by Fuller, the LWCS featured sculptures by Meta Warrick Fuller. It also exhibited the work of painter Lois Mailou Jones.[44] Maude Jenkins, a member of the Junior Division of the LWCS, recalled seeing "a parade of people arriving at 558" to view this exhibition. Jones's teacher was called in from the Museum of Fine Arts School to help mount her art for display. As Jenkins testified, "Lois, as it was not to her liking, had us take all the paintings down. The AKA [sorority] sister who had brought the teacher in was upset and furious."[45] Jones's open disagreement with her teacher on artistic grounds suggests her ability to challenge a white woman's expertise and to assert her aesthetic independence.[46]

Junior Division of the League of Women for Community Service. Courtesy Maude T. Jenkins.

A Singular Event at the Boston Public Library

The most ambitious cultural project spearheaded by members of the league was the "Exhibition of Negro Achievement and Abolition Memorial," intended, on the one hand, to impress white Boston with the outstanding artistic accomplishments of African Americans and expand the public's cultural repertoire. On the other hand, it was meant to honor abolitionist leaders, both white and black Bostonians who had brilliantly advocated for the eradication of slavery. Mounted in January 1922 at the Boston Public Library in Copley Square, the exhibition took place at a time when black artists were still routinely ignored. James Weldon Johnson, the keynote speaker, was a former U.S. consul, songwriter, and the NAACP's first black field secretary. The versatile Johnson was also an eminent poet and literary critic whose classic anthology, *The Book of American Negro Poetry*, would be published that same year.[47] He had already published the bestselling *Autobiography of an Ex-Colored Man* in 1912, although anonymously—the author's name would not be revealed until 1927.[48]

When he accepted the LWCS's invitation to speak at the inauguration of the exhibit, Johnson announced his topic: "The Creative Genius of the American Negro." But he added that all his engagements were contingent on the progress of his lobbying efforts on behalf of the passage of the Dyer anti-lynching bill. Johnson informed the league president that he had to be available to "place urgent calls to Washington," a circumstance that could prevent him from giving his lecture. Nonetheless, he arrived in Boston and delivered his keynote address.[49]

The original plan for the Boston Public Library exhibit of 1922 was to display and publicize the history of the singular achievements of black people, from black abolitionists to artists. By targeting an audience at one of Boston's most hallowed institutions, the women of the LWCS accomplished two objectives: to raise the profile of black participation in the interracial abolitionist movement and to synthesize aspects of dominant and non-dominant culture. Their proposal to showcase African American works of art while raising awareness of past political accomplishments was a radical one. Still, the reaction of one otherwise staunch white ally must have come as a surprise. In a May 16, 1922, letter to Florida Ruffin Ridley, Alexander Mann, the pastor of Trinity Church, the monumental edifice facing the Boston Public Library from across Copley Square, wrote:

> Dear Mrs. Ripley [*sic*]:
> I have your letter of May 15 telling me of the Exhibition of Negro Achievement and Abolition Memorials that you propose to hold next September in the Boston Public Library in the interest of the Maria Baldwin Room. It seems to be a capital idea, and I shall be glad to be of any service I can. So if you wish to make use of my name on your letter heads all right [*sic*]. I do not quite know what you mean by "abolition memorials." The abolition movement of course was a movement of white people, and just how you are going to correlate that with an exhibition of negro achievement, I don't understand.
>
> Yours sincerely,
> Alexander Mann[50]

Strikingly, Reverend Mann, otherwise a strong supporter of the civil rights cause who even addressed the crowds at a 1915 public protest against the racist film *Birth of a Nation*, could not grasp what the exhibit was all about. His assertion that the abolition movement "of course was a movement of white people" is, of course, utterly false. Mann apparently knew nothing of leading black abolitionists such as Lewis Hayden, Maria Stewart, David Walker, and the countless black Bostonians who joined the movement sometimes called the second American Revolution.[51] Mann was one of many who, no matter how highly educated, was uninformed about the legacy that the women of the LWCS and other members of the black elite were working hard to disseminate. In the end, the LWCS had to compromise. The black achievement exhibition, inaugurated on October 8, 1922, focused exclusively on black artistic achievements in art, literature, and music. The women's bid to include a memorial to abolition failed. The abolitionist segment had to be sacrificed as a concession that reveals the force of social constraints preventing black elites from realizing their efforts to shape the scope of legitimate culture.

Nonetheless, the month-long exhibition at the Boston Public Library was an historic triumph. It garnered precisely the sort of critical attention from the white press that the LWCS wished to attract. F. W. Coburn of the *Boston Herald* wrote that "the immediate occasion for display of these outflowerings of negro creativeness [was] to illustrate James Weldon Johnson's lecture on 'The Creative Genius of the American Negro.'"[52] Apart from the curious fact that the *Herald* critic referred to the artwork as "an illustration" attached to the Johnson lecture, he celebrated two painters, Henry Ossawa Tanner (1859–1937) and Meta Warrick Fuller, both of whom would enter the annals of great American art. In 1923, after the Boston exhibition, the French government admitted Tanner to the Légion d'Honneur, and he settled permanently in Paris. Fuller, who like Tanner had studied in France, remained in the Boston area but had to sideline her art due to heavy family responsibilities—raising three sons, an adopted daughter, and two grandchildren, while tending to her ailing husband, Dr. Solomon Fuller, who was losing his sight.

Coburn hailed Tanner's *Flight into Egypt* for its "quiet lyric beauty of painting that is conceived within a narrow range of color values by an artist of much sensibility and good taste." In Fuller's work, represented by several small sculptures—*Future*, *Awakening Ethiopia*, and *A Grandmother*—Coburn appreciated "a flair for symbolic sculpture, delicately conceived."[53] The recognition and praise of critics like Coburn was crucial to black artists and their promoters. Coburn's appreciation of Tanner and Fuller may well be related to their success in producing work consistent with the aesthetic standards of European American elites. Both Fuller and Tanner drew on what French art academies had to offer but each had a repertoire more complex than what their European leanings imply: they creatively transformed prevailing artistic norms by infusing their paintings and sculpture with themes and imagery drawn from the African American experience.

"The historic black achievement exhibition was a great success for the League," wrote Florida Ruffin Ridley, "and it was one that identified the month-long run of the Negro Achievement exhibition as one of its greatest achievements . . . a big undertaking, the biggest and most important thing of its kind ever undertaken in Boston."[54] The exhibit, however, like most of the cultural work done by these black women of the female "Talented Tenth," has been long forgotten.

Although the social constraints imposed on black endeavors surely limited the incentive to pursue artistic and literary ventures, there were internal causes for the decline of active LWCS involvement in the arts: the organization was undercapitalized (it had no endowment), it lacked the social and economic patronage made available to black artists in Manhattan, and it relied on a small group of charismatic women, three of whom died before the dual agenda could be fully realized. However, their most formidable foe was the stock market crash of 1929 and the crisis that followed on its heels. The 1920s were peak years for the New Negro Renaissance, when black authors saw their work published and widely read, and received mainstream acclaim, but the Depression swept away the dreams the LWCS and other small institutions had for the future.

Appreciation for Harlem Renaissance Literature

During their halcyon years the members of the LWCS continued to sponsor many lectures. At the October 24, 1918, league meeting it was announced that W. E. B. Du Bois, having just returned from Europe, was scheduled to speak on April 21, 1919, at the Tremont Temple: it was "a splendid opportunity" to invite him over, one member said, according to the minutes.[55] Maria Baldwin expressed her admiration for Du Bois and recommended that members purchase copies of his *Darkwater: Voices from within the Veil*, in which he called for urgent social, political, and economic reform.[56] Now that significant black-authored works were being published the LWCS started a lending library. George W. Forbes, a librarian at the West End Branch of the Boston Public Library, former coeditor of the Boston *Guardian*, and husband to a league member, used his influence with the War Service to help the league acquire a small collection of books and encyclopedias.[57] They used the proceeds from the Negro Achievement exhibition to add new books to their shelves. This episode illustrates that the cultural entrepreneurs at the LWCS who desired to consolidate a black cultural legacy in the form of recently published books were looking to the future. Like other small private clubs they were short on funds but embarked nevertheless on an ambitious project: the acquisition of books and the staffing of their own library.

A great setback for the LWCS occurred on January 9, 1922, when Maria Baldwin collapsed and died after delivering a speech at the Copley Plaza Hotel. To memorialize their distinguished leader, on December 28, 1923, the LWCS officially dedicated the Maria Baldwin "Memorial Room" at their headquarters. By collecting and discussing works written by African American writers the women honored Baldwin's memory and perpetuated the cultural practices she had promoted. There is no better proof that the LWCS had expanded its identity from one that was originally charitable in nature to one that also emphasized the intrinsic value of cultural endeavors. The establishment of a private library was the capstone of their work.

If not for the documents preserved by the LWCS we would know very little about the history and inner workings of a women's association that merged its social programming with the evolving, distinctively black cultural scene in the city of Boston. From the self-conscious acquisition of property near status markers such as Symphony Hall to the carving out of proprietary spaces from which no one could exclude them, league members transformed the cultural landscape of Boston's South End. Their initiatives constituted an act of resistance at a time when de facto segregation limited the access of blacks to cultural resources. The artistic activities of the LWCS, which centered on the appreciation and production of music, art, literature, and intellectual discourse, flourished for more than a decade, from 1918 to 1930.

The activism of a female Talented Tenth and the presence of a critical mass of creative artists were key to the emergence of a cultural renascence in black Boston. The LWCS, consciously or not, was a participant in the arduous struggle to exhibit and nurture art in a ruthlessly capitalistic society. The women shouldered the arduous task of exhibiting black artistry to audiences that, when not hostile, were unaware of their very presence.

Simultaneously insiders and outsiders, privileged by their socioeconomic status but marginalized by racial discrimination, Boston's elite black women of the interwar period established aesthetic and organizational practices oriented toward black cultural validation. Although it did not have the power to erase the color line, the LWCS certainly challenged its existence. The synthesis accomplished by the league set a high bar for Bostonian elites, whether black or white, working to bridge cultural and racial boundaries. As women steeped in the uplift ideologies developed by the black women's club movement and sustained by Christian faith, they used their influence to translate their aesthetic tastes into a strategy that challenged the cultural boundaries of their era.

As other venues became more welcoming to blacks the LWCS's facilities became less essential to theatre, musical, and other cultural groups.[58] Furthermore, Maud Cuney Hare, with league support and her own entrepreneurial savvy, managed to establish an arts center on Huntington Avenue and opened doors to venues that hitherto had been unavailable to black cultural leaders.

Inevitably, the influence of the LWCS waned along with that of the upper class itself. But the impressive cultural entrepreneurship detailed in this chapter illustrates the fact that black women played an outsized role in fostering a lively cultural scene just as the New Negro movement was being launched in New York. Since it was women who determined distinction and good taste, it is fair to say that the revitalization of black cultural life was largely a female-engendered phenomenon. If it had not been for the Great War, would the Boston black women's clubs have come into existence? And if they had not existed, might there have been no Boston renascence at all?

4

Black Faces on the White Stage

Space and Race, 1925–1930

> It was Mrs. Hare's dream to fulfill—to let people know that there was black talent, and not only dancers and singers, but people who could create beauty in literature and in the dance and in drama.
>
> —Thelma Thornton, Allied Arts Players

In the aftermath of World War I, black Bostonians undertook a variety of cultural projects, some of them attributable to lone artists like Roland Hayes, Lois Mailou Jones, and Allan Rohan Crite. In 1921, Hayes (1887–1977), a lyric tenor, gave a command performance before the king and queen of England at Buckingham Palace, receiving acclaim in Europe before gaining recognition in his own country. Hayes's historic performance on November 16, 1923, at Boston's Symphony Hall under the direction of Pierre Monteux was "probably the first time a Negro sang serious music with a major U.S. orchestra."[1] Not long afterward, Crite (1910–2007) and Jones (1905–98), both trained at the Museum of Fine Arts School, embarked on distinctive careers as painters. Hayes, like Crite and Jones, drew steadfast support from his family, although none was wealthy. Hayes's mother, who had moved to Boston from rural Georgia to be with her son, took in laundry to pay her son's and her own expenses. Crite's mother, Annamae, nurtured Allan's talent with classes at the Museum of Fine Arts, and Jones named her mother as her greatest mentor, patron, and champion.[2]

By and large, however, few aspiring artists could afford to go it alone, and as a result, most cultural projects of the era were the fruit of group collaboration.[3] Black cultural leaders who contended with the complexities of the color line and its spatial dimensions relied on intra-community support and, specifically, on leading black women's clubs. It was precisely this collaboration, strategic planning, and cultural capital that in the mid- to late 1920s enabled the rise of black Boston's "little theatre" movement, led by Maud Cuney Hare.[4] Arts organizers like Hare strategically located their headquarters in the South End, the square mile that had replaced Beacon Hill as the hub of black community life. Of course smaller numbers of African Americans lived in other areas of the city and in surrounding towns, but the demographic clustering of African Americans in the South End proved expedient when it came to recruiting talent and attracting audiences.

Beginning in the mid-1920s and, remarkably, throughout the Great Depression, theatre loomed large on the cultural scene, perhaps more so than any other art form. Hare, a sophisticated musician who was unwavering in her commitment to encourage musical culture in the black community, had assessed the music education available to black children and young adults, concluding that it was inadequate at every level. Her ultimate goal was to win a place for her protégés on the white-dominated stage and attract integrated audiences to their performances. Moreover, her story encapsulates the themes of race, place, and the culture of politics as they played out between the two World Wars. Had it not been for Hare, there would likely have been no little theatre movement in black Boston.

The 1920s saw the spread of new media such as radio, phonographs, and moving pictures. These technological advances placed an extra burden on cultural leaders, who needed to redouble their efforts to attract audiences. Fortunately, live performances still held great appeal for many who were eager to set aside their daily concerns for a few hours of diversion at a modest price. In an age predating electronic communication and social networking, communication took place through encounters, both formal and informal, in settings that ranged from churches and private homes to fraternal clubs and barbershops. These networks were well developed in the cohesive black community of the day. Finding little welcome at the most desirable performance venues, resourceful cultural leaders developed spaces of their own for their startup ventures. In so doing they circumvented racial barriers and created alternate spaces of sociability for mixed-race audiences. Black artistic directors focused on universal themes in the plays and concerts they promoted, raising the awareness of white patrons to their presence in the city. Yet they placed an emphasis on black agency, retaining firm control over every aspect of their productions, from capitalization to artistic design.

The backdrop to these activities was a city whose future seemed bright and its economy healthy. The main streets of the South End bustled with foot traffic as people made their way to church, work places, shops, or one another's homes and porches. Tremont Street, which served as something of a dividing line between the South End to the north and Roxbury to the south, was lined with black-owned businesses: taverns, pharmacies, and southern-style restaurants. William Monroe Trotter, the legendary editor of the weekly Boston *Guardian*, could be seen "pacing the streets, wearing his trademark derby hat and long black coat, his pockets bulging with newspapers," sometimes with his wife, Geraldine, at his side.[5] One of the more atmospheric spots was Slade's, an eatery founded by Remmer Slade, a Virginian who brought with him a winning recipe for barbecue sauce. From the corner of Warrick and Hammond Streets, just south of Tremont, "the scent of good chicken dinners waft[ed] down the block and passersby saw Slade's chefs standing at rotisseries in the front window."[6] Boston had a black-owned bank, the Eureka Co-Operative Bank, and four hotels owned and operated by blacks: Young's, the Pitts, the Carlton, and the Melbourne.[7]

Brothers Silas F. ("Shag") and Balcom S. ("Bal") Taylor, registered pharmacists, were well-known local figures. Their drugstore, the Lincoln Pharmacy on Tremont Street, was a lively meeting place for political debate. At a time when the black community could exert influence but rarely attained elected office in City Hall or the State House, Shag Taylor was a conduit for voicing the concerns of black neighborhoods. During Prohibition spirits could be purchased at the Taylor brothers' pharmacy after hours. Shag was often charged but never convicted for liquor law violations.[8]

Another important community center, the Richard Earle Pioneer Club, established by black train porter Richard Earle, was a haven for black railway workers. The club provided Pullman porters, dining car waiters, and chefs with sleeping quarters, meals, a place to relax, and a space for their musical quartets to play during their layovers in Boston.[9] The red brick, three-story building, located on an alley off Tremont Street, was a late night hangout for both blacks and whites, with impromptu jam sessions and live music featuring famous musicians who came by after their shows in Boston.[10] In fact, the popular music scene developed parallel to the rise of little theatre. From about 1925 through 1933, George Tynes led what was probably the city's first black big band to record with a major label.[11] Eddy Deas, a drummer and vocalist who began his career with Tynes, started his own band, the Boston Brownies Orchestra, which was well known from the late 1920s through 1934.[12]

A wave of migration from the South introduced formerly insular black cultures to each other: Virginians, Alabamians, Texans, and Georgians brought their southern drawls and folkways, while West Indians brought clipped British colonial accents, high teas, and cricket matches. The "Roaring Twenties" women, newly empowered to vote, exchanged Victorian high necks for sleeveless flapper dresses with hemlines below the knee. Black and white women alike styled their hair in emulation of screen and stage idols and could be seen strolling down the streets amid the buzz of commercial activity. Dorothy West, who in 1948 would publish her acclaimed novel *The Living Is Easy*, deeply admired white dancers Irene and Vernon Castle for their artistry but also for their courage in choosing black orchestras as accompanists.[13] The Castles traveled with James Reese Europe's Society Orchestra and issued records of his music at a time when close interracial contact was frowned upon. On the dark side of the decade stood fierce anti-immigrant sentiment, a resurgent Ku Klux Klan, racial violence, rumblings of anticommunist agitation, and crackdowns on homosexuals.

Few studies have focused on the tenor and texture of African American life in 1920s Boston, but the absence of writing on the rise of black theatre is particularly noticeable. Apart from cultural consumption—attendance at cultural events, both mainstream and black—black Bostonians were active producers, as I discovered by interviewing knowledgeable elders and family members, from documents and photographs entrusted to me, and from archival sources.[14] Public performance, a major avenue of self-expression for black Bostonians, surged in the late 1920s, but its antecedents lay in the previous century. In 1879, for example, the Hopkins Family Colored Troubadours drew white and Negro spectators alike to their outdoor performances of "Slaves' Escape; or, The Underground Railroad."[15] An admiring *Boston Herald* review described Pauline Elizabeth Hopkins as "a young colored lady of this city, who has written several other dramatic pieces of merit, and who has orders for a number more that will be produced during the coming season."[16] But black performance art in Boston dates back even earlier, to William Wells Brown, the noted abolitionist, historian, and writer who in 1858 wrote *The Escape; or, A Leap for Freedom*.[17] Consciously or not, the black Bostonians of the 1920s and 1930s would privilege this specific genre and establish its primacy at the core of their cultural production.

The black theatre of the 1920s was in no way a sequel to Brown's lively satires or the Hopkins Troubadours' suspense-filled enactments of narrow escapes from bondage. Instead, Maud Cuney Hare, Ralf Coleman, and James Henderson, their twentieth-century successors, founded their own companies to stage plays with themes and techniques that would appeal to forward-looking audiences. Unfortunately, the "little theatres" of black Boston have been forgotten, remembered only by dwindling numbers of their contemporaries and descendants. My own awareness of these pioneering groups initially came from reading a memoir by Allan Rohan Crite. Crite, who would become renowned for his paintings of Lower Roxbury and South End scenes, described the Allied Arts Players, the first black theatre group established in twentieth-century Boston, founded by Maud Hare, as "one of the amateur groups that were dealing with the cultural heritage of [b]lack people."[18] Crite was a set designer and an occasional bit-part actor in some of Hare's plays.

Maud Cuney Hare and Female Agency in 1920s Boston

Cuney (later Hare, after her 1904 marriage) was a striking sixteen-year-old when she first arrived in Boston to enroll in the New England Conservatory of Music.[19] A frequently reproduced photograph of the young woman from Galveston, Texas, shows her standing proudly in the splendid attire she used for her lecture-concerts.[20] At the conservatory she specialized in the pianoforte, an instrument not known for its ease of use, as well as piano. She emerged as a scholar-performer who would devote the next twenty years to research on black music. Cuney became the first to bring the Creole songs of New Orleans to the attention of musicologists and cultivated urban audiences, and her reviews appeared in major musicological journals as well as in Boston's *Christian Science Monitor*, a highly respected weekly. These were remarkable feats for a black person of her time, let alone a woman. She joined forces with black Nova Scotian baritone and pianist William Richardson, giving illustrated lectures across the Northeast with Richardson as her accompanist. From 1905 through the early 1920s, the duo traveled as far west as Ohio as well as in New England and New York. Classical European pieces and music from the black diaspora were fixtures of the Hare and Richardson repertoire. One of their remarkable concerts was held at the elegant Copley Plaza Hotel, frequented by the cream of the white elite of Boston.[21]

A Sudden Change of Course

In 1925, Hare sidelined her musical pursuits to try her hand at theatre production, a field in which she had no prior experience. But her appreciation for the theatre ran deep—as a child she had often traveled with her family to attend shows in Boston. When Hare recruited more than twenty young black Bostonians to form the Allied Arts Players, she was reviving a field that had lain fallow since the days of the Hopkins Family Colored Troubadours.

Why, after some twenty years of accomplished lecture and concerts, did this successful musician suddenly redirect her energy toward theatre production? Most illuminating in this regard is her correspondence with W. E. B. Du Bois. Written between 1925 and 1930, their letters, never published, offer a glimpse of Hare's day-to-day artistic concerns.[22] The interchanges contained therein reveal the organizational dynamics behind Hare's efforts to establish an arts center while also allowing us to trace the genesis of her involvement in black theatre. The evidence suggests that Du Bois's famous proclamations on theatre and his own incursions into stage production in Harlem were catalytic: they likely prompted Hare to organize a group of her own on Boston turf. Yet it was not Du Bois's influence alone that set Hare on this particular path. First of all, the Harlem Renaissance was in full swing.[23] She was already well informed about the groundbreaking innovations introduced in Russia, where the stage was a hotbed of experimentation in stage design; Ireland, where the folk play reigned supreme; and the mainstream little theatre movement in the United States.[24] But Du Bois was an enabling confidant and advisor even though his end of the correspondence was less expressive than Hare's—his letters were terse and typed by a secretary, while Hare's were handwritten. The preservation of their correspondence makes it possible to uncover the story of Hare's pioneering theatre project. Additionally, it enables us to trace evolving notions of the New Negro era, itself a nexus of influences that extended beyond the geography of uptown Manhattan.

Maud Cuney Hare and W. E. B. Du Bois: "Much More than Friends"

The relationship between Cuney and Du Bois, who was six years Cuney's senior, began in the fall of 1890, at the start of her first semester at the New England Conservatory of Music.[25] Du Bois, a graduate student at nearby Harvard University, was well acquainted, at least by reputation, with Maud's father, Norris Wright Cuney (1846–97), who led the Texas Republican Party during Reconstruction and after. The most powerful African American leader in nineteenth-century Texas, Cuney was at the zenith of his political career when his daughter entered the conservatory. At the time Beacon Hill was still the hub of Boston's black community and Josephine St. Pierre Ruffin, the prominent editor of the monthly *Women's Era*, presided over regular gatherings of black intellectuals at her Charles Street home.

Du Bois was a Ph.D. candidate in history "and what would have been Sociology if Harvard had yet recognized such a field."[26] In one of his autobiographies, Du Bois described the weekly gatherings held by Ruffin, the widow of the eminent Judge George Ruffin, "and her beautiful daughter 'Birdie' [Florida]." Du Bois was a promising young intellectual who had yet to publish *The Souls of Black Folks* in 1903.[27] At these soirées, the "high and mighty freeborn families [of Boston]—Grimkés, Pindells, Trotters and others"—spent "literary evenings salted with the poetry of Browning (whose antecedents were widely believed to be 'mixed') and musicales featuring Brahms or the Chevalier de St. George (about whose mixed antecedents there was no question)."[28] At the Charles Street soirées, as Du Bois recalled, he encountered "many educated and well-to-do folks, many young people studying or planning to study, many charming young women," all of whom "met and ate, danced and argued and planned a new world."[29] He was particularly captivated by Maud Cuney, whom he would later describe as a "tall imperious brunette, with gold-bronze skin, brilliant eyes and coils of black hair. . . . She reigned in Colored Boston, with me among the hosts of young men bowing before her throne."[30] Maud was one of only two black students at the conservatory—the other was Florida L. Desverney (or Des Verney) of Savannah, Georgia. The two women settled into the school dormitory, which was located in the same building where classes were held.[31] But one month into the semester the parents of Cuney and Desverney received a letter stating that because the conservatory had "a large number of pupils who [were] affected by race prejudices," the girls would need to "make their home with friends outside."[32]

Maud's father would not cooperate with the conservatory and neither would Maud.[33] The elder Cuney fired off a letter as elegant as it was indignant, invoking the great Bostonians who had struggled ceaselessly in the cause of Abolition: "You request my cooperation in surrendering to the demands of prejudice, by withdrawing my daughter; I cannot help you. Ask Massachusetts; ask her mighty dead; ask her living sons and daughters. They will co-operate with you, if you cannot solve the problem, and render your Institution illustrious throughout all ages."[34] Desverney withdrew from the conservatory, continuing to study with her teachers privately.[35]

Maud Cuney proceeded to seek the support of black students studying at nearby universities. Du Bois was among those who "rushed to her defense" when the conservatory "tried to 'jim-crow' her in the dormitory."[36] The Colored National League threatened to have the school closed.[37] The Cuneys and their allies prevailed, so Maud remained in the dormitory for the rest of the school year despite being "subjected to" what she called "many petty indignities" of a sort we can only imagine.[38] She did not return to the conservatory the following year. Instead, like Desverney, she resumed her studies with private teachers.[39]

For his part, Du Bois recalled, "I fell deeply in love with her and we were engaged."[40] The two had in common that they were born during the dark days of Reconstruction and came from families with mixed racial heritage. Cuney's family tree included two white grandfathers who had families with slaves on their plantations. In this regard she was positioned more closely to the mainstream race than was Du Bois, with his remote Dutch, French Huguenot, and Bantu ancestry but, he insisted, "thank God! no 'Anglo-Saxon.'"[41] This difference in racial ancestry is arguably a crucial one: it could account for Cuney's assiduous pursuit of a career that straddled both worlds, in contrast with Du Bois's turn toward separatism and a permanent departure from the United States, his country of birth. But meanwhile, Du Bois "found happiness with Maud in the Boston

African-American community, release from the pressures and challenge to seek more than marginal social presence in white Cambridge."[42]

Maud and "Du," as she called him in their correspondence, playing on the familiar form of "you" in German, never married. In 1892, Du Bois was awarded a fellowship that funded his advanced studies in Germany. The fortunate young scholar accounted for their parting in vague terms, saying that he had "study plans to hold [him] back" from his "serious dreams of love and marriage" as well as other "curious reasons" for not marrying. Historian David Levering Lewis suggests that Du Bois sacrificed his relationship with Cuney for the sake of his career: "That he would also be leaving Maud Cuney behind if the fund recognized his claim, was the bittersweet price of destiny."[43] Elsewhere Du Bois claimed that he would not marry a woman whose face did not show her African heritage. Cuney was fair-skinned, with European features—to one of her young black protégées she "looked Egyptian."[44] Du Bois omits mention of the emotional dynamics surrounding the separation, but he recalled that when in 1892 he embarked on his *Lehrejahre* in Germany, "Maud Cuney stood on the top rung of happiness and accomplishment, with music dripping from her fingers."[45] The two remained friends. Over the next four decades, Maud endured both misfortunes and triumphs and shared them with Du Bois through their correspondence, which was interrupted only by her death.

A careful examination of the Hare–Du Bois correspondence raises questions about the precise nature of their relationship. In his biography, Lewis writes that "[Maud Cuney] and Du Bois would remain much more than friends through the years of her companionable marriage to a well-connected black Bostonian." In their correspondence no particular terms of endearment are in evidence. When I contacted Lewis to clarify the nature of the Hare–Du Bois connection he responded that the relationship was indeed an intimate one.[46] Whatever the private nature of Hare's relationship with Du Bois, the two were in constant communication to the end, and Du Bois proved to be an important influence on the direction of her career.

Interlude: Texas, Chicago, and a Return to Boston

Around 1897—the exact date is difficult to ascertain—Maud Cuney left Boston, as Du Bois had done five years earlier. Perhaps (and this is likely) she had been unable to find employment at a rank befitting her credentials. In any case, she took a position as musical director at the Deaf, Dumb, and Blind Institute for Colored Youths in Austin, Texas. Perhaps the greatest incentive to return to Texas was to be close to her beloved father during what would be the last year of his life.[47] Norris Wright Cuney was Maud's role model: he had worked tirelessly for black education and equal opportunity. She was at her father's bedside when he died in 1897.[48]

Maud hoped to launch a career as a concert artist, but white supremacy was on the rise in the former Confederacy. Hostility to black aspirations was pervasive. Her teacher Edmund Ludwig scheduled a piano concert for her at the Austin Opera House, but the authorities refused to seat blacks and whites together. Cuney canceled her contract with the Opera House, moving the performance to the institution where she taught and garnered lavish reviews, thereby outmaneuvering the racists.[49] But the price of victory was the loss of the wider public exposure that would have resulted from an appearance at the Opera House. This incident would have made it crystal clear to Cuney that her chances for a successful career as a professional musician in Texas were nil.

After her father's death Cuney married Dr. J. Frank McKinley, a physician whom Du Bois described as being "quite as old as her father."[50] It was a decision made in haste—she was in mourning and may have perceived McKinley as a father figure. McKinley, for his part, would have been eager to acquire a wife of Cuney's prestigious lineage and beauty—a trophy wife. After the couple moved to Chicago, where Maud worked at a black social agency, she discovered—to her horror—that McKinley "wanted as little as possible to be bracketed with the Colored world." Both he and Maud were fair-skinned and could pass as "Spanish-Americans," and McKinley exploited this happenstance to hide their racial identity. But Maud refused to pass for white, even involuntarily.

Not so Dr. McKinley. When in 1900 Maud gave birth to their daughter, Vera, McKinley registered the baby's race as "white."[51] Maud never disclosed this very personal information in writing, but after her death Du Bois revealed that leaving her husband "to his devices," Maud moved to Texas with her young daughter.[52] Removing the child from Illinois was ill-advised, as it led to her losing custody in court. After years of filing lawsuits, she scored a partial victory and won partial custody: three months per year in the summer. Hare shared her jubilation over this news with Du

Bois.[53] But her joy was short-lived, for McKinley remarried and regained full custody.[54]

Once divorced from McKinley, Maud left for Boston and never returned to Chicago. According to Florida Ruffin Ridley, her close friend and fellow member of the League of Women for Community Service, Cuney, "from the first, made herself a part of Boston life."[55] On August 10, 1904, Maud married William Parker Hare, who was employed by the U.S. Postal Service. At the time marriage conferred middle-class status on women, and the title "Mrs." was a mark of respectability. As a married woman Maud also stood a better chance at regaining child custody than as a divorcée.

William Hare's reliable salary, his support for his wife's nascent career, and his pension allowed Maud to freely pursue her intellectual and musical interests. Her newfound security also provided an opportunity for her to challenge the color line, as she had done at the New England Conservatory. The Hares purchased a home at 43 Sheridan Street in Jamaica Plain, a predominantly white section of Boston.[56] Not content with this successful crossing of the color line, Maud set her sights on buying a lot in nearby Squantum (part of the city of Quincy) where she could build a small home studio. This she achieved, over the objections of the neighbors.[57] On July 18, 1930, she wrote to Du Bois,

> My Dear "Du"—It really looks now as if I shall have a little Studio Home at Squantum by Fall, so I will get some rest in September. The house would have been up by August first had not the color question been rampant. I unwittingly disposed of my first lot, and then came the fun—I partly owned three other lots within 3 weeks time. "Murder" was out before the last papers were signed, but just as fast as one cut up on my hands, I tried another. I made up my mind that that was the section I wanted to live in and laughable the whole matter was. Each succeeding lot was better than the first and this one is the prettiest of all, and right in the midst of pretty cottages—all the year round home owners. So! When they wake up, they will wish they had allowed me to land in the first place where there were a few vacant lots to separate us. I have rights too, to the private bathing beach. I was quite unprepared for such an outcry. I hope you have a happy Summer. Sincerely, Maud.[58]

In 1908, a telegram from Chicago brought the news that Hare's daughter, Vera, had died. Hare communicated the sad news to Du Bois, who also endured the death of his first child—in the spring of 1899, Du Bois's two-year-old son, Burghardt, had died of diphtheria. Hare surely sought consolation from religion—she and William Hare had joined the Christian Science Church. Submerging her grief in work, Hare set about writing a biography of her father, which would finally be published in 1913, and other books. In 1918, she would publish *The Message of the Trees*, an edited anthology of poems, which bore the dedication "To My Little Daughter Vera, 1900–1908." Surprisingly, the anthology includes only one black poet, Paul Laurence Dunbar, a favorite of both whites and blacks at the time.[59] Hare's failure to include more African American poets is difficult to reconcile with the fierce race pride she expressed in all her other publications. It is possible that Maud had some ambivalence about her dual identity as an African American who was often perceived as a white woman and sometimes "passed" involuntarily. In her biography of her father, the sole printed source of information about Maud's early life and education, Hare recounts "an amusing" incident in which she corrected a woman who misidentified her as Spanish—"But you and your father must be Spanish! No? Then Creole—surely you can not be colored."[60]

Hare also launched a successful program of lecture-performances with William H. Richardson. In 1919, Hare and Richardson, a baritone, presented a concert-lecture at the Boston Public Library, the first by a musician of color in the library's series. Hare surely took great satisfaction in breaching another color line.[61] Another successful event was an October 24, 1924, performance at the Brooklyn Academy of Music in New York, which was "jammed to capacity."[62] Following this and other positive receptions, Hare and Richardson expanded their circuit in academic and musical circles, appearing in such cities as New Haven and Cleveland.

These individualistic pursuits occupied Hare well into the New Negro era that would transform African American consciousness and set its artistic expressions before the world. Hare was well aware of these stirrings—she reviewed Alain Locke's *The New Negro* for the *Christian Science Monitor*, but oddly enough, with little enthusiasm. However, she did agree with Locke that it was time to put a stop to "liberal minds peer[ing] with sympathetic curiosity into the darkened Ghetto of a segregated race life."[63] It was for African Americans, not European Americans, to define themselves and make their voices heard across the nation, Hare insisted vehemently.

The Continuing Influence of W. E. B. Du Bois

After returning from Europe Du Bois taught history, sociology, and economics at Atlanta University, where he met and married Nina Gomer, a student, and embarked on a peripatetic career as a professor and civil rights crusader. He had established his literary credentials in 1903 with the publication of *The Souls of Black Folks*.[64] In 1909, he cofounded the National Association for the Advancement of Colored People (NAACP) and became the founding editor of the *Crisis*. In his editorial capacity Du Bois made public his views on many subjects, among them the function of black theatre. Drama, he declared, could serve as an instrument to "assail the ears of the nation."[65] He also spearheaded the *Crisis*-sponsored literary contests in the categories of poetry, fiction, nonfiction, and—most significantly for Hare—drama, where entries were required to deal with some aspect of Negro history or the black experience.

In January 1924, Hare informed Du Bois that she was writing a play called *Antar of Araby* for the *Crisis* contest. A year later it was complete, and by February 23, 1925, the script was in the mail. "My Dear Du," she wrote, "Will you please read my play, a diamond in the rough, and tell me when I come through New York March 4–5 if you think it worth submitting to the *Crisis*. If so, I shall have a stenographer copy it neatly."[66] No response is included in the archived correspondence, but Hare certainly would have been disappointed if Du Bois failed to lend her encouragement. Meanwhile, the drama prize for that year went to two women, one from Missouri and another from Arkansas.

On October 19, Hare wrote that she had been "miserably ill for six months, hospitalized with 'a breakdown.'" Might Du Bois have given *Antar* a negative review when he met Maud in New York that March? If so, the disappointment could have precipitated her health crisis. But the resilient Hare would move forward with the play, with or without Du Bois's blessing. "The young folks" of the Allied Arts Centre had encouraged her, she wrote pointedly, and she would "attempt" to stage her play in December 1925.[67]

Antar of Araby: "Black in Face and Fair in Deeds"

Antar came on the heels of a series of successful one-act plays and would earn Hare recognition from black intellectuals far beyond Boston.[68] Willis

Richardson, the distinguished author of *The Chip Woman's Fortune,* the first musical production by an African American on Broadway, publicly recognized Hare as "one of the leading spirits in the Allied Arts Theater Group which mothers the Negro drama in the New England capital."[69] Richardson's use of the word "mother" as a verb might be construed as belittlement, but it captures the importance of Hare's generative role. Her initiative was personal and proprietary, unlike some of the other efforts of the time. As an ensemble, the Allied Arts Players would become the most influential small black theatre group launched in Boston, or for that matter in New England during the 1920s.

The premiere of Hare's four-act *Antar* took place on December 14, 1925, at the Fine Arts Theatre on Norway Street, adjacent to the massive Symphony Hall building.[70] Until then, few plays portraying blacks in a dignified light had graced the Boston stage. Only a few theatres, including the Gaiety on Washington Street in Chinatown and the Casino in Scollay Square in downtown Boston, occasionally featured black shows, some with integrated casts, but these were mostly burlesques featuring popular dances, trendy music, broad comedy, and musical revues with black casts, which often propagated crude racial stereotypes.[71] Du Bois called such popular musical comedies "decadent stories about clowning people."[72] A serious, all-black play was a rarity.

For this first performance of *Antar* Hare assembled a cast of thirty actors, among them Charles Burroughs, a New York associate of Du Bois, who took the leading role, and Bernice Martin, another New Yorker, who played the female lead.[73] Almost all the other cast members were black Bostonians, including Benjamin (1904–96), Henry (1906–96), and Lorenzo Quarles (1907–99), the sons of a subway porter who went on to distinguished careers. Benjamin would become a distinguished historian, Henry would rise to the ranks of Boston's most prominent black attorneys, and Lorenzo became the stage manager for director Ralf Coleman in the Federal Theatre Project (1935–39).[74] Other native-born Bostonians participated as well: Lois Mailou Jones, then a fledgling painter, designed the costumes. Mildred Davenport, a future dancer in Broadway musicals during the 1930s, was also part of the production.[75]

For *Antar* Hare drew on the talent of men and women who, like herself, had moved to Boston, drawn in by its cultural life. Estelle Ancrum Foster, a North Carolinian who founded the Ancrum School of Music in the

Antar of Araby, by Maud Cuney Hare. Courtesy Thelma Thornton Wynn.

South End, was her pianist, and Hare's stage designer was Meta Warrick Fuller. Finally, Hare cast Eugene Gordon (1890–1974), a Florida-born journalist, in the role of the Arabian King.[76] Fuller, who sculpted the race-conscious *Ethiopia Awakening* and the politically charged *Mary Turner: A Silent Protest against Mob Violence*, is also known to have executed a small bust of Maud Cuney Hare. The two were kindred spirits, black women who forged their own careers despite prevailing notions of domesticity. In mounting this ambitious, large-scale production, Hare was investing her resources and her hopes, but also sacrificing her chances for a career as a concert pianist.

The Arabian hero recreated in Hare's play was inspired by fifth-century poet-warrior Antar(ah) ibn Shaddad, or Shedad. His saga, well known in Arabian popular culture, was introduced to Europe in the early nineteenth century and celebrated in a symphony by Nikolai Rimsky-Korsakov, as Hare explained in an article she published in the *Crisis*. Hare wrote that she was drawn to Antar for two reasons: The first was that his tribe "cultivated oratory and excelled in poetry" and "recognized a kinship between poetry and music." The other was more political—Antar was the biracial son of an Ethiopian woman kidnapped and enslaved by an Arabian chief. Antar's victories on the battlefield and his poetic gifts freed him from slavery.[77] When Westerners first encountered the Antar epic in the nineteenth century, "they swooned, proclaiming it the Arabic *Iliad*."[78] This story held deep personal meaning for Hare, whose beloved father was the biracial son of an enslaved woman and a white plantation owner (who saw to it that his children were well educated).

Based on the stage directions, it may be inferred that Hare's play was a magnificent spectacle. The set was an idyllic desert oasis that served as the backdrop to Antar's story of enslavement. Antar is seen standing guard in front of the royal palace while the story of his mother's capture, sugarcoated to suppress any intimations of rape, unfolds. Antar's burning desire to gain freedom and full recognition of his royal blood and the rejection of his entreaties drives the action. When Antar proves his superiority by fighting off an army of attackers, his grandfather the king, and Prince Shedad, his father, grant him "the rank and dignity of an Arab."[79] Prince Shedad also allows Antar to marry the princess (never mind that they are half-brother and half-sister).

Hare's script, extremely stilted and formulaic to contemporary ears, focuses on the issue of race in a way that makes the play suitable for high school and college audiences—that is, Hare's aim was pedagogical, to teach while entertaining with spectacular visuals and music. The narrator describes Antar, the "son of the black-faced Zebeeba, who met the foe and won his love at point of spear." Hare notes that Antar becomes the target of racial taunts: "Black skin, thou lookest vastly miserable indeed." Hare divides her characters schematically into two groups: the "prejudiced" and those who are "without prejudice" but "to some extent appreciative of talent." The king's embrace of Antar at the play's end may be viewed as a metaphor for the acceptance of biracial children. Hare's stage directions accentuate this idea by specifying that the actor "must be of dark complexion." Through Antar, Hare alludes to those who, like her father, were descendants of slaves but through successful careers rose to political power.[80]

Also embedded in the play is a defense of blackness on aesthetic grounds: black is the color of fragrant ambergris, the precious substance from tropical seas that is used to make exquisite perfumes.[81] Blackness is also seen as the natural complement of the presumably white-skinned princess, the darkness of whose hair reflects the complexion of her African-descended suitor. Hare's interest in biracial figures led her to identify another Middle Eastern figure, the musician Mabed, the singer of the hero's praises and scribe of the court. Elaborating on the commonalities of Antar and Mabed, Hare writes that one was a poet of humble birth and the other a singer: "Mabed, the date of whose birth is wanting, was born a slave, the *son of a Negro father and he, himself a mulatto.*" Both men "won their freedom because of their marked superiority and extraordinary gifts."[82] Similarly, many black leaders of Hare's time believed that through their attainments, as much in the arts and literature as in politics, African Americans could be agents of nonviolent social change. Hare herself should be viewed as part of a female Talented Tenth.

Other outstanding black figures in this production were Hare's friends Montague Ring, the Afro-British female composer, who dedicated her *Four Moorish Pictures* to Hare;[83] Clarence Cameron ("Carlo") White, who wrote the overture; and William Richardson, Hare's concert partner, who was the principal singer. As shown above, a professional photographer of the era captured the visual richness of the spectacle, enhanced by the main characters' long embroidered robes and elaborate headdresses, Antar's dark complexion, and the contrasting lighter skin of the princess.

Hare agreed with James Weldon Johnson, the poet, composer, and anthologist, who contended (perhaps naively) that "the final measure of the greatness of all people is the amount and standard of the literature and art they have produced." Going out on a limb, Johnson argued that "no people that has produced great literature and art has even been looked upon by the world as distinctly inferior."[84] But Hare, ever the educator, also was cognizant of the budget constraints of the black communities where the play would be performed, and wisely specified that if "a gilded chair be unavailable for the king's seat," boxes covered with rugs could serve as props. "Imitation jewels," she added, were meant only to give "an impression of wealth and magnificence." In her own recital performances Hare wore elaborate costumes, headdresses, and long, beaded earrings, as seen in surviving photographs.[85]

Hare's emphasis on message as well as spectacle—ornate costumes, evocative music and dance—appealed to her racially integrated and politically progressive audience, many of whom were steeped in abolitionist memories. Hare's approach to the breaking of the color line was not through oratory or protest but through a shared affinity for high culture. Black spectators who knew that the terms "Egypt" and "Ethiopia" were code for black nationalism would have been in even a better position than whites to grasp the deeper meaning of the play.[86] Writing to Du Bois, Hare celebrated a "wholly positive" critical reception and a "flattering" success on May 15, 1928, opening night of the second production of *Antar:* "A full house—not only colored spectators—but an appreciative audience drawn from Boston's most cultured circles" was in attendance.[87] The *Boston Traveler* reviewer wrote admiringly that *Antar of Araby* "would be a difficult achievement [even] for professional players," and lavished praise on Thelma Thornton in her role as the princess, and Ralf Coleman, who played the king. Coleman would soon part ways with Hare to establish his own performing group.[88]

Du Bois and the Doctrine of a "Real Negro" Theatre

In the June 1926 issue of the *Crisis,* Du Bois published his definition of "a real Negro theatre," which would address "a Negro audience desiring to see its own life depicted by its own writers and actors." His prescription contained the famous phrase "About, By, For, and Near us."[89] Plays were to be "written by blacks and deal honestly with black life." The term "edutainment," coined by scholar Remi Omodele, aptly describes Du Bois's brand of engagé theatre, exemplified by Krigwa, the little theatre group he founded at the 135th Street Branch of the New York Public Library.[90] Hare, however, must have realized the Du Bois model was not feasible in Boston, a city with an exceedingly small black population, limited resources, and no institution that would extend a welcome like that of the New York Public Library.

The Debut of the Allied Arts Centre

In December 1926, Hare shared with Du Bois an idea she had for promoting black artistry in Boston: "I am hoping to have an opportunity to talk with you about a project which is close to my heart. . . . I want a Music School Centre that will embrace an experimental children's Little Theatre."[91] In focusing her attention on the needs of black children Hare was reaffirming the educational mission she had embraced soon after her graduation from the New England Conservatory. In a letter to Henry Gilbert (1868–1930), a composer and proponent of musical nationalism who would join her board of directors, Hare wrote that her Music School Centre "[would] welcome talented children of any race, station or creed and at the same time offer *opportunity to colored children who are now proscribed against and are shut out* from the advantages that a Music settlement offers to those who can't afford to pay professional tuition rates."[92] Hare's desire to found a school was fueled as much by a determination to break the back of segregation as by artistic aims. The following January, she told Du Bois she had succeeded in opening "the closed doors of the South [End] Music School."[93]

In fact, Hare originally hoped to open a music school that would include an experimental children's little theatre but soon envisioned something grander: an independent school, the Allied Arts Centre, where she would promote a synthesis of music, dance, and pictorial art in performance. Du Bois promised to call her when he arrived in Boston the following week. There is no record of their conversation, but Hare probably received Du Bois's encouragement, or at least his tacit approval, which would have sufficed to spur her on. As her plans continued to evolve, Hare again solicited Du Bois's advice and expressed the hope that they would meet when he stopped in Boston or when she visited New York. On January 30, 1927, Hare announced that she was "about to inaugurate for the League of Women for Community Service an Art Centre that will care for the cultural needs of the colored child."[94] Evidently, the LWCS, of which Hare was a prominent member, had "come around as to possibilities, through my efforts for a Music School Centre," and was offering her "a large room and the house facilities where I can carry out my plans for an Art Centre. . . . We have a delightful small auditorium you know—room for 150 chairs. I am doing this under the League's name—not independently—and while under my sole direction I want it known as the Art Centre of the LWCS."[95]

This statement confirms the generative role played by the League of Women for Community Service. On Hare's stationery the LWCS letterhead is merged with the Allied Arts Centre's logo, an indication that she used the clout of this black women's club to legitimize her work.[96]

As a proponent of racial integration at all levels, Hare wanted to avoid the perception that her arts center was "a segregated movement . . . sponsored by colored women."[97] Hare was engaging in the debate about the best strategy for achieving civil rights and social equality. Should blacks "amalgamate" with whites? If so, in what sense and to what extent? Voluntary segregation, which had waxed and waned in the mid- to late nineteenth century, still had considerable support in the North, but anti-segregation, or integrationist, forces were on the ascendance. And yet Hare's resolutely integrationist arts center was all black. Even William Monroe Trotter, the fiery anti-segregationist, founded an all-black institution, the Boston *Guardian*. The contradiction was a calculated one, appropriate to that particular stage of the civil rights movement.

Hare needed a larger space than the one the LWCS could offer, and she took care to locate it in mainstream white territory.[98] She found such a space on Huntington Avenue, directly across the street from her alma mater, the New England Conservatory of Music. Writing to African educator Adelaide Casely Hayford (1868–1960), whom Du Bois had visited in Africa, Hare described the new location: "At last I have found a small house tucked in between larger ones right in the artist section of Boston proper. It is near the downtown section in a rapidly growing quarter for fine hotels, theaters, etc., with . . . attractive shops, interior decorators, student studios . . . tucked between, all are white. . . . *I abhor the segregated districts.*"[99]

The "small house" was the not-so-small Gainesboro Building at 295 Huntington Avenue, where she rented space.[100] The attractive three-story brick edifice remains intact today, with high stairwells, stamped tin ceilings, and a steep wooden staircase redolent of a past era. Musical instrument makers, photographic studios, a bookstore featuring classical sheet music, and the offices of the Boston Philharmonic Orchestra currently fill its second- and third-floor suites. Allied Arts member Ralf Coleman, who would succeed Hare as the doyen of little black theatre, remembered the space as one large room: "We had to block it off with sheets and all that sort of thing so that the individual groups could do their thing."[101]

Huntington Avenue was the elegant thoroughfare flanked by such venerable Bostonian institutions as Symphony Hall and the Museum of Fine Arts. To the south lay the strongly black districts of the South End and Roxbury. In locating her center on the north side of the avenue, Hare was challenging what black Bostonian James Guilford, Jr., once referred to as "the Maginot line" dividing white districts from black.[102] That she could do so at a time of a stealthy growth of Jim Crow practices—being turned away from theatres and restaurants, for example, or running up against race-based quotas at universities—further confirms that for Hare the connection between art and social engagement was ironclad.[103]

Whereas Du Bois called for theatres located in predominantly black neighborhoods "near the mass of ordinary Negro people," Hare staged her performances on the Avenue of the Arts, breaking the color line and essentially redefining the location as a race-neutral zone. It would have been difficult to implement Du Bois's provision that "the theatre must cater primarily to Negro audiences and be supported and sustained by their entertainment and approval."[104] The smallness of the Boston black community and of its cultured elite rendered such prospects unrealistic. Yet the location Hare chose was sufficiently close to the heart of the community that black Bostonians could take advantage of the Allied Arts Centre's offerings.

Indeed, the center encouraged many talented African Americans who lacked mainstream opportunities. At the new site Hare would produce a dozen dramas, creating the sense that something innovative and exciting had come to black Boston.[105] Her repertoire was as eclectic as one might expect from someone as sophisticated as Hare. One early production was *The Boor*, a light European classic by Anton Chekhov that would have made for an entertaining evening while also providing an excellent training experience for fledgling actors. Another production was *The No 'Count Boy*, a one-act folk comedy by Paul Green (1894–1981), which, like the Chekhov play, dealt with a thwarted country courtship.[106] Hare also staged *Plumes* by Georgia Douglas Johnson, a now-classic tragedy that turns on a terrible choice faced by an impoverished mother: to spend her life savings on the cost of needed surgery for her child or on a beautiful funeral (the girl dies before the mother can make a decision). The "plumes" of the title are the headdresses worn by the horses at "a shore 'nuff funeral, everything grand—with plumes!"[107] This play fulfills Du Bois's criteria for black authorship and realistic engagement with black life but could not have been easy for Hare to stage, after the death of her own young daughter.[108]

To sustain her arts center Hare relied on allies and friends who supported the arts and black causes. For example, at a tea held to honor artist Louis Windsor Brooks, Meta Warrick Fuller exhibited some of her sculptures, baritone William Richardson added music to the program, and Brooks exhibited some of her own work, which including pastels depicting "racial types."[109] While Hare was able to finance her own research trips to Puerto Rico and St. Thomas, Virgin Islands, at some point she appears to have run out of funds. Thus, in a letter to Du Bois she wrote, "My Dear Du, I am looking for work which I must have immediately. Is there anything I can do on The *Crisis*, either in the office or at this distance—since one can now 'commute' by bus at reduced round-trip rates! Temporary work at a stated salary is my present need." Hare added this disquieting statement: "It may be that there is no place for me in the 'colored' world and that I had best turn my efforts in the opposite direction. That I must soon determine."[110] Coming from a woman who was proud of being black and refused to "pass" as white, her statement is surprising. In answer to her inquiry about employment, Du Bois replied sympathetically but with regrets: "I certainly wish there was some way in which I could use your services, but I see nothing in sight now. With the severe competition to which we are continually subjected we have to expand slowly and hire only the absolutely necessary force. That was, of course, one of the strong reasons for letting Miss [Jessie] Fauset go. Of course, whenever there is the slightest chance of helping you I shall do so."[111]

A year later Hare had evidently recovered enough to begin work on a new production, *Tree Fantasy*, a medley of narrative and dance drawn from Hare's anthology, *A Message from the Trees*. The venue was "The Barn," a converted carriage house at 36 Joy Street on Beacon Hill used by local amateur theatre groups. It was owned by Hare's friend Catharine Huntington, a bohemian from a Brahmin family.[112] Hare was thrilled by the result, telling Du Bois, "You should have seen the tree dancers, Mildred Davenport as 'Pan' and later as the African girl worshiping under the fetish tree. . . . Please note that I selected trees that would easily lend themselves to the spirit of the darker races."[113] The inclusion of an African girl in this work would have appealed to Alain Locke, who exhorted young artists to turn their gaze to Africa. Hare enjoyed her success: "Since our beautiful 'Tree Fantasy' given at the Barn last Wednesday night, I have received no end of praise for the program and for the young folk that took part. Patronesses continue to telephone and show interest that is most encouraging for the future."[114]

Du Bois responded that he would be glad to include a picture of the *Tree Fantasy* set in an upcoming number of *Crisis* magazine but made no further comment. It may be that this fanciful work did not fit his definition of black theatre. Regardless, Hare still harbored dreams of becoming a playwright: "I have two fertile plot ideas: am waiting for your word about 'Bathesda' before attempting any more."[115] The nature of the script she references is unknown. It would seem that the famously icy Du Bois did not give Hare the encouragement she sought. Nine months later she canceled the lecture that he was slated to give at the Allied Arts Centre. Only a few days prior to the date Hare let Du Bois know that she could not "get a grip on" herself and was "unable to go through with the planned address and reception."[116] Whether or not Du Bois's failure to encourage her ideas triggered Hare's relapse we do not know.

Five months later Hare had recovered and was ready to recommence her labors. On May 15, 1928, she staged a second performance of *Antar* having made changes in the cast. Perhaps not so coincidentally, she replaced the two New Yorkers, Charles Burroughs (an associate of Du Bois) and Bernice Hughes Martin, with two Bostonians: Lucien Ayers, a student of voice, and Thelma Thornton, a student at Emerson College. With this gesture Hare signaled her readiness to rely on her own instincts, rather than on the precepts of Du Bois.[117] She also cast Ralf Coleman in the role previously played by Eugene Gordon (for reasons unknown).

Antar proved to be the high point of 1928 for Hare. She reported to Du Bois, "The days and nights have been crowded. . . . My experiment in the Allied Arts is winning sympathy and our play receipts will provide for our Studio maintenance until late Fall."[118] Another indication that Hare had ceased trying to please Du Bois was a letter saying explicitly that she was "making plans for . . . an art theatre which differs from the 'Harlem idea.' *I have my own vision* and as I am unsalaried and am making personal sacrifices to establish the work, am free to try my wings. Of course, they may get broken, but we do not look forward to any serious falls."[119]

Hare was charting her own course. Her success in building an interracial audience made up almost evenly of blacks and whites—an authentic feat—emboldened her to further distance herself from her mentor's prescriptions. In fact, she had done so even earlier. On November 23, 1928, the curtain rose on Hare's original *Ivory, Ebony and Gold: A Hand-Glass of Fact and Fantasy*, a play infused with cross-cultural themes reflective of Hare's research interests.[120] A blend of drama and comedy with a cast of some twenty actors, *Ivory, Ebony and Gold* was made up of three vignettes, of which the second and third merit attention. "From the Other Side of the South," the second segment, takes place in the western Sahara, where a Sudanese freed slave tells his story of captivity. An American traveler recognizes in the mysterious song chanted by the freed man the melody of "John Brown's Body," sung by General William Sherman's troops on their march to Atlanta. Hare, ever the musicologist, was surely calling attention to the links between African music and traditional American songs, while also denouncing colonialist racism (a white Englishman derides the Sudanese, claiming that they are in need of discipline and initiation into what he calls "civilization").[121]

The most notable segment, however, is the third, "An Ancient Papyrus," which links Africa (represented by Egypt) to black America. Hare had recently attended a lecture that made her quite angry. Writing to Du Bois, she fumed that George A. Reisner, an archaeologist and Harvard professor, erroneously asserted that the creators of the artifacts he found could not have been black. Hare made a habit of challenging such unfounded assertions throughout her career.

In *Ivory, Ebony and Gold* Hare again indulged her affinity for exotic settings, times, and places, not out of any "orientalist" bent but because she was determined to showcase black talent in the context of a splendid heritage and a lush setting. The playbill describes a confluence of rich costuming, music, and dance. With Meta Warrick Fuller's sets, elaborately costumed actors, and lyrical music composed by London-based Montague Ring, Hare used all the devices at her disposal to forge an "alliance," that is, a synthesis of the performing arts, the better to expand her Boston audience's frame of cultural reference. In pursuing her ideal, Hare set Du Bois's prescriptions aside. In the process she distanced herself from her mentor's contention that black theatre should deal directly with (be "about") black life. An additional sign of Hare's and Du Bois's divergent views was her appeal to a racially inclusive audience, the polar opposite of the segregated theatre model demanded by Du Bois. At this point in her career Hare was leaning toward the ideas of Alain Locke, who did not court controversy but encouraged the performance of folk plays for interracial audiences.[122]

Locke's presence at the third anniversary celebration of the Allied Arts Centre shows that Hare had his seal of approval. Dedicating the program to Locke, she featured a scene from *Tambour* by the well-known black composer John Matheus and a complement of Haitian dances.[123] An appreciative Locke applauded "the cultural value to be gleaned from such a movement as the Allied Arts Center," adding the knowing comment that "New England with its puritanical inhibitions is apt to miss the beauty in real art."[124] With the production of *Tambour*, an act of expression wholly in accordance with Locke's championing of art inspired by black folk life, Hare, the transplanted Texan, stood at the peak of her Boston success.

It is perhaps surprising, given that almost all of Hare's productions had featured racial themes and promoted the ideal of racial equality, that the Allied Arts' next production, presented only days later, had no racial focus at all: *Invisible Threads* (*Los intereses creados*), a three-act comedy by the Spanish playwright and Nobel Prize winner Jacinto Benavente (1866–1954), which opened at the Allied Arts Centre studio on February 25, 1930. In the first scene two penniless fugitives from justice arrive at an inn, passing themselves off as a master and his servant. Amusingly plotted around a thicket of deceptions and marriage proposals to an heiress, *Invisible Threads* delivers a conventional message: the invisible thread is love, "which makes these men and women . . . almost divine."[125] The cast of this unabashedly romantic play included such stalwarts of the Allied Arts Players as Alvira Hazzard, a substitute teacher in the Boston public schools, who also published two plays in the *Saturday Evening Quill*, and Granville Stewart, a concert tenor who worked at the elegant Lenox Hotel. Avon Long (1910–84), a highly successful Broadway actor from Baltimore who studied at the New England Conservatory of Music, would become famous in the role of "Sportin' Life" in the 1942 *Porgy and Bess*.[126]

Allan Crite, the painter, created the set described by Hare as "the design of a futuristic inn" and a garden.[127] Crite also played two bit parts, one as a secretary and the other as one of the "ruffians."[128] An ensemble of violins, viola, and cello played pieces by Montague Ring, Anton Rubinstein, Sergei Rachmaninoff—pairing the African-descended Ring with white composers—in the second and third acts and between acts. Hare's success with this production is all the more noteworthy when we consider that the stock market had crashed only a few months earlier.

Hare had apparently hit the soft spot in staid Boston's heart. To her mentor, she wrote glowingly, "Du, I wish I could describe the success of our play at the AA Centre last night! Such an audience—professors from Harvard College, a magazine editor, writers and musicians from the world proper; many in evening dress, a regular first-night at the opera. [I am] perfectly enraptured and surprised. *There were almost as many colored as white in attendance.*"[129]

In May of that same year the Allied Arts Players prepared to perform what should have been the jewel in the crown of the Allied Arts Players: *Dessalines, a Dramatic Tale: A Single Chapter from Haiti's History.*[130] The play celebrates Jean-Jacques Dessalines, the plantation slave turned revolutionary whose troops defeated Napoleon's army, the most powerful in Europe and a prominent figure in the pantheon of black historical and literary heroes. In 1874, black Bostonian William Wells Brown noted that "nearly all historians have set him down as a bloodthirsty monster, who delighted in the sufferings of his fellow-creatures," and in Dessalines's defense added, "They do not rightly consider the circumstances that surrounded him, and the foe that he had to deal with."[131] For this production Hare changed the original title to the more provocative *Dessalines, Black Emperor of Haiti.*

The cast of *Dessalines* included five seasoned Hare protégés: Avon Long as a voodoo priest and Granville Stewart in the lead role of Dessalines. Alvira Hazzard was Dessalines's wife. Allan Crite played "Pétou, a schemer." In *Dessalines* as in *Antar,* a black man of low social rank achieves victory and high social status. Both plays end with the marriage of a former slave to a prominent white woman, a parallel that makes an existential connection between Africa and the Americas. All three of Hare's large productions contained this global motif, and while they make no overt reference to America's race problem, the implications are present. Under the cover of rich visual, musical, and dramatic spectacles such as *Antar, Ivory, Ebony and Gold,* and *Dessalines,* Hare sent a political message across the color line. The accomplished black protagonists defy the association of blackness with negative traits, even as their achievements imply that there is no justification for segregation.

But the Boston critics knew that the historical Dessalines rescued the Haitian people from oppression through anti-white violence and bloodshed. For Norris Wright Cuney, Maud's father and a friend of the playwright, Dessalines was a great warrior who "possessed the ferocity of the Nubian lion, the undaunted heroism of the Spartan, *and an unquenchable hatred of the whites.*"[132] In her decision to stage this play Hare's instinct for public relations failed her. She likely did not take into account that influential black leaders, frustrated by stalled progress, were advocating for radical solutions to the race problem. Marcus Garvey and his nationalistic movement, whose influence peaked in 1924, was still strong among his numerous followers in Boston.[133] Before producing *Dessalines,* Hare had kept a prudent distance from radical ideas and politics—unlike the left-leaning Du Bois, who would leave America never to return. The celebration of Dessalines as an example of black heroism was hardly in keeping with someone who had always worked to build alliances with like-minded white (as well as black) Bostonian integrationists. Hare was unprepared for the backlash, indicating some naiveté on her part: perhaps she should have anticipated trouble when she changed the title.

For the first time, Hare noticed, "the leading newspapers were silent, with no reviews. The *Boston Globe* mentioned the presentation, but although we advertised as before in the *Herald* and the Evening *Transcript,* they would not touch the play."[134]

> There were many advance notices—the radio [station] W.E.E.I. gave me the privilege of broadcasting a story of Haitian heroism—full fifteen minutes. My music publisher graciously displayed for one week a collection of music, flags, (French and Haitian—I had to make a Haitian flag), a West Indian instrument and other data and mementoes that I had assembled for the window exhibit. The Negro papers gave mention of the play only when paid and followed this with very short and scant reviews. The colored people were the most difficult to interest and yet we had a fine patronage—an audience of almost three-quarters white. No one walked out so the strong lines of the play could not have offended. There *was* someone there from the *Herald* because he spoke to me, but the review was mysteriously omitted. . . . I had no idea that a play of Haiti in the Napoleonic period written 30 years ago would be taboo.[135]

The *Boston Traveler* and the *Christian Science Monitor*, both of which had praised *Antar*, made no comment on *Dessalines*. Even the *Boston Chronicle*, founded by two West Indians presumably interested in Caribbean themes, did not review it. The local editors, both white and black, on whom Hare had come to rely shunned the inflammatory play—and in genteel Boston, silence had the weight of sanction.

Hare was stung but carried on, undeterred from her mission of opening theatre doors to black performers and spectators of both races. Just before Christmas of 1930 she staged her final play at the Allied Arts Centre, with results that fulfilled her high hopes. The players presented *Cinda*, by Jack Bates, to "a distinguished audience."[136] Not unlike editor William Monroe Trotter, who sacrificed his wealth for a greater cause, Hare held fast to her avowed purpose—"that the Centre remain a workshop where the unknown writer may learn his technique—tho we lose."[137]

Conclusion

The little theatre movement of black Boston, having originated in the mid-1920s as the brainchild of Maud Cuney Hare, kindled a renascence of black theatre, which had long been dormant in 1920s Boston. Hare gave up a promising lecture and performance career to try her hand at theatre, with results that would have fallen into complete obscurity had it not been for the correspondence she conducted with W. E. B. Du Bois and the testimony of Allan Rohan Crite. The Hare–Du Bois correspondence reveals the arduous work Hare undertook to fulfill her dream of an all-black theatre company with appeal for integrated audiences. Initially inspired by Du Bois, who led the way by founding the Krigwa Players, and by working to gain the support of the League of Women in Community Service, Hare created the Allied Arts Centre in the heart of Boston's high-culture district. Like Du Bois, James Weldon Johnson, Alain Locke, and other black intellectuals, Hare believed that art must be enlisted as a weapon in the war against white supremacy. So inspired, she cannily navigated the politics of race, place, and space in her segregated city. From small-scale studio performances to ambitious productions at white-owned theatre venues, Hare showcased Afro-Bostonian artists and asserted their right to full equality in the arts as well as in American society.

5

Writing While Black

The Saturday Evening Quill, *1925–1930*

> We Negro writers, just by being black, have been on the blacklist all our lives. Censorship for us begins at the color line.
>
> —Langston Hughes

New York's Harlem was incandescent with creativity during the interwar era, and while Boston could not hold a candle to New York, known to many as the cultural capital of black America, the proud city on a hill witnessed its own modest renascence. Sculptor Meta Warrick Fuller designed sets for black theatre productions, painters Lois Mailou Jones and Allan Rohan Crite launched their careers, and local black musicians George Tynes and Eddy Deas were introducing jazz to the general public.[1] The mid-1920s also saw the emergence of a group of young, socially engaged black Bostonians who identified writing as their primary outlet for self-expression.

In 1925, Eugene Gordon (1891–1970), a journalist with the *Boston Post*, invited some of these promising people to form a literary workshop. With few other outlets available to them locally and with mainstream publishers unreceptive to the work of black authors, the invitees welcomed the opportunity to attend weekly meetings of the Saturday Evening Quill Club. The group convened initially at the Women's Service Club and other times at the comfortable home of Gordon and his wife, Edythe Mae, in Cambridge. The following year, Gwendolyn Bennett hailed Boston's Quill Club in "The Ebony Flute," her respected column in *Opportunity* magazine, noting that literary activities outside Harlem often escaped notice: "We who clink our cups over New York fireplaces are wont to miss the fact that little knots of literary devotees are in like manner sipping their cup o' warmth in this or that city of 'the provinces.'"[2]

In 1928, Eugene Gordon published the initial annual issue of the *Saturday Evening Quill*. This was the only such publication by blacks in the city since the *Colored American Magazine*, edited by Pauline Elizabeth Hopkins, was transferred to New York in 1904 and also the first since *New Era* magazine, likewise spearheaded by Hopkins, ceased publication in 1916.[3] Alain Locke, looking back on the 1928 literary year, announced jubilantly, "Beauty has spread to the provinces."[4] Of course the Athens of America was hardly a "province," having nurtured African American literature since the 1773 publication of Phillis Wheatley's first volume of poetry, but its twentieth-century record had been lackluster. This chapter reveals for the first time the breadth and depth of black literary production as reflected in the *Saturday Evening Quill*, the magazine originated and conducted by Eugene Gordon without the intervention of white sponsors.

The Quill Club was among the many literary salons, each inflected by its geographic location and culture, that thrived during the first and second phases of the Harlem Renaissance.[5] Among the most noteworthy clubs were the Saturday Nighters of Washington, D.C.; the Ink Slingers of California; the Ethiopian Guild of Indianapolis; the Book and Bench in Topeka; and the Scribblers of Baltimore. However, few of these clubs published their own "little magazines," a term used to describe smaller, not-for-profit (as opposed to older, established) magazines.[6] The *Saturday Evening Quill* of Boston began publication in June 1928, on the heels of *Black Opals*, a Philadelphia magazine whose first issue had appeared in the spring of 1927 and its last in June 1928. But *Black Opals*, conceived as "an outlet for young Philadelphians," was short-lived and localized. The *Quill*, by contrast, became the voice of black Bostonians and the only publication of its kind in New England.[7]

Although scholars have identified the *Saturday Evening Quill* as a key site of New Negro creativity, few have explored its contents in any depth.[8] The merits of the *Quill* are best appreciated when placed in the historical context of other arenas of artistic expression in black Boston. The launching of the *Quill* in 1928, for example, coincided with the peak years of Boston's little theatre movement. The overlapping theatre and literature activities furnish concrete evidence that a cultural renascence was brewing in black Boston.[9] The two projects had the common goal of promoting talented young black Bostonians faced with a lack of outlets for their work.

The Saturday Evening Quill, cover, June 1930 issue.

Moreover, the close association among the members of the two groups facilitated the participation of *Quill* writers in little theatre and vice versa. They differed sharply, however, with respect to the thematic terrain they covered: while Maud Cuney Hare's work focused on the heroic figures and cultural riches of the black diaspora, the *Quill* championed young writers' unfettered aesthetic expression and allowed for their engagement with the darker side of black life in America.

The Leadership of Eugene Gordon

The *Quill*'s success must be attributed to Eugene Gordon, without whom the aspiring writers and artists, all Bostonians either by birth or adoption, surely would not have come together. A writer of editorials and columns for the mainstream white *Boston Post*, he was superlatively qualified to lead the club and design a publishable magazine. Gordon, however, downplayed his qualifications, and in the first issue of the *Quill* told readers that his prime credentials were his personal contacts with prominent writers and many years of voracious reading: "And I?," he wrote in *Quill*'s second issue, "Oh, but I am not a critic at all! I am only a reporter describing what I have observed. It chances, however, that through years of reading almost everything Negroes published, to say nothing of close personal association with many of the writers, I have acquired a fairly accurate knowledge of their accomplishments as well as a gage for their capabilities."[10] (In fact, Gordon was an excellent writer of short fiction pieces, some of which appeared in the *Quill*.) His outstanding leadership as the editor of the *Quill* set a strong example for one club member, Dorothy West, a twenty-one year old who would go on to found *Challenge*, a magazine featuring black writing during the last phase of the Harlem Renaissance.

Unlike the Boston-born and -bred West, Gordon was a native Floridian who had lived in three of the five states in the Deep South. He was born in Oviedo in Seminole County, some eleven miles from Eatonville, the town made famous by Zora Neale Hurston. Gordon and Hurston were born within a year of each other, yet Hurston was destined for literary fame while Gordon would vanish into near obscurity. There is at least one other similarity: Hurston depicted life in her town with affection and humor, and Gordon evoked fondly the orange groves of his early childhood. His earliest memories of Oviedo are idyllic: "Rocking chair, the front porch and the harmonica which keeps time to the creaking rockers . . . Garden of weeds a forest in which to hunt wildcat and pantha with a wooden gun . . . Limitless white beach whose breakers alternately bring and remove an interminable line of silver fish."[11] Using lyrical language that is uncharacteristic of his writing, Gordon's unfinished manuscript conjures up what was for him a childhood paradise.

That paradise was lost when he was three years old and his family left Oviedo, traveling by steamer to New Orleans. In that sultry southern city the family shared a wooden cottage with a pastor and his wife, and Eugene's father preached "an occasional sermon as a coming Baptist minister," but his days were consumed by grueling labor on the levees. Gordon's family also ran a shop selling ice, coal, and wood, with vegetables and fruit on the side. But work on the levee was so onerous that the elder Gordon became a junk collector with a horse-drawn wagon. The Gordons stayed in New Orleans for seven years, an experience that left Eugene with more idyllic memories: tasty Creole food, blacks who spoke French, and colorful street scenes at Mardi Gras. Sanitation was primitive, however, and the gutters "were filled with running water, minnows, leeches and filth." Violence in the city, including street shootings, riots, and a mob takeover, led the Gordons to hastily decamp for Hawkinsville, Georgia, where Eugene's paternal grandfather owned a plantation.[12] By contrast with the diversity of New Orleans, it was a "black world without a white face."

When the ten-year-old Gordon first met his grandfather, he was astonished to see the man riding on horseback across his plantation and giving orders to the black people who toiled for him. Living conditions improved: for the first time the Gordons lived in their own house, a short distance from their grandparents. To attend a school that followed "the tradition of the 'best [black] people,'" Eugene walked many miles. But the family's peace of mind was disturbed when "rumors of terror and bloodshed reached [their] secluded black world." An attempt to set the Gordons' home on fire was followed by the lynching of a black preacher known to the family. Amid the violence—Gordon would later incorporate scenes of mayhem and perversion in his stories—the Gordon family nonetheless remained in Hawkinsville.

Gordon continued on at the local school until the improbable age of twenty. At that point his family bought him a train ticket to Washington, D.C., and gathered to bid him goodbye at the station. He fully intended to matriculate at Howard University but learned that his schooling was woefully inadequate. Instead, he had to enroll at Howard's high school. He was admitted to the university later on but found himself without money. He dropped out of school and worked as a janitor, eventually returning to Howard—when and for how long is unknown. In 1916, Gordon married Edythe Mae Chapman, a Washingtonian whose family was no better off than his own.[13]

In 1917, while in his junior year at Howard University, Gordon was drafted and sent for officer's training, first to Camp Devens near Boston and later to Camp Upton on Long Island. He and his regiment shipped out from Hoboken, New Jersey, to enter combat on the front lines in France. In 1919, Gordon was awarded the Croix de Guerre for valor in combat.[14] Returning to the United States, and at the suggestion of one of his brothers, Eugene and Edythe moved to Boston, home to a congenial and vibrant black community. Remarkably, Gordon was hired by the editorial department of the *Boston Post* even though his only relevant experience in journalism was founding and editing the *Bayonet*, the official publication for the 2nd Separate Battalion of the Massachusetts National Guard. For an African American to hold a position at a prominent mainstream newspaper was virtually unheard of at the time. At the *Post* Gordon was advanced from copyeditor in the feature department to editor of short stories and serials, seemingly undeterred by race prejudice.[15]

Ten years later, in 1938, however, when Gordon returned from a three-year stay in the Soviet Union, he stated publicly that he had been denied investigative assignments for which he believed himself fully qualified. Interviewed by the New York *Amsterdam News*, Gordon compared his experience as a journalist in Boston to the one he had in the Soviet Union: "I went to the Soviet Union after fifteen years on the *Boston Post*, where I was a sub-editor in the feature department. . . . While on the *Post*, although doing responsible work, my possibilities were very much limited owing to racial prejudice in the country." By contrast, in the Soviet Union, "no limits were placed on my field of activity. . . . I was assigned to interview many leading people in the country."[16]

In 1920s Boston, notwithstanding his hardscrabble southern background, Gordon and the Quill Club members were part of what Charles S. Johnson, the editor of *Opportunity* magazine, called the "small, articulate group" in black America that would make "conscious contributions to arts and letters."[17] That there was considerable talent to be found in the community is evidenced by the U.S. Census of Boston. As early as 1900, the census for Boston identified a sizeable number of blacks who were artists and teachers of art, musicians and teachers of music, actors and performers, as well as literary and scientific men and women.[18] The figures for 1920 are similar, and it is likely that Gordon drew his writers from this demographic. But writing to Gwendolyn Bennett, who spread the news about the club's debut in "The Ebony Flute," Gordon singled out two members, both female, as superior talents:

> Eugene Gordon of Boston makes the pleasing gesture of an enthusiasm which calls forth two letters. . . . He throws us this delicious sweetmeat:

"Helene Johnson is a member of the Saturday Evening Quill Club (of which I happened to be president), as is also Dorothy West, whose story was printed in the July *Opportunity*. These girls are cousins and are both so modest that they do not speak of their work even at Quill Club meetings, where such matters are supposed to be discussed, until formal demand is made of them."[19]

Gordon was correct (and prescient) in singling out Helene Johnson and Dorothy West for special distinction.[20] Each of the young women, not yet twenty years old, would go on to become well known in the Harlem Renaissance circles of New York, Helene as a poet and Dorothy as a short fiction writer.

Literary Patronage and Self-Funding

Many of the Harlem Renaissance writers benefited from personal patronage and from foundation fellowships funded by white supporters. Critics have argued that white money coopted and distorted black art and diverted its development away from the potential to grow organically. In contrast, the Boston group had no such sponsors, white or otherwise, and relied almost exclusively on funds the club members themselves contributed to the cause.[21] Gordon made this point when he wrote that the Quill Club members had paid for their "little folly . . . out of own pockets and purses," and owed no money or other debts to anyone.[22] "Evidently," write scholars Abby Arthur Johnson and Ronald M. Johnson, "[the *Quill's*] pockets were more full than those of [Wallace] Thurman and his associates, since they could sustain their effort for three years."[23] Remarkably, the *Quill* was beholden to no one and had no creditors—it was black-authored and -edited, as well as black-financed. When Dorothy West founded *Challenge* magazine six years later, she would hone to the same model.

Gordon disarmingly described the writers as having "no exalted opinion of their work" and no particular idea of it being "wonderful," "remarkable," "extraordinary," "unusual," or even "promising"—their intended audience was limited to their own circle of friends.[24] However, "Motto," a poem appearing on the inside of the cover, expresses higher expectations. George Reginald Margetson (1877–1951), a poet from the Caribbean island of St. Kitts and, as such, the only West Indian–born member in the group, characterized the writers as iconoclastic "crusaders of the quill . . . reaching for immortality" and "literary glory." Reading between the lines, one gathers that while Margetson recognized that societal bias against skin color would keep them from rising high, the young writers could still enjoy equal rights among their own: "We gather cordially / And strive the goal to win / *Of art's democracy*."[25]

Indeed, leading black intellectuals signaled that the arts were a territory where new and positive images of African Americans might be generated. The differing perspectives of Margetson and Gordon may be explained by a generation gap: Margetson was born in 1877, during the Victorian era, and Gordon in 1890, the nadir of the black experience in the post-Reconstruction era. Margetson wrote in a stilted, neo-Victorian style while Gordon favored a New Negro aesthetic.

The Critics and the *Quill*

Widespread public acclaim poured in from admiring critics, including the most prominent of black intellectuals, W. E. B. Du Bois. Writing in the *Crisis* magazine, Du Bois deemed the inaugural issue "the most interesting and best of the 'booklets' issued by young Negro writers in New York, Philadelphia, and elsewhere, for its handsome presentation and for its maintenance of a 'high mark of excellence.'"[26] From another quarter—the independent lay Catholic journal *Commonweal*—came praise for "an admirable absence of jazz and Harlem posturings in this publication of the Boston Afro-Americans."[27]

On the inside cover of the 1929 issue of the *Quill*, Gordon proudly listed additional commendations from large-circulation white newspapers such as the *Boston Herald* and the *Washington Tribune*. Edward J. O'Brien, a white anthologist, selected two stories by Eugene Gordon ("Alien" and "Rootbound") and one by Dorothy West ("An Unimportant Man") for mention on his "List II"; another by Eugene Gordon ("Cold-Blooded") on "List III" of his Roll of Honor; and one by Edythe Mae Gordon ("Subversion") on "List V." (Honor Roll stories were listed, but not included, in the volume, with List I being the highest category and List V the lowest.)[28] The following year the Boston *Transcript* joined the chorus, going so far as to suggest that aspiring white writers should emulate the Afro-Bostonians: "It may well be wished that a group of ambitious young whites would get out a paper in which they do as well, at least in the serious muse, as these Negroes do."[29] Gordon reiterated in the second issue that the *Quill* was intended only for consumption by club members and their friends, but he must have sent out quite a few sample copies, considering the many plaudits that he culled and printed on the inside cover of the 1929 issue, which could hardly have been spontaneous. The magazine would eventually reach a circulation of some five hundred copies.

The *Quill* Writers: A Collective Profile

Most of the writers had been born at the turn of the twentieth century, during the infamous era known as the "nadir" of black history.[30] Gordon playfully challenged his readers to guess their ages: "You who would like to know more may amuse yourselves by fitting authors to ages 60-odd and 22."[31] It is easily deduced that Florida Ruffin Ridley, age sixty-seven, was a member the "Old Negro" generation, and George Reginald Margetson was fifty-one. At the opposite end of the spectrum was William Edward Harrison, a Boston-born nineteen-year-old who was in his sophomore year at Harvard. Gordon himself was thirty-eight, almost twenty years Harrison's senior. Given his experience in the army, his service in France, and his position at the *Post*, Gordon was seen as an elder statesmen by his colleagues, even though Margetson and Ridley were considerably older. Many of the members were also neighbors, living in the South End, the heart of the black community; in Roxbury, which was becoming more prominent as an area of black residence; and in Cambridge, which had a strong black population.

With regard to race, Gordon stated quite plainly that those involved with the magazine were black but qualified that statement, saying they were only "*incidentally* Negroes" and "anybody who is eligible may become a member."[32] Gordon reemphasized this stance (albeit without the curious term "incidentally") in the 1930 *Quill* issue, which would be the magazine's last, though he surely did not know it at the time: "Although its membership is composed wholly of Negroes, *there is nothing in the Club's constitution against admitting others.*"[33] Gordon's open-door policy was not unusual for the era: The *Crisis* and other Renaissance journals often published articles, stories, and poems by white writers without necessarily identifying them by race. This gesture of inclusivity, so characteristic of integrationist (that

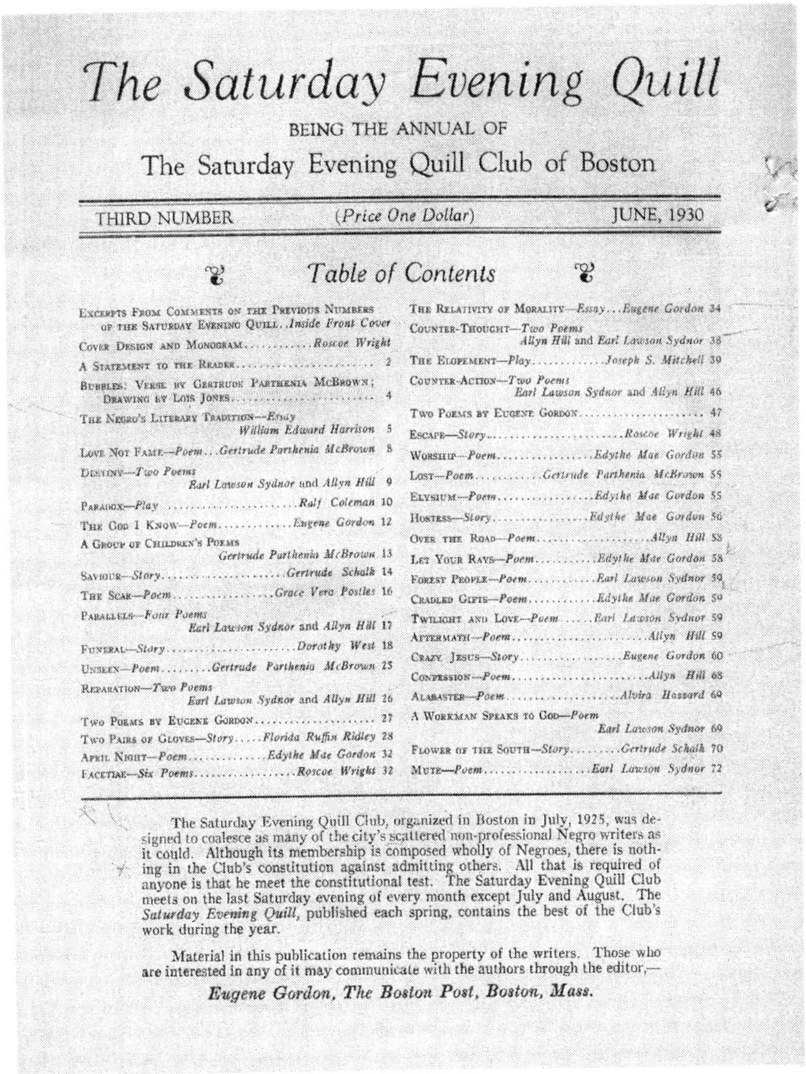

The Saturday Evening Quill

BEING THE ANNUAL OF

The Saturday Evening Quill Club of Boston

THIRD NUMBER (*Price One Dollar*) JUNE, 1930

Table of Contents

The Saturday Evening Quill Club, organized in Boston in July, 1925, was designed to coalesce as many of the city's scattered non-professional Negro writers as it could. Although its membership is composed wholly of Negroes, there is nothing in the Club's constitution against admitting others. All that is required of anyone is that he meet the constitutional test. The Saturday Evening Quill Club meets on the last Saturday evening of every month except July and August. The *Saturday Evening Quill*, published each spring, contains the best of the Club's work during the year.

Material in this publication remains the property of the writers. Those who are interested in any of it may communicate with the authors through the editor,—

Eugene Gordon, The Boston Post, Boston, Mass.

The Saturday Evening Quill, table of contents, June 1930 issue.

is, anti-segregationist) thinking, is significant when one considers that a few years later, Gordon would embrace communism, an ideology that minimized the importance of race and maximized that of class.

Some club members were novices, but others—among them Helene Johnson, Dorothy West, and Eugene Gordon—had already connected to the New Negro Renaissance in Harlem (Johnson and West had already moved there), then at its apogee, and had won prizes in literary competitions sponsored by the *Crisis* and *Opportunity*.[34] Some sources state that Dorothy West published in the *Boston Globe* or the *Boston Chronicle*, which is unlikely (but not impossible)—the latter, a black weekly, does not seem to have published creative writing. It is more likely that West's and Johnson's work came out in the *Boston Post*, where Gordon had some influence, although this has yet to be substantiated.

One of the chief commonalities among the members was their high level of educational attainment. This should not come as a surprise when many scholars, among them David Levering Lewis, have remarked that the Harlem Renaissance itself was "an elitist response on the part of a tiny group of mostly second-generation, college-education, and generally affluent Afro-Americans—a response, first, to the increasingly raw racism of the times, second, to the frightening Black Zionism of the Garveyites, and finally, to the remote, but no less frightening, appeal of Marxism."[35] At a time when only a small percentage of Americans and even fewer women, let alone blacks, earned college degrees, most of the Boston writers had college experience, with some earning degrees from area liberal arts colleges and universities, others obtaining graduate degrees, and still others pursuing their education at extension courses offered by local institutions. Poet George Margetson, not having received higher education, used the intellectual forums of Boston advantageously, while William Harrison, the Harvard student, also took advantage of them—especially the progressive Ford Hall Forum and other venues open to the public, participating in its lively debates. Joseph S. Mitchell received his J.D. from Boston University Law School. Edythe Mae Gordon received an M.A. from Boston University.[36] Marion Conover earned degrees from both Simmons College's School of Social Work and the Portia Law School. Florence Marion Harmon graduated from Gordon College, a Christian institution in Wenham, Massachusetts, north of Boston. Joshua H. Jones, Jr., who published poetry in the *Quill* as well as an estimable novel, was an alumnus of Brown University in Providence, Rhode Island.[37]

Those with strong backgrounds from classical liberal arts institutions and, in some cases, professional schools would have created a common language as well as shared perspectives among the club members. Black students who studied at white institutions in the North were often satisfied with their education despite many racial slights and the fact the curricula were invariably Eurocentric.[38] For African Americans higher education constituted cultural capital, although it could not shield them from the kind of discrimination that relegated many to underemployment and deprived society of the fruits of their talents.[39] As Du Bois famously put it, black men and women were shut out from the white world by a thick veil.

Aside from their commonalities, the *Quill* members were noticeably different in their geographical origins, which ranged from the Deep South to the North. The northerners, in turn, were evenly divided between a core of "black Yankees," including Dorothy West, Helene Johnson, and Lois Mailou Jones, all born and raised in Boston, and others who came from elsewhere in the North, such as New Jersey and Pennsylvania. The southerners, including Alabamian Joseph S. Mitchell and the Floridian Gordon, were drawn to Boston by the city's cultural mystique and the possibilities they believed to exist in the Athens of America.[40] Other aspiring young people attracted to Boston were Earl Sydnor, who arrived from Orange, New Jersey, and Waring Cuney, who came north to attend the New England Conservatory of Music, believing, as did many, that education was a hedge against racism. Even as they wrote in a black Yankee voice, the *Quill* members drew on the diversity of their backgrounds, thus infusing their particular perspectives into their work. Another source of difference may be found in religious affiliation, where diversity reigned: Maud Cuney Hare was a Christian Scientist, Allan Crite and Gertrude "Toki" Schalk were Episcopalians, Florida Ruffin Ridley was a Unitarian, and Ralf Coleman was a Congregationalist, to cite only a few examples.[41] Eugene Gordon alone emerges as an extreme iconoclast and a critic of all creeds. Gordon and his views notwithstanding, for the majority of black Bostonians, Christian faith was a bedrock and source of strength in the presence of adversity. Its importance should never be underestimated.

Reading the *Quill:* A Bird's-Eye View of Its Overarching Themes

Within the covers of the *Quill* one finds a thematic spectrum ranging from hypercritical assessments of black literary traditions and pointed critiques of American capitalism to lyrical meditations on love and death. Positioned at the fringes of the American literary mainstream, the *Quill*'s unique perspectives are reflected in many pieces that remain fresh and stimulating for a twenty-first-century reader.

The concerns expressed by the writers are so diverse as to resist generalization, but they may be grouped under four headings: iconoclasm and dissent, race consciousness, portrayals of agency, and responses to the New Negro movement in New York. The leading exponent of iconoclastic views, without doubt, was Eugene Gordon. On organized religion, for example, he conveyed his adversarial stance in one particularly intense short story.[42] "Crazy Jesus" takes sharp aim at religious demagogues who promise salvation to unsuspecting black believers.[43] The protagonist is a self-proclaimed black "messiah" calling himself Jesus, who arrives in a southern black community with promises to heal the sick and raise the dead. His devotees dress in flowing white robes and live in a tent colony made from rough-hewn planks. He has the black folk convinced that being "lower in the scale of humanity than their fellow-men of other races," they must look to him for salvation. But one fateful Sunday a "boisterous, cynical, heretical, unruly lot" of black college students arrive from the North to challenge the preacher publicly. He discredits the students, whose heads "are stuffed with useless information about astronomy, evolution, higher mathematics, and foreign languages" (63), but he cannot quell their protests.

In the climactic final scene the reporters rush to the colony to behold the erstwhile messiah nailed to a cross, flanked by two followers, all crucified and silhouetted against "the white-gold disc of the moon" (68). The colony's leader, upon investigation, is revealed as an impostor, a white man with a complexion just dusky enough to pass for black. The story reflects Gordon's aversion for those who exploit the innocent in the name of religion and his view of religion itself as a primitive superstition. Further evidence of Gordon's iconoclasm comes in his poem "The God I Know," which dismisses the belief in a merciful Creator: "Not the kind and benevolent father / Of a hapless race is the God I know," but "a blind and stupid force, / Albeit powerful—ruthless as floods / Unharnessed, or windwhipped fires in canebrakes."[44] Gordon's scorn for religion was manifested in a sweeping negation of God, an intriguing turnabout for the son of a Baptist preacher.

Moving to the realm of politics, the iconoclastic Gordon took aim at the

U.S. Senate. "The Relativity of Morality," an essay, recklessly disputes the intelligence of senators whom "tests have shown to average only a shade or so above the moronic" and whose election he attributed to the votes of "overwhelmingly moronic majorities." The real-life senator Reed Smoot (1862–1941), who rose before the Senate to exhibit "fifty books which he said were obscene, and therefore, are unfit for you and me to read," became a target of Gordon's ire, but any other moralistic advocate of censorship would have served Gordon's purpose.[45] Reasserting his extremely antireligious views (and extremist views in general), Gordon, the World War I army hero, broadened his assault on what he saw as sanctimoniousness to include hypocrisy—churches that send young men to die on the battlefields without a qualm while preaching that murder is a sin.[46]

It is useful to compare Gordon's antiwar stance with Dorothy West's more nuanced presentation. In West's "An Unimportant Man," the main character opposes black participation in the segregated U.S. military and is glad to have escaped being drafted into a white man's war. But when he finds himself "caught in a cheering crowd . . . watching a [black] regiment march by, . . . his bitterness [i]s swept away in the beauty of a tall, black boy, straight and fine and gloriously eager, marching sternly on because he was free and proud."[47]

Gordon's iconoclasm extended to another realm, as seen in "Sarcophagus," one of his strongest short stories.[48] In a lecture hall at "Boston University," a "wizened, grayish, sharp-featured Professor of Egyptian History" delivers a lecture to a class of sixty white graduate students when, much to his chagrin, a stranger seated at the rear of the hall interrupts him. A "bald, nose-spectacled, goateed black man" introduces himself as Hezekiah Thompson, a former professor of history from a Baptist college in Macon, Georgia. The southern academician charges that white professors of history are "in league to ignore the black man's contribution to civilization" (36). When African achievements are perceived as "ordinary" they are acknowledged as "Negro," he claims, but when they make significant contributions to knowledge they are not identified by race. The professor, Niles, summarily dismisses Thompson's claims—they are motivated, he declares, by "some deep-seated grievance against white folk in general and against me in particular." Thompson then confronts Niles with a passage from a book authored by Niles himself, *The Glory of Cheops*, which argues that the ancient Ethiopians, as well as the Yemenites and

Ethiopians were "mixed races, dark-colored people, but . . . not, African [N]egroes" (38). In response, Niles sends Thompson to the Museum of Fine Arts (with which the black professor is already fully acquainted). He insists that when Thompson reaches the Egyptian gallery, he must "get down inside" a massive granite sarcophagus. There he will see that no African features are detectable on the carvings.

Thompson follows Niles out of the room and to the brink of the stairwell, where he pushes the white professor down: "A body shot out, shrieking, sprawling, whirling, descending. . . . A moment later there came the sound of an object striking the hardwood floor" (38). The agitated black man rushes to the Egyptian gallery of the museum, where much to his satisfaction, he confirms that the faces carved on the ancient sarcophagus are indeed "Negroid." He lifts the granite lid and climbs inside, as Niles had instructed him, but, propped against a ledge, the lid falls closed. Thompson's cries for help are smothered, and he is destined to suffocate in the same ancient artifact that would have supported his argument for the "Negro" origins in ancient Egyptian art. The text is open to extensive interpretation, but on its face it indicates not only the arrogance of white men high in the academic hierarchy but that madness that can be an outcome of continuous racial oppression.

How the *Quill*'s readers reacted to this story is difficult to gauge—perhaps it struck them as far-fetched or perhaps it offered a confirmation of their own experiences with white academia. It is significant that a half-century later, an erudite, three-volume study entitled *Black Athena* argued on semantic, historical, and aesthetic grounds that ancient Egyptians, many of whom were black, contributed significantly to the development of Greek civilization. European scholars of the nineteenth century, author Martin Bernal has argued, were responsible for suppressing all traces of black influence.[49] In critiquing biased and self-interested constructions of knowledge Eugene Gordon was well ahead of his time. Maud Cuney Hare, theatre producer and black intellectual, also disputed the claims of the real-life "Professor Niles." Eight years before Gordon published "Sarcophagus," Hare attended a lecture given by Harvard professor George A. Reisner.[50] In a letter to W. E. B. Du Bois, her former fiancé, Hare took vehement exception to Reisner's assertions that the Ethiopian artifacts discovered by his team did not depict black people: "He says the people were not at all Negro Africans," seethed Hare, "and then proceeded to show a statue on the screen of a Negro Prince and Princess. Evidently the Negro royalty had no children!"[51]

Like Gordon, Hare was incensed by the erasure of black achievements. The denial of black contributions to the cultures of ancient Africa was intolerable to her, as it was to Gordon. "Sarcophagus" exposes the white intellectual establishment's sanguine suppression of historical evidence. Some scholars have described Gordon as "conservative," a man who "carefully separated himself from radical positions in literature and politics," but this textual evidence (plus the matter of his communist leanings) should put the matter to rest.[52] Gordon boldly decried hypocritical pieties, institutional racism, and the claims of scholars who believed themselves to be objective.

Race Consciousness as a Recurrent Theme in the *Quill*

One of the chief projects of the Harlem Renaissance was dismantling stereotypes of blackness by displaying black excellence in the creative arts. The *Quill* strongly supported that goal. Indeed, the Boston *Transcript* correctly identified one of the dominant themes of the 1930 issue as the "group life of the Negro, and the injustice with which he is treated by whites."[53] Race consciousness, coupled with social conscience, found abundant expression in the *Quill*. Both Alain Locke and Walter White signaled race consciousness as a result of racism and warned that it could spur greater efforts to overcome racial oppression. Charles S. Johnson, however, took for granted that repression and exclusion were a fact of life. Historian David Levering Lewis points out that the one area that had not been proscribed was the arts. Consequently, "the sole battle plan affording both high visibility and low vulnerability" had to involve literature, visual art, and performance. The black intelligentsia achieved what assimilation it could "through copyright, concerts, and exhibitions."[54]

References to racial identity from various perspectives abound in the *Quill*, perhaps most strikingly in "I Am Not Proud" by Helene Johnson. The first two lines of this poem take the reader aback by appearing to reject blackness: "I am not proud that I am bold / Or proud that I am black." In the final two lines, the poem reverses course: "Color was given to me as a gage / And boldness came with that."[55] By using the archaic word "gage" (a valuable object deposited as a guarantee of good faith), the speaker likens black heritage to an ancient amulet that bestows courage on the bearer—a powerful articulation of race pride. The poem concludes by redefining blackness as a priceless treasure.

Florida Ruffin Ridley asserted a racial consciousness that was deeply rooted in her upper-class identity. In "Preface: Other Bostonians," part essay and part memoir, the narrator described a handcrafted box that held documents related to her mother's family, whose history "stretches back into colonial New England."[56] In this skillfully crafted piece Ridley gloried in the mingling of Native American, Anglo-American, and African American blood, notwithstanding the fact that a society governed by the "one drop rule" views racial mixture only as a negative.[57] Ironically, none of the documents referenced in Ridley's nonfiction piece have survived. Also found in the *Quill* is another Ridley story, "He Must Think It Out," about a man whose discovery that he has black forbears is cause for panic rather than celebration.[58] Henry, a white attorney, is jubilant when he learns that he will soon receive an inheritance, but when it emerges that his benefactor is a black relation previously unknown to him, his reaction goes from joy to panic: "Tied up with a black family! 'No, no!' he almost shrieked, as he threw down the papers and rushed to open the window. 'Damn him, no, no!' So violent was his instinctive reaction that a feeling of nausea overcame him as he leaned against the open window seeking air. . . . He—'a nigger' and Irene, his Irene, his gay lovely daughter. . . . It was a lie! A lie!" (7). Henry, a man of high status in white society, knows that in a racist society his blackness is a stigma. If he is no longer "a white man," then his daughter, a colored woman, will face "doors closed everywhere and on every side—in schools and stores and churches and homes!" There is no resolution possible: Henry "must think it out. He must think it out alone" (8).

If Ridley viewed race consciousness from two opposing perspectives, for Earl Lawson Sydnor such awareness led to a confrontation with history. His poem "Mute" opens with a description of winter's frigid beauty: "I see the winter's gale / Curl silver whips on silent hills." The image of a whip leads to thoughts of the brutality unleashed against black people. The narrator recoils but cannot stop hearing "the echoed lashes / Spent on Negroes' backs." Turning his back is useless because the speaker hears

> *the wind moan spirituals*
> *Through bare brown branches,*

And fail to recognize
A black man's password to eternity.

At the end sound gives way to silence and a strong image of the wind spattered in "vivid red":

I see the sun deserting day,
And wildly scatter vivid red upon the wind . . .
I have no thought
That this might cheapen blood.[59]

The speaker's insouciance gives way to revulsion, thus heightening the impact of Sydnor's poem.

Agency, Resilience, and Spiritual Strength

The term "agency" is useful when applied to the energy of literary characters who seek to extricate themselves from adverse situations. Such characters, endowed with a degree of autonomy, can function to propel the flow of a narrative or to forestall a negative outcome. Conversely, a lack of propulsive energy often foreshadows a tragic ending. The phenomenon of suppressed female agency in particular strongly reflects the subordination and oppression of women living in a sexist society. This phenomenon surfaces prominently in "Black Madness" and "Saviour," both by Gertrude Schalk.

In "Black Madness," Angy, who once was an attractive woman, is now "just another colored scrubber, neither better-looking nor worse-looking than the average." Despite ill-health, Angy soldiers on, washing "miles of" marble steps in office buildings while her feckless husband, Jim, engages in drinking, smoking, playing the numbers game, and pursuing women—"a good-for-nothing n——," Angy admits—but she cannot bring herself to confront him, until one night when Angy oversleeps, missing her work shift. She awakens, startled by "the scraping of chairs and rattling of glasses [and] coarse voices" in the adjacent room. One of the voices is female. "It had never dawned on her that Jim would bring women into her home when she was out" (58). Still, Angy refrains from confronting Jim for fear he will leave her. She could "shoot them both, but they wouldn't suffer enough. . . . Cut them? Disfigure them? Better, but she had no knife.

Suddenly she almost laughed aloud: superstitious colored people. . . . That was the way" (59). Angy conceals herself in the bedclothes, stretches out, and suppresses her breathing. This act is so effective that when Jim approaches the bed he finds Angy's body rigid to the touch: "With a violent motion he leaped from the bed. The woman was behind him, screaming" (59). Angy's death is real enough (the reader surmises that her weak heart has given out). Although it strains credibility, the story vividly portrays an exploited woman who summons the courage to take an action that destroys her.[60]

Surprisingly, or perhaps not, Gertrude Schalk depicts, almost exclusively, women who fail to challenge their exploiters. The short story "Saviour" features another black woman beset by adversity who ultimately cannot extricate herself from entrapment. Coerced into prostitution at an early age, Minnie longs to escape from the "rough sailors and stokers . . . all rarin' to go." Her desperation makes her vulnerable to the blandishments of a man at the brothel who tells her that she is different from the rest: "I knowed you was different the first minute." Minnie surrenders to his flattery and eagerly accepts a train ticket that will presumably carry her to safety with his family: he is her savior, "like an old-time saint in modern dress." It is only as she nears her destination that she examines the envelope he has given her more closely: it is addressed to Susie Jackson, the owner of a notorious brothel just a few train stops down the line. In the end, "there was nothing to show whether the girl on the platform had slipped or jumped." The reader must decide whether Minnie loses her balance as she stands on the platform or jumps to her death. In this controversial story, Schalk's protagonist believes herself powerless to act on her own behalf.[61]

In contrast to this pessimistic outcome, Roscoe Wright's "Washwoman" features a black woman with "calloused dark hands" and "ginger brown arms" whose remarkable determination thwarts her exploiter. In this story, set in Washington, D.C., Amy launders other people's clothes while her live-in boyfriend, Jackson Scott, pursues studies in medicine.[62] Amy is sustained by the certainty that he will marry her "when his ship c[omes] in," but the omniscient narrator comments darkly that "this mythical vessel always remained far at sea" (57). When Amy discovers that the wedding ring she has helped Jack purchase is not for her but for a black New York socialite, she devises a scheme that proves more effective than Angy's passive resistance. Traveling to New York and storming Jack's wedding ceremony, the infuriated Amy publicly objects to the marriage. In the (somewhat implausible) ending, the preacher forces Jack to honor his promise to marry Amy. Remarkably, it is a male writer whose protagonist fights on her own behalf, vividly demonstrating the potential of a strong-willed female agent.

Just as Roscoe Wright's "Washwoman" provides a counterpoint to Schalk's "Black Madness" and "Saviour," another of his pieces, "Escape-A Story," displays an alternative to the tragic outcomes seen in Schalk's stories.[63] Betty is an attractive girl living in a small New England town where the African American population is "exactly two"—Betty and her father, who are seemingly untouched by outright racism because "New England tolerance always prevailed on the surface" and "people were good Christians" (52). Betty and her father had never experienced outright insults or abuse. When Betty endures daily taunts from passersby (one man, a recent arrival from the South, sees her from across the street and calls her a "colored wench"), her father advises her, "White folks are funny, but you shouldn't mind them, chile! Just go along as ef it didn't bother you a bit" (49). Betty's brief romance with a white boy results in shunning by the community, and she takes refuge in fantasies of escape. The Pullman porters and dining car chefs who pass through her town give her an inkling of her options, and their vivid tales of New York's Harlem nurture her dream of escape. Betty "had once heard that Negroes . . . lived in tall, handsome apartment houses with imposing entrances, elevators, and all modern conveniences" (49).

Fueled by illusion, Betty packs a suitcase and is walking to the train station when a silver and black Rolls Royce pulls over. The chauffeur, a black man, engages Betty in conversation: she is "the prettiest brownskin girl" he has ever seen. Charmed, and oblivious to the man's lascivious gaze, Betty throws caution to the winds and steps into the limousine, bound for Harlem. As she leaves town she looks back at the townspeople with "her Afroid nose high in the air." Seeing a road sign that invites visitors to "come again to the town," Betty whispers "to her satisfied self, 'Come again like Hell, I will'" (54). Wright's protagonist makes this choice even at considerable risk to her physical and moral integrity. But the open ending of this richly detailed story allows the reader to surmise that Betty's decision will change her life for the better: Harlem symbolizes a sense of possibility and freedom.

Wright's stories, with their glimmers of optimism, may be fruitfully compared to "Blind Alley" by Alvirah Hazzard, who worked in the Boston schools as a substitute teacher and was a member of the Allied Players, directed by Maud Cuney Hare.[64] This story is a marvel of precision: in a mere two pages the author successfully depicts the fortunes of Betts, a woman who has moved up from a table-waiting job in "a dive" to a position at a hospital, albeit at a menial level: "Maybe if she went to night school and got a certificate . . . she could be a real nurse and not just a ward maid" (73). Phil, the man in her life, also struggles to improve his lot. But Betts's roommate intercepts messages from Phil (whom she labels "a gutter snipe") and derides Betts for being a "dickty girl," using the slang word for pretentious. Betts and Phil, however, refuse to be dragged down. In the final scene Phil enters a smoky poolroom, "vile with fetid smoke and the odor of perspiration." One of the men taunts him for being "uppity," and Phil, "fired with rage and pent-up emotion," strikes him on the chin and walks out, "with the coolness and disdain of a victorious gladiator," leaving the men "electrified." At the end of her story Hazzard reverses the paradigm of defeat: "There was hope in the afternoon air" (74).

The protagonist of another Schalk story, "Flower of the South," displays the exercise of female agency in a most disturbing way.[65] The story opens as a white Englishman arrives at a "huge white mansion" somewhere in the South to court Betty Lee, the daughter of a "liberal" senator. Hugh, the Englishman, is deeply in love with this southern belle, whose "sparkling dark eyes . . . cause his usually staid and well-behaved heart to jump about like a skittish colt." He knows that the people of the South, "so charming, so beautiful, seemingly, in spirit," have a murky past, but he is still taken aback when he learns that many southern "gentlemen" have shadow families. Among the dark-skinned servants in Senator Lee's household are "three or four fair-skinned boys and girls who looked with knowing eyes whenever he came near them" (70).

A local "mammy" informs him that it is common for white masters to sire children with a black servant: "Shuah, suh, we ain't none of us without de white streak," the woman asserts. "Chile, ah's old, mos' a hundred, an' done had twelve chillum—all of um by my mahster." Her own daughters have married "inter the bes' families in de South. Dey's so white dey's passin'. Chile, iffen dem white folks knowed dey was half colured . . . !"[66] Hugh does not know the term "passing" until he discovers the sinister side of the South. Still, he continues to believe that "from all the intrigues of this beautiful South, Betty alone stood clean and pure" (70).

In a devastating climax, news arrives that a black man has been accused of raping a white woman. With his daughter's British suitor in tow, Senator Lee rushes to the scene, only to find that a mob has tied the black man to a stake. Hugh is sickened by the sight of the instigators throwing wood at flames beneath the man's feet. He now sees that the southerner is but a "barbarous creature who boasted of being the flower of American aristocracy; this *Thing* who burned men alive yet preached freedom and culture." Suddenly Hugh hears the voice of a woman who is egging on the crowd to set the victim on fire: "Across the hazy space, Hugh's eyes, momentarily clear, leaped to meet the bloody gaze of Betty Lee. Her arm still aloft, and her dress stained with gasoline, she stood there in all her flaming southern beauty" (72). This moment explains the full meaning of the opening passage: "The two weeks [Hugh] had spent at the Manor as guest of the Lees had been one succession of *things he should remember and things he should remember to forget.* It seemed that *there were more things to remember to forget than there were to remember.* In that moment something died in Hugh; something that never again would blossom" (70, emphasis added). The story's last sentence encapsulates the disillusioned Englishman's sentiments: "God, he was ashamed" (72).

It is highly ironic that the only autonomous female in Schalk's *Quill* stories exercises her power in the most perverted way imaginable. Schalk artfully peeled away the veneer of gentility that serves as a camouflage for criminal acts. "Flower of the South," in exposing the atrocities of lynching, implicitly indicted Congress for repeatedly failing to pass an antilynching bill.[67] In reality, the story was a protest. Schalk, like other black writers, many of whom militated in the cause of racial justice, manifested her indignation even as she achieved literary excellence. As an educated black woman from Boston, a city of relative safety, Schalk used her art to denounce injustice. Neither she nor her peers ignored the fact that half of the black Bostonian population was southern-born and had fled from Jim Crow, segregation, white supremacy, and violence.

But nowhere does the ability of egotistical females to crush and devastate comes across as clearly as in the writing of Dorothy West, the best known of the *Quill* writers. Even as West situated her fiction in the North, she highlighted the close connection of black Bostonians to the

South. Mining the autobiographical tales of her parents, both southern migrants, West crafted unique stories of middle-class life in Boston. In her cast of characters are strong-willed females who wield power in the domestic realm and manipulate their kin for their own selfish ends. One of her prototypes is the narcissist who withholds affection from her husband and controls the lives of her family. The most prominent example is Cleo, the protagonist of West's novel *The Living Is Easy*, published in 1948 when the New Negro Renaissance was but a distant memory.[68] Two out of the three stories West contributed to the *Quill* illustrate the workings of perverted female agency. One of them, "Prologue to a Life" does not measure up to the level of craftsmanship seen in many West stories—it deserves mention only as a strong example of West's emphasis on female dominance.

"An Unimportant Man," which shows that West was developing her craft, visits the unhappy lot of a husband whose status-hungry wife rejects him.[69] The story is remarkable for its infusion of positive female agency through the insertion of a child with redemptive powers. Zebediah Jenkins works by day as a cook and by night studies law in the (unrealistic) hope of becoming an attorney. His pride and joy is his little daughter, Esther, likely a stand-in for Dorothy West as a child. "He was glad, rather fiercely glad, that she knew enough to stand up to people. No one would ever—must ever—shape the course of Esther's life" (22). Quite confident that she can become anything she desires, "Essie" declares that she will be a dancer or a singer: "I'd just as lief do anything—beautiful" (27). While "Prologue" and "An Unimportant Man" highlight perverted female agency, the child who is intent on doing "something beautiful" serves as a counterweight to that sad spectacle. Dorothy West herself would do "beautiful" things, including serving a brief stint as a supernumerary in the cast for the Broadway show *Porgy*, traveling to London, taking an enlightening trip to the Soviet Union, and completing two landmark novels.[70]

But the black female protagonists portrayed by *Quill* writers are trapped by adverse circumstances beyond their control. Their lack of formal education relegates them to menial labor, and consequently they see no choices and have little control over the course of their lives. As portrayed in the *Quill* these failures are no fault of the characters. Instead, they highlight pervasive discrimination against black people, denial of opportunity, and suppression of their aspirations. In this sense, the stories serve to alert readers to the ravages of double jeopardy—the discrimination inflicted on black women because of their race as well as their gender.

While the *Quill* was published in the relatively prosperous 1920s, an era of furious debate about women's rights and the idea of "the New Woman," these stories do not reflect that sweeping changes were taking place: women won the right to vote, they bobbed their hair, shortened their skirts, dreamed of having careers, and imagined new life choices. However, due to their intimate knowledge of the difference skin color made for black women, the *Quill* writers were more concerned with exposing a socioeconomic order shot through with gender, class, and race prejudice than on pointing to signs of progress.

Black Boston developed its own divergent aesthetic bent, quite different from the expansive range of taste in Harlem. The *Quill* did not encourage truly experimental writing nor did it care for the African-inflected art that emanated from Harlem and Paris. Eugene Gordon chafed at critics who expect blacks to write out of their African origins: "There is no reason under heaven why an Aframerican, whose ancestors came here more than three centuries ago, should be swayed by jungle influences."[71] William Edward Harrison, the youngest Quill Club member, may well have been following the lead of his editor and mentor when he dismissed the literature emanating from Harlem. In his essay entitled "The Negro's Literary Tradition," Harrison claimed that depictions of "the negro quarter of New York" by Harlem writers such as the brilliant playwright and novelist Wallace Thurman were "the epitome of the bizarre and the unregenerate asylum of Vice."[72] Born and raised in tight-lipped Boston, Harrison bridled at graphic descriptions of black society, its street life, its bars, and the use of explicit descriptions of sex, declaring, far too prematurely—and perhaps puritanically—that the Harlem theme was "stale."[73] Likewise, the search for inspiration in an idealized Africa, a strong theme of the Harlem Renaissance, left Harrison unmoved. He was not alone: most *Quill* writers would have responded with little enthusiasm to the rhetorical question famously posed by Countee Cullen, "What is Africa to me?" or the idea that Harlem Renaissance artists represented them.[74]

And yet the exciting events of Harlem were not far from the thoughts of Afro-Bostonians. The mystique of Harlem as a black cultural capital is embedded in the *Quill*, although Eugene Gordon's critique of Claude McKay's novel *Home to Harlem* reflects some ambivalence: Although, on the one hand he reveals his repugnance for McKay's depictions of characters belonging to "the lowest stratum of Harlem," on the other hand he finds that the novel "traps the flavor and the color and the odor of Harlem's cabarets and her teeming horde of flat dwellers, and he successfully transmits these elusive ingredients to the book."[75] Gordon himself would later move to Harlem, where he continued his work in journalism and became active in the Communist Party, which he joined in 1930.[76] The simultaneous disapproval of Harlem-centered themes, expressed at various points in his writing, as well as occasional nods to its mystique, suggest that Gordon felt attraction as well as quasi-puritanical repugnance.

There is no better example than Roscoe Wright's Betty, who in "Escape—A Story"surrenders to the lure of Harlem and abandons her New England home. In a drawing by Wright published in the 1929 issue of the *Quill*, an elegant black figure is depicted in modernistic 1920s style.[77] In other examples, Ralf Coleman's play *The Girl from Back Home*, is set in Harlem, and Waring Cuney mimicked the rhythms of jazz in many of his poems.[78]

Similarly, Helene Johnson's most celebrated poems are linked to New Negro themes. "Regalia" powerfully evokes the intersection of race and tragedy. Big Sam, a janitor from the South, relishes life in the North. He makes "good money," enough to pay for his son's schooling and spare his wife from day work. The anchor of this man's identity is his fraternal lodge, with its joyful street parades and brightly colored uniforms. The lodge means so much to Sam that

> *he would have rather gone without his vittles*
> *Than not pay his lodge dues,*
> *Than not march in the lodge parade,*
> *Than not wear his uniform of blue and gold and orange,*
> *And high white plumes and yellow braid and gold epaulets*
> *And snow-white gloves and shining black shoes and tassels.*[79]

These vivid images are reminiscent of the spectacular parades held in New York by Marcus Garvey's Universal Negro Improvement Association, an inspirational mass movement that fueled black pride internationally and was particularly strong in New York, Atlanta, and Boston.[80]

But Sam's happiness is short-lived. His dour pastor warns of divine disapproval: "God don't like that. . . . God wants mourning / And wailing and dark clothes. . . . He don't want all that / Regalia." Tortured by visions conjured by the gloomy pastor, Sam suddenly strips himself of his regalia and collapses on the street:

It was hard to make him out in all that flood of color.
He seemed so little and tired and bent and dark and humble.
He looked so funny, beating his breast that way.
In fact, he looked more like the little colored janitor
Who stoked stoves,
And emptied garbage,
And piled ashcans,
And scrubbed stairs
In a big apartment in Harlem.

This compassionate portrayal of a black man's struggle for pride of racial identity indicates that Johnson as well as other *Quill* writers, even those of genteel backgrounds—and Johnson's was quite genteel—identified with the vast majority of black people, many of whom were sometimes uplifted and other times oppressed by their religious leaders.

While Johnson drew inspiration from the culture of 1920s Harlem, Waring Cuney delighted in folk religion, music, and dialect, thus balancing the earnestness of other *Quill* selections.[81] When he was at the New England Conservatory of Music, Cuney studied European American musical forms, but he resonated more with what Locke described as "nascent movements of folk-expression and self-determination."[82] Cuney would later move to Harlem, where his stylized black vernacular won him a place in the ranks of eminent New Negro poets. The four poems he published in the debut issue of the *Quill* have been anthologized and appreciated for their resonance with the rhythms of the blues.[83] "Jes' Moochin' Along" is a witty lyric meant to be recited or sung before an audience. The chorus,

Jes' Moochin' Along,
Down de road.
Jes moochin' along,
Wid ma load

is repeated five times, and between repetitions the speaker exhorts us to "Turn to de Bible" (Daniel in the lions' den, Mary Magdalene) to see

"Down an' out folks / Like you an' me." Cuney's folk idiom and music are coordinated with tales of ordinary people:

Dere was po' Mary
A low down gal,
Jesus tol' her
I'm yo' pal.[84]

In this poet's hands, folk religion merges with the black vernacular enshrined in New Negro literature.[85] Notwithstanding Eugene Gordon's disavowal of Harlem's relevance to Afro-Bostonian literary expression and the predilection of Afro-Bostonian writers for their own evolving aesthetics, the Harlem mystique casts a soft but distinctive shadow over the pages of the *Quill.*

The Demise of the *Quill*

The last annual issue of the *Quill* was published in June 1930, having endured longer than some of the comparable little magazines launched at the peak of the New Negro Renaissance. Eugene Gordon continued to work in journalism, cultivating painting as a sideline.[86] Some of his star writers, like Helene Johnson, Dorothy West, and Waring Cuney, went on to become recognized as Harlem Renaissance writers. Only four years after the *Quill* ceased publication, the ambitious West founded her own little magazine, *Challenge*, intending to revive the Harlem Renaissance. To launch the magazine West invested her own personal funds—including three hundred dollars that she received from a film company that employed twenty-two African Americans to make a movie in Russia, and perhaps a small inheritance from her father.[87]

West believed that "new" New Negro writers could raise the Renaissance from its ashes during the bleak 1930s. Like Gordon, West had no white sponsors because, one assumes, she was unwilling to be patronized, literally or figuratively, by anyone. Similarly, recalling Gordon's statement that although all of his club members were black, non-blacks were welcome to join, West was glad that "most of the authors [in the May 1935 issue] were new and not all of them were Negroes." West hoped that "*Challenge* [would] showcase and discover writers of promise and encourage the kind of literary exchange she found so critical in her own experiences as a fledgling writer. Eugene Gordon's Saturday Evening Quill Club encouraged West's early fiction, and some of her first publications appeared in his journal.[88]

West expended considerable effort to recruit new talent and published submissions from a number of "South Side Writers" from Chicago, but the results were disappointing—the New Negro Renaissance stubbornly refused to be revived. It is puzzling that West did not reach out to the Boston writers and artists she knew from the Saturday Evening Quill Club. Gertrude Schalk, Roscoe Wright, Alvirah Hazzard, and poets like Earl Sydnor would have surpassed in quality the contributions West received. Scholar Cherene Sherrard-Johnson also finds it surprising that West did not solicit art from her Boston friend Lois Mailou Jones.[90] Roscoe Wright could have contributed illustrations as well, as he had done for the *Quill*. The most conspicuous absence, however, is Eugene Gordon himself, West's first professional mentor, a well-known journalist, and a prize-winning author of short fiction.[89]

Perhaps West's head was turned by Marian Minus, her coeditor and longtime partner, who focused on collaborating with the Chicago writers emerging at the time. West supported Minus's ideas, and as Sherrard-Johnson puts it, was "excited to publish her cousins" in the Midwest.[91] At her own peril West set her black Yankee roots aside and missed an opportunity to mine a rich trove of proven talent.

Hoping to change course, but still opting not to include members from her Boston peer group, in 1937 West started *New Challenge*, a revamped installment of the magazine under a new name. To infuse it with new energy she engaged the brilliant young Richard Wright as associate editor and published his groundbreaking essay, "A Blueprint for Negro Writing," in *New Challenge*.[92] Nonetheless, West's personal "challenge" turned out to be her confrontations with emergent black radicalism and the demand for politically informed social realism. Besides, West's collaboration with Wright was stormy. When it became clear to her that he and the other Chicago writers intended to take over the magazine, she shut it down completely.[93]

Years later West returned to Massachusetts to live year-round in her family's summer cottage on Martha's Vineyard. She enjoyed a remarkable second act when Jacqueline Kennedy Onassis, the widow of President John F. Kennedy and an editor at Doubleday, read West's columns in the *Vineyard Gazette* and encouraged her to complete an unfinished manuscript.[94] Before West's death at the age of ninety-one, Doubleday published *The Wedding* and a collection entitled *The Richer, the Poorer.*[95] Both books have been chosen as required reading by countless book clubs across the country.

6

The Boston Players

Broadway Bound, 1930–1935

> There is no monument to them, not even a book about their lives, struggles, and successes during the quest for expression in theatre arts.
>
> —Ralf Coleman

Cultural leaders in black Boston were far from Harlem, the veritable mecca where a flourishing New York theatre scene was a significant part of the 1920s expansion of black artistry, most famously on Broadway. For the first time audiences saw a string of all-black shows, like *Shuffle Along* and *Blackbirds*, that become smash hits. Those years were also fruitful ones for black theatre artists in Boston, especially for Maud Cuney Hare and her Allied Arts Players, who created their own modest renascence on the stage.

The stock market crashed on Tuesday, October 29, 1929, but the panic in financial markets did not show its magnitude at first; the realization that the country's economy was nearing the brink of collapse was delayed. As late as two months after "Black Tuesday," U.S. Secretary of the Treasury Andrew Mellon was still predicting a year of healthy growth: "Nothing in the present situation is either menacing or warrant[s] pessimism," he proclaimed.[1] But no corner of the country was exempt from disaster. The Boston experience of the Great Depression was similar to that of other major cities, where the consequences for African Americans were even more dire than than for other ethno-racial groups.[2] By 1932 the percentage of unemployed African Americans far exceeded the numbers among whites—up to 25 percent for urban unemployment. As one historian notes, "Negro workers in the South End and Roxbury—almost none of them in unions, over 70 percent of them unskilled, and with a tuberculosis death rate four times higher than that of whites—experienced an unemployment rate some 15 to 18 percent above the city average." Growing numbers of men in the South End and Roxbury faced a Christmas season without jobs.[3]

In 1930, prospects for the stage were particularly bleak. Langston Hughes lamented the closing of theatres in Manhattan and the disappearance of what had been a fertile field of opportunities for leading black creative artists: "Colored actors began to go hungry, publishers politely rejected new manuscripts, and patrons found other uses for their money. The generous 1920's were over."[4] While Boston's cultural scene can hardly be compared to Harlem's, a parallel may be drawn between downward spirals in both places. Harlem had a raft of literary magazines, some of them small and short-lived, like Wallace Thurman's *Fire!!*. Black Boston had the far less influential *Saturday Evening Quill* magazine, with its rich trove of black writing in all genres by men and women alike, but it produced its last issue in June 1930. Soon afterward Maud Cuney Hare was compelled to close the doors of her Allied Arts Center and disbanded her theatre group. Only a visionary leader of stature could revive Boston's little theatre movement in black.

The Rise of a New Cultural Vision

Ralf Meshack Coleman, a thirty-one-year-old protégé of Hare, fit that description. Under Hare's direction he played the male lead in the second production of *Antar of Araby*, but in 1929 he parted company with the venerable Hare to start his own performing group, the Boston Players.[5] Rejecting the high-culture model of Hare's predilection, Coleman fixed his attention on a flurry of prize-winning plays about black life that were gaining favor on the New York stage. He also hoped to create the kind of theatre that would help dispirited black Bostonians endure the Great Depression. The tall and lanky Coleman, endowed with seemingly boundless energy, was determined to keep the spirit of noncommercial theatre alive. In the five years following the demise of the Allied Arts Players Ralf Coleman's name would become familiar to aficionados of amateur theatre, including both blacks and whites, many of whom had little previous exposure to black artistry.

Coleman was an unlikely successor to the aristocratic Hare, but he made up in charisma, talent, and intelligence what he lacked in privileged upbringing and prestigious family connections. Ralf and his younger brother Warren, both theatre enthusiasts, were the sons of a Baptist minister, Meshack Coleman, and his wife, Ellen Johnson Coleman.[6] Ralf was born in 1897 in Newark, New Jersey, and came of age during what is known as the Progressive era. Ironically, it was a time when African Americans saw precious little progress and derived scant benefits. Instead, disenfranchisement, extralegal violence, and the rollback of gains made during Reconstruction were earmarks of what historian Rayford Logan identified as "the nadir" of black history.[7] It is true that African Americans in the North did not experience the same level of oppression that plagued their counterparts in the South—in fact, the southern black presence in Boston was a result of their flight from the racial atrocities in the region of their birth—but racism was still institutionalized and pervasive. Community organizer Ed Cooper, a native of North Carolina who moved to Boston in 1928, remembered "very distinctly and very vividly that ninety-nine percent of the blacks who worked for the 'the Bery'" (that is, the Boston Elevated Railway, also known as "the El") were porters and janitors. "I remember going down to see the Director in an effort to get blacks driving the streetcars," Cooper told an interviewer with an oral history project. He had come to Boston to matriculate at Boston University's School of Business Administration, only to be told that the quota for colored people had been filled through 1932. The sting of that experience motivated him to devote himself to the struggle for equal rights.[8]

Under circumstances that are unknown, in 1910 Ralf and his brother Warren were adopted by Baptist minister O. Paul Thompson and his wife, Carmelite, who lived in Richmond, Virginia.[9] The teenaged boys were sent to the New Jersey Industrial and Manual Training School for Colored Youth (sometimes called the Bordentown School, but also known as "the Tuskegee of the North") in southern New Jersey. An African American minister had founded this historic boarding school, known affectionately to its alumni as "Mother Ironsides," in 1876. Its curriculum was initially vocational, modeled on the principles of Booker T. Washington, rather than academically oriented. The male students received training in manual arts and agriculture while the girls studied dressmaking and domestic science. Fortunately for the Coleman brothers, however, Bordentown had expanded its curriculum prior to their arrival and was also offering college preparatory courses. It was at Bordentown that an English teacher lit the first spark of a lifelong passion for theatre for Ralf. He would long remember the joy of memorizing and acting out scenes from Shakespeare. A decade later he would direct his own all-black *Macbeth* in a production that predated by six months the celebrated *Voodoo Macbeth* produced in New York by Orson Welles. For his part Warren Coleman would write original one-act plays and experience considerable success on the stage.

After graduating from Bordentown the brothers moved back in with the Thompsons, who now resided in West Newton, Massachusetts, a well-to-do Boston suburb with an historic black community and an equally historic black church, the Myrtle Baptist.[10] Reverend Thompson may have hoped that at least one of the Coleman brothers would follow him (and their biological father) into the ministry, but the young men had other intentions: to live the life of the stage. Through this medium they would also contribute to the advancement of their people in a field to which blacks had limited access. Thompson thoroughly disapproved of theatre and dancing as forms of entertainment, but he evidently came to accept the inevitable, judging by the warm relationship he and his wife sustained with their adopted sons. In years to come Ralf; his wife, Luella; and their children, Riche and Leona ("Nonie"), would be frequent guests for Sunday dinners at the Thompsons'.[11] Nonie remembers Reverend Thompson as a hard-shelled Baptist who "prayed forever and the food would get cold. He was so strict that you couldn't even read the funnies."[12] When Nonie asked her father why the son of a minister would go into acting he answered, "There's not too much difference between religion and acting."[13]

Newton's tiny black community had little to offer in the way of the lively arts, but nearby Boston, with its distinctive black history and a city of culture, beckoned to the Coleman brothers. At the heart of the black community of the time was the South End, a vibrant neighborhood where new arrivals from the South and the Caribbean islands diversified the small black Yankee population. The West Indians had their own social circles, and black Yankees did not always warmly welcome the southerners, but overall the community was close-knit, its strong black institutions providing fertile ground for a variety of new initiatives, including arts-related projects.

An added draw for Coleman was the proximity of Boston's renowned and distinguished cultural institutions: the Boston Public Library was open to all comers, and virtually anyone could take night classes at certain area colleges and universities. Moreover, the downtown theatre district was easily reachable by public transportation from anywhere in the city and even Cambridge, across the river. The city of Boston directory for 1920 lists "Ralph Coleman" as a twenty-one-year-old printer residing at 466 Massachusetts Avenue, South End, where the Women's Service Center (WSC) had established its headquarters.[14] It is perhaps no coincidence that Ralf stayed there for a time and listed the premises as his address, as he would hold his first rehearsals at this location.

Coleman first became involved in the arts through the Soldiers' Comfort Unit (SCU), the forerunner to the WSC and the League for Women in Community Service (LWCS).[15] The entertainment committee of the SCU, as Coleman recalled, "was always looking up skits and songs and dances and refreshments, anything to entertain the boys."[16] The effectiveness of this strong female association with an ambitious agenda illustrates the level of social cohesion that can exist in minority communities like that of black Boston at the time.

In the aftermath of World War I, as Coleman would later recall, "most of the young people from the hut, having had a little taste of show business, answered the call to take part in *The Open Door*," an elaborate pageant depicting the historic progress of blacks after emancipation from slavery.[17] The pageant, written by the wife of Atlanta University's president and a benefit performance for the university, was staged at Symphony Hall on December 8, 1920. It is truly remarkable that a black theatre ensemble could occupy the stage of Symphony Hall, one of Boston's "palaces" of high culture," at a time when de facto segregation was part of business as usual. *The Open Door* was a series of narrated tableaux, an immensely popular art form in the 1920s. White cultural leaders like Eva Whiting White (1885–1974), a leader in the settlement house movement, produced "a seemingly endless stream" of them, including "racial pageants" featuring Chinese, Italians, Irish, and Jews performing songs and dances outdoors. One such play, *The Beacon*, consisting of a series of market scenes representing the West Indies, Tripoli, Morocco, and the East Indies, was performed as late as 1930 on the Boston Common. Such public shows, notes historian Charles H. Trout, "enacted a racial and ethnic harmony that was

Ralf Coleman and Luella Coleman. Courtesy Jocelyn Coleman Walton and Gretchen Coleman-Thomas.

more wished for than present," serving as a mask for the interethnic and -racial conflicts of the time.[18]

The producers "combed the city for a man with a voice that could carry," and chose Ralf Coleman to be the narrator of *The Open Door*.[19] Many years later, Coleman described this production, which toured to Providence, Springfield, and New Haven, and listed the names of some of the performers: "All of us stage-struck youngsters were in it: Jack Bates, Lola Wilson, Mildred Davenport, Emma Jane Rountree, Gladys McAdoo, and many others."[20] The *Boston Globe*'s advance description of the Symphony

Hall production noted that all the parts, mostly allegorical figures, "in this moving spectacle" would be "played by Negroes," but did not mention that the celebrated black violinist Clarence Cameron White would lead the orchestra in a performance of Afro-Canadian composer Nathaniel Dett's *Juba*.[21] Since Boston audiences had little exposure to manifestations of black high culture and were unaccustomed to seeing black people perform on the stage, *The Open Door* was without doubt a milestone event.

In the early 1920s, Coleman took night courses in theatre at area colleges to increase his expertise. At Harvard he studied with Henry W. Longfellow Dana, a champion of progressive causes, and at Emerson College his instructor was Belford Forrest, a professor of theatre arts with a strong interest in black culture.[22] By his own account Coleman kept up a full schedule of activities, working with the Boston Experimental Theatre and the Provincetown Wharf Theatre while working to support himself and his family. In his own words, Coleman was "build[ing him]self up as an actor and possibly then as a director."[23] Working by day as a presser in the garment industry, he gave public recitals on his own time of poems by such Harlem Renaissance–era poets as Langston Hughes and Countee Cullen, and sang spirituals during intermissions at concerts for groups like the Charles Henry Quartet. The high-energy Coleman also recited at Sunday afternoon literary gatherings at the WSC and at churches—in short, he took advantage of all venues available to black people and picked up extra money in the process.

In 1925, Maud Cuney Hare established the Allied Arts Centre, where Coleman found an opportunity to try out his acting skills. The studio—Hare billed it as "the studio at the gay green door"—occupied a prime location opposite the New England Conservatory, Hare's alma mater. It would soon become known as "the black center of the arts in Boston"—a place where "the theatre, the dance, costume making, and sculpture were all encouraged."[24] Hare cast Coleman in the lead role of the second performance of *Antar of Araby* and became his mentor. She also assigned him parts in other productions, including *Ivory, Ebony and Gold*, another of Hare's originals. But Coleman chafed at Hare's strict discipline and had a different vision of what black theatre should be; ultimately the gap could not be bridged. Hare's ideas seemed Victorian to Coleman, and, indeed, the elegant and sophisticated musicologist, born in 1874, had been educated along classical lines during the late nineteenth century. The daughter of a prominent Texas politician who grew up with all the cultural advantages of the elites, by all reports Hare carried herself like a grande dame. She moved in black elite circles and was close with Mary Evans Wilson, the president of the WSC, whose daughter, Lola Wilson, a little girl at the time, got the distinct impression that her mother's good friend "had airs."[25]

Hare's discipline seemed excessive not only to Coleman but to quite a few of the other actors who came of age during the dynamic and permissive "roaring twenties." Nevertheless, many an actor got his or her stage legs thanks to the sophisticated Texan who had quickly made Boston her home and become a black Yankee. For Coleman in particular the apprenticeship with Hare was transformative. The Baptist clergyman's son observed in awe as Hare, seemingly impervious to the color line, took the decisive steps necessary to introduce black faces to the white-dominated stage. Coleman would apply these lessons later on, finding ingenious ways to bring black-themed plays from New York to Boston—even in the depths of the Depression.

Meanwhile, working at a small garment factory on Kneeland Street, the charismatic and congenial devotee of the stage was elected president of his (predominantly Jewish) union and felt "equal to anyone," as he recalled in 1972.[26] After a day's work, his daughter Leona remembered, "He'd be in his den, surrounded by his books. From the smell of cigar you could tell he was home."[27] Many years later Coleman confided to his granddaughters that he hated the work: his lifeblood was the theatre, a medium that he said "could create life out of the cold pages of a book."[28]

Entering into the thick of his community's cultural life, Coleman developed a loyal following, attracting audiences that included white as well as black people. At his job, in the South End, in Roxbury, and in the theatre milieu, Coleman enjoyed cordial relations with a wide circle of like-minded individuals and his social life included people from a variety of socioeconomic levels. Family members affirm that Ralf never forgot that he came from "humble beginnings," nor did he identify with the elite "Four Hundred," although many perceived them as such.[29]

In building their careers, minority cultural leaders like Coleman faced a major challenge in addition to those confronting amateur groups in general: most mainstream venues did not rent their rehearsal and performance facilities to black people. De facto segregation was so egregious that William Monroe Trotter, the famed editor of the Boston *Guardian*, joined the battle to successfully desegregate the Boston Keith-Albee Theatre in 1926. He also challenged the Jim Crow policies of other establishments and institutions including hotels and schools, and prevented a YMCA from opening on the grounds that it was racially segregated.[30]

Even in New York, aspiring black thespians faced a scarcity of venues because many institutions would not have blacks making use of their premises. W. E. B. Du Bois lamented that only "now and then" was a church in the city "liberal enough to house a play." Finding that many suitable venues had a policy of "no blacks need apply," Ernestine Rose, the (white) head librarian at the Harlem branch of the New York Public Library, assisted Du Bois when he started his little theatre movement, the Krigwa Players, at the library.[31] In Boston, black cultural entrepreneurs like Hare and Coleman were on their own when it came to finding venues where race-based restrictions did not apply. Such "free zones" were few in the Jim Crow era, as segregation was the core feature undergirding racial inequality.[32]

Just as Hare had relied on the LWCS in the 1920s, in 1930 Coleman approached the WSC at 464 Massachusetts Avenue with a request to use their headquarters: he was launching his own group, the Boston Players. In fact, one of Coleman's first independent productions took place at 464: *Cinda*, by fellow black Bostonian Jack Bates, was a black version of the Cinderella story that had already been staged at the Allied Arts Center. When Hare learned that Bates had defected from her center to join Coleman, she expressed her disappointment in a letter to W. E. B. Du Bois: "The amateur playwright we furthered has now had Baker Co. accept one of the plays for publication. By my devoting my time to enable him to work out his technic and gain experience, he is in a position to do something worthwhile. And so, he has turned to 'The Boston Players' to have them repeat his 'Cinda.' "[33]

The WSC, like the LWCS, was among the three key institutions that served as a lifeline to black artists during the 1920s and 1930s. The third was the Robert Gould Shaw House, founded in 1908 with the support of Boston's Episcopal Diocese of Massachusetts as part of a social movement that flourished in the early twentieth century. Its express purpose was to provide opportunities for Boston's black population, excluded by such institutions as the segregated YMCA. By making space available for meetings, rehearsals, performances, classes, and all manner of social functions, these three institutions were instrumental in sustaining black artistry during the Depression.[34]

The Robert Gould Shaw House's second director described the place informally called "the Shaw" as "a neighborhood house located in a section largely settled by colored people, and [which] therefore concerns itself chiefly with the activities desired by the people who are its chief constituents." The institution's philosophy embraced "justice and equal opportunity for all, irrespective of race, color, or other arbitrary distinctions . . . and the promotion of a just and amicable relation between the white and colored people."[35] In 1930, Julian Steele, an urbane Harvard graduate, became the Shaw's first black director. Steele greatly expanded programming at the interracial settlement house so as to reflect the makeup of the community. On his staff were twenty-six white and twenty-seven black workers, one of whom was Constance Ridley (the daughter of Florida Ruffin Ridley and granddaughter of Judge George L. Ruffin and Josephine St. Pierre Ruffin). Reverend Michael Haynes, a prominent minister and state legislator who during his youth participated in activities at the Shaw, asserts that "almost nothing of cultural significance occurred that did not involve the Shaw House." The musical and dramatic activities organized by the Shaw further strengthened identity and community bonds and boosted the confidence of countless talented black children and adults through the early 1970s.[36]

The first production by the Boston Players outside the black community took place in a converted stable called the Barn. Maud Cuney Hare had paved the way to this venue, located at 36 Joy Street on Beacon Hill, and she staged her original poetic piece *Tree Fantasy* there in 1927. Fittingly, the Barn stood only a few blocks from the historic black district on Beacon Hill that had been a beehive of antislavery activity in the previous century. Coleman gave other productions under the auspices of the Ford Hall Forum, a private institution widely known for its lecture series.[37] The liberal forum held debates on controversial issues such as socialism, women's suffrage, and reproductive rights. Coleman established "a lasting friendship with the Ford Hall people, and especially with program director David K. Niles, who was on the Boston NAACP's Executive Committee and had a keen interest in Negro theater."[38] "At the Forum there was no color line," Coleman stated with satisfaction.[39]

Well on a path to greater success, in late February 1930, the Boston Players entered a tournament sponsored by the Curtain Call Club. The Players were the only black company competing in a field of nine, and they took the prize with their performance of *The Dreamy Kid* by Eugene

O'Neill, who embraced the noncommercial little theatre and, most significantly, the black folk play form.[40] *The Dreamy Kid* deals forthrightly with gangster life, focusing on a young fugitive from the law who, swayed by the moral influence of his grandmother, turns himself in to authorities.

Coleman had admired O'Neill ever since seeing *The Emperor Jones* at Boston's old Castle Square Theater, with famed Broadway actor Charles Gilpin in the starring role.[41] On November 1, 1930, the Boston Players presented O'Neill's *All God's Chillun Got Wings,* which featured an interracial relationship. Controversy swirled around this play, particularly because it defied the rule that black and white actors were not permitted to touch each other on the stage.[42] This production was directed not by Coleman but by a white enthusiast of black theatre named Charles Flato, who would direct another two plays with Coleman's actors and cowrite two more with Warren Coleman before disappearing into anonymity.[43]

That same year Coleman and his company, billed as the Ford Hall Players, staged *The Rider of Dreams,* which was part of the groundbreaking trilogy, *Three Plays for a Negro Theater,* by Ridgley Torrence, a prominent white New York poet. Coleman went on to present the remaining two parts of the trilogy, *Granny Maumee* and *Simon the Cyrenian.*[44] Torrence was hailed for breathing new life into the American theatre, which prior to World War I had featured far more musical comedy and melodrama than serious dramas.

Unlike other directors, who routinely used white actors made up in blackface, the Ohio-born playwright Torrence specified that the actors in his plays must be "colored." In order to make his plays more authentic he incorporated theatrical gestures drawn from black traditions even as he drew attention to the unequal status of African Americans.[45] Torrence's major innovations—all-black casts and more authentic portrayals of black characters than American audiences had previously seen—advanced two major causes at one time: theatrical innovation and civil rights. Many black critics welcomed his plays, as they did those of Paul Green and Eugene O'Neill, although some, like Ralph Matthews, the drama critic of the Baltimore *Afro-American,* fulminated against "dramas that flowed from the pens of white playwrights" and deplored what "could not conscientiously be classed as Negro Theatre." Matthews claimed that "an unconscious strain of Ofay [white-skinned] psychology" prevented non-black playwrights from portraying the African American "as he sees himself." Rather, "he is seen through the condescending eyes of the detached observer."[46] Carter Woodson, the great black historian, was equally suspicious of white dramatists like Green, O'Neill, and Marc Connelly because "they could not think black."[47] Coleman, on the other hand, valued their pioneering plays and proceeded to stage even more plays by O'Neill and Green.

On May 5, 1930, even as the 1929 crash was wreaking havoc, Coleman presented his original play *Paradox, a One Act Play of Negro Life* at the Barn.[48] The "paradox" of the title refers to the plight of aspiring blacks, even those with Harvard degrees, who could not crack the color line. It was well known that educated men and women, if they were black, were automatically eliminated from applicant pools and could rarely secure employment commensurate with their education. In *Paradox* Coleman's main character, Daniel Patterson, is a Harvard graduate working at Boston's South Station, where black redcaps complained that white supervisors "drove them like slaves."[49] In the first scene, set at the station, a commuter berates a porter with these harsh words: "You damn niggers are all alike—too dumb to live. If I had you down South I'd fix you." This line, which graphically conveys the viciousness of white racism, probably shocked the demure Beacon Hill audience at the Barn. To be terrorized on a daily basis was part of the black experience, no matter one's skin tone or social class.

The tide of the play turns when Dan's one-time girlfriend, Charlotte, recognizes him and demands to know "what on earth . . . a Harvard graduate, a man of letters, with education, opportunity, and youth is doing here." Charlotte is about to board a train to Alabama where a teaching position awaits her. She urges Dan, who is trapped in a marriage to a deceitful woman, to cut loose and join her: "I know you've always hated the South, but it's the only place you're going to get the chance you deserve." At that moment a fellow redcap bursts onto the stage with the good news that Dan's wife has eloped with the true father of her baby. "Here, boy is yo' bill of divorcement! . . . You sho' ought to send dat 'Sporty' guy a box of cigars. Dat's what I call a friend in need."

Despite its contrived and abrupt ending, Coleman's play succeeds in bringing out a cold truth: the best Boston had to offer a black man was semi-skilled labor. The irony would not have escaped the Boston audience: Dan agrees to join Charlotte and start a new life in Alabama, a dangerous place for blacks, to escape discrimination in Boston. But this was precisely

Coleman's point: the golden city attracted many talented and hopeful blacks only to disappoint them.

Coleman surely drew his material from conversations with many who, like Dan, worked beneath their education level and wasted their talents. Dean K. Denniston, Sr., who, like the Coleman family, summered at Oak Bluffs on Martha's Vineyard Island, found no teaching opportunities in Boston despite his master's degree in education from Boston University, so he followed his sisters south to Georgia and became the principal of a segregated boarding school.[50]

For many decades well-meaning educators, both black and white, advised black graduates to go south. Such was the experience of Lois Mailou Jones, who also spent summers on Martha's Vineyard. The young painter, who would rise to international prominence, described her distress at being advised to leave Boston to an interviewer for the Radcliffe Oral History Project:

> Because I had been praised so highly having been the winner of the Susan Minot Lane scholarships and the first awards in design, and I felt that maybe they could use me I went to talk with the director of the Museum School [of the Museum of Fine Arts]. I asked Henry Hunt Clarke, the director, if there was any chance for me to perhaps work as an assistant. And I remember his very beautiful cold blue eyes staring at me and hearing him say, "Well, we have no opening here, but why don't you think of going South to help your people?" Well, I was just shocked. To go south to help my people. If you know anything about Boston people you will know that they probably knew about Fisk or Tuskegee, that is the younger ones of us, but to go south was sort of, in a way, insulting. We had been exposed to Harvard University, to Tufts College, to Simmons College, to Radcliffe, but to go south to help my people was just something that was not to be thought of.[51]

But Jones did go south, first to teach at the Palmer Memorial Institute in Sedalia, North Carolina, and finally to Howard University in Washington, D.C., her stepping-stone to a brilliant career. Denniston too left Boston for Georgia but soon returned, preferring to be a dining car waiter on the Boston to Washington line of the New Haven Railroad rather than living with Jim Crow. He loved classical music: for four decades he and his wife held season tickets to the Boston Symphony Orchestra and their son Donald became an accomplished composer and conductor.[52] Like many black Bostonians the Dennistons partook of the high-culture events of their city, deftly circumventing its more subtle forms of discrimination. Coleman knew Denniston and Jones well as neighbors in his summer community and as peers in Boston's black cultural circles.

Educated black women faced an equally formidable but somewhat different set of obstacles. If they were dark skinned, for example, few avenues other than domestic work were within their grasp. The women could be elevator operators or work at a department store counter only if they passed "the paper bag" test, meaning having a light skin tone. At one point Leona "Nonie" Coleman, Ralf Coleman's fair-skinned daughter, participated in an experiment devised by the Urban League. She and a dark-skinned friend were sent out—separately—to apply for the same job at Gilchrist's, a well-known department store in downtown Boston. The dark-skinned applicant was told that the job was filled, but when Leona showed up, they offered her the position on the spot. This experiment corroborated charges of employment discrimination against Gilchrist's and provided evidence that was used in court.[53] Bostonian Cynthia Belgrave, who would become a well-known producer and actor in New York, was the first black woman hired and assigned to serve customers at a counter in Gilchrist's.[54]

The life stories of Afro-Bostonians like Jones, Denniston, and Belgrave add substance to the historical record, highlighting the strategies they devised to reach their goals. Ralf Coleman leveraged his success with the Ford Hall Players to gain sufficient credibility to aim for larger mainstream venues. One was the Fine Arts Theatre, with a more central location than the Barn. Maud Cuney Hare had again paved the way, staging two of her large-scale productions there. Coleman followed Hare's lead. He was determined to transform the white-dominated stage into a platform for people of all races. On February 2, 1930, he staged Paul Green's *In Abraham's Bosom: The Biography of a Negro in Seven Scenes,* thereby contesting racial segregation in local theatres.[55]

The main character in Green's folk play is a black farm worker with minimum education (we see him struggling with simple math) and unrealistic expectations. When provoked by his abusive white half-brother, he responds with violence. It goes without saying that he will be killed in retaliation and the killer will be held blameless. The scene epitomizes the oppression suffered by African Americans, and not only in the South. *In Abraham's Bosom*, like other plays produced by Coleman, was staged as a benefit for the Boston Urban League, which had worked to break employment barriers in Boston since 1917. Coleman did not accept payment for this play or for his other benefit performances because he regarded his productions, even those that were seemingly apolitical, as "protest plays"—weapons in the equal rights struggle.[56]

Over a period of five years, from 1929 to 1934, Coleman staged nearly a dozen plays, ranging from folk plays to Broadway comedies. The Boston Players went on tour to Worcester and Springfield, Massachusetts, and Providence, Rhode Island, for repeat performances.[57] Depression-era audiences were only too happy to escape their troubles by going to the theatre. Some plays were light fare and unrelated to black concerns, but such was not the case with *Scarlet Sister Mary*, based on a controversial novel that was banned in Boston.

Scarlet Sister Mary: A Stepping-Stone to Broadway

Coleman signaled his return to serious, black-themed drama with *Scarlet Sister Mary*, one of the most successful of his incursions into mainstream theatre. In this play, set in a Gullah community off the coast of Georgia, Mary is an orphan raised by her aunts on an abandoned plantation, far from white racism but subject to judgment by the church brothers and sisters.[58] Mary, with her eight children from as many fathers and all born out of wedlock, meets with disapproval, which accounts for the word "scarlet" (sinful) in the title. But she is a resourceful woman who appeals to the churchmen's better instincts, avoids excommunication, and is welcomed back into the good graces of her spiritual community.[59]

Years before the Boston Players took it on, the play had debuted on Broadway with Ethel Barrymore and a full cast of white men and women made up in blackface. After its debut on November 25, 1930, the *New York Times* drama critic Brooks Atkinson fumed, "Most of us will never understand why Ethel Barrymore has chosen to appear in 'Scarlet Sister Mary.' It merely reminds us that Negroes are the best actors of plays about Negro life."[60] Barrymore freely acknowledged that her New York friends were displeased enough not to attend the performance.[61] Langston Hughes was indignant that Barrymore would appropriate a role that by rights should have gone to Rose McClendon, the leading black actress on the Broadway stage. Hughes's indignation prompted him to write the satirical work *Scarlet Sister Barry*, a parody featuring white actors who fail pathetically in their attempt to portray blacks.[62] In November 1930, the blackface *Scarlet Sister Mary* traveled to Boston, where a large and expectant crowd awaited the arrival of the famed Barrymore. Apparently, the Boston theatregoers were no more impressed than the New Yorkers.

Coleman staged *Scarlet Sister Mary* at the Fine Arts Theatre with an all-black cast on April 15, 1934. News of the all-black Boston production reached Broadway producer Margaret Hewes, who immediately traveled to Boston to see a performance. Afterward Hewes went backstage and asked the company, "Would you folks like to go on Broadway?"[63] They quickly agreed, for, as Coleman explained, "an actor's dream at that time was to be on Broadway: that was the pinnacle of success. Hollywood didn't matter in those days. New York was the center of entertainment."[64] Hewes proceeded to sign Coleman and all thirty-five Boston Players, including a sixteen-person choir, for the world premiere of a new Paul Green play, *Potter's Field*.[65]

Potter's Field Debuts in Boston

On April 16, 1934, after months of rehearsing at the WSC, Paul Green's *Potter's Field: A Symphonic Play of the Negro People* opened at the Plymouth Theatre in a tryout. Green himself traveled to Boston to oversee rehearsals of his play.[66] The *Boston Globe* vividly described the opening scene of this socially conscious play set in a poverty-stricken black settlement: "The curtain rises to disclose a boarding house keeper lolling indolently before her ramshackle hut in the sweltering heat of a late Saturday afternoon. She is surrounded by sundry of her boarders, who chatter and cut up joyously, or sit in bitter silence offering a few grim comments on the hopelessness of their lot. . . . From time to time there are heard rumblings of a chain gang building a new road."[67] John Henry, a stranger, arrives in the guise of a preacher, but unbeknownst to the town, there is a warrant out for his arrest. The female lead is Millie Wilson, who lives with Tom Sterling, a boarder, while her husband, Bantam, a convict, works on a chain gang. Bantam returns and threatens to kill Sterling but is killed by him instead. The play closes with a stirring scene in which John Henry, from center stage, begins a hypnotic folk chant. The police stand motionless as the members of a chain gang, inspired by the chant, drift into an illuminated circle and join in the singing. In the final scene the gang returns to its labors, steamrolling the village shanties to clear the way for the new road. Even as the dispossession and ruination of black people in the hostile South are poignantly displayed, hope rings in the air.

Coleman's cast included his brother Warren in the role of John Henry, and James Henderson, who had his own little theatre in Boston and would live to be a centenarian but did not continue with the play when it left town because he was staging his own production, *Invisible Empire*, in Boston.[68] Dolphe Martin, about whom next to nothing is known, composed the musical score and directed the chorus, who sang from the orchestra pit. Coleman's production of Paul Green's magnificent blend of choral music and drama worked its magic on audiences and critics alike. The sheer number of reviews suggests that the play caught hold of the imagination of the Boston audience. Most of the city's major dailies gave it glowing reviews, a remarkable event for an all-black production in a segregated city. The *Boston Post* pronounced *Potter's Field* "one of the most moving and extraordinary dramas that the theatre ha[d] offered within present memory," while the *Boston Globe* marveled at this "strange, haunting, unusual play" that had "the comedy, the pathos, and the futility of a subject race, free in name, but actually still enslaved to ignorance, poverty, the dominant white man and his law."[69] An exception to the positive reviews was an anonymous critic for the *Boston Globe* who expressed distaste for a play that exhibits "a crusader's zeal about what he evidently considers a social blemish: the pitiable plight of a small colony of Southern Negroes 'squatting' wretchedly in Potter's Field." It is possible that this critic would have been averse to any drama placed in the service of political protest. Even so, the critic echoed the praise of the *Transcript*, describing the characters in the final scene as "grasp[ing] hopefully at a symbolic ray of light."[70]

The Coleman brothers and their close associate Luoneal Mason must have been elated by their specific mentions by one reviewer, who described Warren as "an actor [whose] exceptional abilities have been revealed." For Ralf as Tom Sterling and Luoneal Mason as Tom's rival, Bantam, the review had praise for adding "great illusion to their characterizations of . . . the leading roles."[71] With such admiration expressed for a black play steeped in folk culture, there was every reason to believe that the receptivity to black artistry would continue indefinitely. Instead, the enthusiasm evaporated in just a few years.

The Boston Players' success in the theatre district would have been a great accomplishment for any amateur company, but for a Negro troupe, it was also a well-aimed blow at the color line—an advance in the struggle for black actors to gain space on the white stage. *Potter's Field* had a one-week run, prompting the *Herald* reviewer to express deep frustration: "It speaks poorly for those who have clamored to the high heavens for more and better plays in this city that it was withdrawn last evening after eight performances." *Potter's Field* deserved more, the reviewer asserted, adding pointedly that "[we] can only hope that the play has a second chance, not here, where it seems more and more that audiences demand big names in actors and producers, but in New York, where there is a willing public for boldly experimental adult drama."[72] It seemed that there were good prospects for a positive reception for *Potter's Field* in New York.

In September 1934, the play opened for a second tryout at the Pabst Theater in Milwaukee, Wisconsin. It was renamed with the more upbeat title *Roll Sweet Chariot*, perhaps to evoke the spiritual "Swing Low, Sweet Chariot."[73] Ralf Coleman again starred as the romantic lead, Sterling. The *Milwaukee Sentinel* praised the play's "seamless merging of words and music" and lavished compliments on both Ralf Coleman, "the fiery man who loves and kills," and his brother Warren, for his "tremendous basso" and "a capital portrayal of a counterfeit preacher and later a genuine member of a slave gang." Approving "cries of Bravo! and Author!" were heard from the back of the house, wrote the reviewer, but he also predicted that *Roll Sweet Chariot* would "cause a stir in the town" and provoke "furious debate as to its worth."[74] Could this comment have been a veiled allusion to the play's protest theme? Ultimately, the Milwaukee experience was a tryout without a triumph. Perhaps a political play featuring an all-black cast proved to be too much for the Midwestern reviewer.

Roll Sweet Chariot Opens in New York

Upon the company's arrival in New York the Boston Players learned that Margaret Hewes had added two great Broadway stars, Frank Wilson and Rose McClendon, to the cast (in minor roles, with Wilson as one of the boarders and McClendon as Bantam's mother). On October 2, 1934, the play opened at the Cort Theatre at 138 West 48th Street but to mixed reviews. The *Chicago Defender* reported that Broadway had liked *Roll Sweet Chariot* but Brooks Atkinson, a champion of black theatre, found the opening performance "tragically bad" and only marginally better three nights later. The fault lay with Paul Green's "imperfect sense of theatre tempo," Atkinson ventured, and consequently some minor scenes were overly protracted. Another issue Atkinson noted was diction: "Excepting the speech of Frank Wilson, Warren Coleman, and Rose McClendon . . . the accents were more Harlem than [southern] Negro." And yet, he wrote, "No chronicle of current drama would be complete without a discussion of Paul Green's stirring drama."[75]

After seven performances the play was closed down. Its failure must have come as a surprise to the company, given the rave reviews seen in Boston. But the historical record leans in favor of a positive assessment. In an authoritative book, esteemed drama critic Edith Isaacs pronounced *Roll Sweet Chariot* a strong forerunner to a long line of "music-plays" to come—among them *Jonny Johnson, Knickerbocker Holiday,* and *Oklahoma!* Dolphe Martin's score, wrote Isaacs, "made music as integral a part of the play's sound and meaning as the words."[76] In an enthusiastic article published in *Theatre Arts,* the New York critic also delivered a superlative review:

> The critic who loves the theatre has had a mighty good time in NY this month. . . . If he happened to see the first night of Paul Green's "Roll," he had the thrilling experience of coming unexpectedly upon a great production. The clear, high talent expressed in Paul Green's earlier work, and the advance news of the unusual quality of this "symphonic play" of the Negro people (coming in from a road tryout that was probably not completely in hand) gave no hint of the actual achievement. . . . For years there has been a looking forward to the time someone would make a play of words and music, not separately but jointly, so that the music should be as integral a part of the play's sound and meaning as the words.[77]

After the closing of *Roll Sweet Chariot* Warren Coleman stayed on in New York to create the role of Crown, the villain of *Porgy and Bess,* but Ralf never thought about staying: "I never waited around for a job in New York, where there were thousands of other unemployed actors. Boston has been my home base," he declared without hesitation.[78] In 1944, however, he would return to New York, called to tour professionally as stage manager for *Anna Lucasta*, a Broadway hit featuring an all-black cast.[79]

Other Black Theatre Directors of the Era

Coleman was not the only black theatre producer-director who continued to thrive during the Depression. William Frederick Fisher and James Henderson also stimulated and invigorated black theatre, but of this we would have no inkling if not for the encyclopedic memory of Reverend Michael Haynes. As Haynes recounts, Fisher arrived in Boston from North Carolina with a doctorate in theology and a passion for the stage. Haynes recalls that year after year Fisher attracted large crowds to his "wildly popular performances" of *The Open Tomb* at Symphony Hall, a passion and resurrection play in which Fisher himself played Jesus. Haynes further asserts that one cannot discuss drama and culture without taking into account Dr. William Frederick Fisher, a theologian who majored in theatre at the traditionally black Livingston College in North Carolina, and his theatre group. "In 1934 or 1935 we stood in line at Symphony Hall at 4 a.m. Easter morning to see *The Open Tomb* in which Fisher portrayed Jesus." Later moved to Jordan Hall (at the New England Conservatory of Music), *The Open Tomb* was regarded as a Boston tradition. Haynes vividly recalls the crowds lining up at the ticket booth hours early to see Fisher's one-man show.[80]

James Henderson was, according to Haynes, "a distinguished, dark-skinned man, short and stocky in appearance, easy to relate to and good-humored. He wore a goatee and a fedora and always carried a briefcase."[81] He was born in 1894 in Elizabeth, New Jersey, majored in theatre at the Thyne Institute in Virginia and Livingston College in North Carolina, and taught English and drama at Nansemond Collegiate Institute in Suffolk, Virginia, before heading north. He wrote, produced, and directed his first Boston plays at the Robert Gould Shaw House, where he worked part-time. During the summers Henderson was a volunteer drama specialist at Camp Breezy Meadows, the summer camp associated with the Shaw. Like Coleman, Henderson furthered his studies in expression and acting through evening classes at Harvard and Boston University, concentrating his studies on Shakespearean drama and playwriting, and perfecting his art through private lessons with an elocution teacher.[82] In the mid-1920s Henderson teamed up with Ralf Coleman to cowrite *Color Line*, for which no script survives. The two men put on this show and others in the gymnasium of St. Mark's Congregational Church in Roxbury, where Coleman was a member. Ruby Henderson, James's wife, was the leading coach for these productions.[83]

An excellent opportunity came Henderson's way when a Miss Wagner, the director of an agency called Community Services, approached him about starting a black theatre group: "Why couldn't we have a Negro theater in Boston, a professional one?" she asked Henderson, to which he immediately replied, "Why couldn't we?" Wagner asked eagerly if he could "get [her] ten professional Negro actors." Henderson immediately promised her twenty. In fact, as he later confessed, "I didn't know but two, besides myself and Ralf Coleman." But he brought in Frank Silvera and others who "had talent and had been in quite a number of plays." In collaboration with Coleman, Henderson founded "Company C" to perform a pageant called *The Black Man's Gift*. Two decades later the title would cause an uproar in the black community, according to Coleman, because only "colored" or "Negro" were acceptable. Coleman, Henderson's codirector, testified, "Half the colored people in Boston wanted to lynch me for using the word 'Black.' It was anathema then."[84]

On his own Henderson produced an original play, *The Invisible Empire*, of which little is known other than its probable performance year—1934—and the involvement in it of white actors. Reminiscing about his experiences, Henderson commented that he had started off "with a white director, but eventually we got Ralf Coleman to direct the play. I had seven white and eight black actors, some of whom worked at Community Services."[85] The play was produced at the Peabody Playhouse, whose location remains to be identified. Henderson took pride in *The Invisible Empire*, which was not financially succesful but made a great impression, resulting in Henderson's incorporation into the Federal Theatre Project in 1935.

Other grassroots theatre initiatives contributed to the vitality of Afro-Bostonian culture. Thelma Thornton, a protégé of Maud Cuney Hare, formed the University City Players for children interested in acting.[86] Initiatives such as those spearheaded by Henderson, Fisher, Coleman, and

Thornton call attention to the fact that racial and economic hurdles did not deter black cultural leaders from showcasing black talent and expanding the scope of the city's offerings beyond monoculturalism. Fledgling amateur groups would soon have to compete with moving pictures for attention, but in what was still the golden age of radio, live performance had all the advantage in popular entertainment.

The theatrically inclined cohorts of black Boston persisted in the pursuit of their goals. Coleman and the Boston Players provided the momentum to tide over the little theatre movement until 1935. Coleman turned a reversal of fortune into an opportunity by staging both serious black dramas and up-to-date Broadway plays that could entertain Bostonian audiences during the city's darkest days. In so doing, he awakened local audiences to the cultural contributions of African-descended people. With a string of successfully produced plays and a cast of talented literary and musical people, Coleman demonstrated that the color line was not impermeable, even as he set an example to be emulated by upcoming actors. Coleman and other black directors kept the spirit of noncommercial black theatre alive by virtue of their charisma, unflagging enthusiasm, and powers of persuasion. That year saw the arrival of the Federal Theatre Project (FTP). This unprecedented and never duplicated federally funded program would bear fruits for African Americans and for other ethno-racial groups in America.

Between 1930 and 1935 Coleman extended his reach to include white as well as black patrons. *Scarlet Sister Mary*, performed at a mainstream theatre on Huntington Avenue, and *Potter's Field*, staged in the theatre district, were major breakthroughs. Equally significant was Coleman's break with blackface, the notorious practice of covering the faces of white actors in grease paint and displacing black actors in the process. The Broadway run of *Potter's Field* (as *Roll Sweet Chariot*) was an illustration of how much the American stage could benefit from the integration of black artists into the entertainment industry. Coleman's passion for theatre, his leadership, and his dedication to the racial struggle were the driving force that inspired the black Bostonian showmen and -women to press on to success. But charisma and boundless energy alone would have been insufficient had it not been for the rich pool of talented Afro-Bostonians who acted—literally and figuratively—on their artistic dreams. Dozens of gifted black dancers, choreographers, costumers, playwrights, designers, and actors worked relentlessly to accomplish the artistic and politically conscious goals that meant so much to them.[87]

Supported by black institutions such as the Women's Service Club, and taking full advantage of the venue of the Robert Gould Shaw House as brick-and-mortar rehearsal and performance venues, Coleman and his cohort chipped away at the exclusionary policies that had stunted the aspirations of countless black Bostonians. These two institutions, in addition to the League of Women for Community Service, helped to sustain aspiring black people and eased the transition from the optimistic 1920s to the rough 1930s.

On October 5, 1975, Boston Mayor Kevin White recognized Ralf Coleman by awarding him the official title of "Dean of Boston's Black Theatre," honoring his four decades of significant contributions to the enhancement of cultural life in the city.[88] By extending black performance art into the 1930s, Coleman, though he could have not known this, was preparing fertile ground for the arrival of the FTP. In 1935, he received an appointment as director the Boston unit of the FTP, the project's only black unit that was free of white control. But Coleman, never one to dwell on his personal triumphs, pressed the point that the pioneering African Americans with whom he collaborated had been forgotten: "There is no monument to them," he insisted, "not even a book about their lives, struggles, and successes during the quest for expression in theater arts."[89]

7

The New Deal for Boston's Black Theatre

Four Golden Years, 1935–1939

> In reality, the Great Depression was not depressing.
>
> —Matthew Josephson

In mid-October 1934, when Ralf Coleman and the Boston Players returned to Boston flush with their Broadway experience, the Great Depression was taking a heavy toll. Years later Coleman would describe the country as "a mortally wounded animal, staggering, foundering, until in 1935 it fell flat on its face."[1] Amid labor protests and with unemployment rates soaring to 25 percent, Boston's Mayor James Michael Curley branded all public demonstrations as communist-inspired.[2] Bread lines, soup kitchens, roving panhandlers, and unemployed men selling apples on street corners were common sights in the city, and "Brother, Can You Spare a Dime?" was a signature song that echoed throughout the 1930s.

On the cultural front, where there had been vibrancy, came decline. Theatres went dark: actors, musicians, technical assistants, chauffeurs, and other industry workers joined the ranks of the unemployed. Unsurprisingly, prospects for reviving an independent theatre company like the Boston Players faded along with the city's fortunes. The activities identified with the Harlem Renaissance diminished noticeably, but historians note that the movement was still very much alive. In 1933, at the behest of Franklin Delano Roosevelt, Congress passed massive legislation for a

"New Deal" composed of a vast network of antipoverty programs. "Federal One" was the collective name for five divisions charged with providing relief for unemployed professional artists: the Federal Art Project, the Federal Music Project, the Federal Theatre Project (FTP), the Federal Writers' Project, and the Historical Records Survey.[3] Roosevelt named Harry Hopkins, the director of the Federal Emergency Relief Administration (FERA) and one of the president's closest advisors, to oversee Federal One's unique experiment in social engineering. Never before had cultural workers—visual artists, musicians, writers, researchers, and theatre professionals—drawn their salaries directly from the federal payroll. The most controversial of the five programs was the FTP, directed by Vassar College professor Hallie Flanagan.[4] Its left-leaning productions incurred the ire of so many U.S. congressmen that its days were numbered from the start. Still, Flanagan fearlessly confronted the opposition and fought tooth and nail for the FTP, without conceding the fight until the end.

In retrospect it is not obvious why the federal government developed and promoted a comprehensive arts program, until we consider the conditions of this unprecedented crisis and the fact that the central and most persistent feature of the Depression was massive unemployment, which affected hundreds of thousands of unemployed artists. Flanagan later described the plight of theatre workers and the case she made for inclusiveness during the planning phases of the FTP: "The people of the theatre—directors, actors, designers, costumers, stagehands—turned to any sort of job that could be found, however temporary, however poorly paid. They were willing to dig ditches and they did dig ditches, but unskilled labor was also unemployed and could dig better ditches. A violinist, a circus clown, a sculptor, a stagehand—these people are trained in one profession and one profession only. Try as they would, they could find no recourse except charity."[5]

Despite the absence in the United States of a tradition of federal support for the arts, the Roosevelt administration and First Lady Eleanor Roosevelt embraced the notion that artists and writers—white, black, or any other ethno-racial minority—were an integral part of national identity and must be included in the grand scheme of the first New Deal.[6] Hopkins chose Flanagan to head the FTP for many reasons. The first female recipient of a Guggenheim Fellowship, she had studied populist theatre movements in Europe and published a book on the latest innovations.[7] Described by John Houseman of the New York FTP as a "wild little woman who believed and publicly stated her conviction that the theatre is more than a private enterprise; it is also a public interest which, properly fostered, might come to be a social and educative force," Flanagan would need every bit of her tenaciousness to confront formidable opposition.[8] Harry Hopkins and Flanagan, who had in common their strong populist leanings, conferred in Washington, D.C., and devised a plan that would bring a relief program to thousands of professional actors. A second and equally important goal was to entertain low-income families with plays that met specific criteria of social relevance. Americans with little or no experience to live art would have opportunities that had previously been beyond their reach.

While in Washington Flanagan learned to her delight that Eleanor Roosevelt was "interested in all these art projects."[9] She met with the first lady, who encouraged her to accept the extraordinary challenge of establishing a national theatre through a network of theatre production units in major cities across the nation.[10] In the first two years of its operation the project held performances at no charge to schools, orphanages, homes for the aged, veterans' hospitals, sailors' havens, and other venues. This was not theatre for the elites but "people's theatre," wrote Willson Whitman, a participant in the enterprise. When Whitman published his enthusiastic book on the subject in 1937, he could not have foreseen that the FTP would be terminated two years later.[11]

By August 1935, the FTP entered the final stage of planning. Flanagan spread out a map of the United States to identify cities that could host "five [later six] great regional theatres . . . each one a production center for a professional company; each a retraining center for the actors . . . , each a service, research, and playwriting center for its own region . . . [to] do new plays and classical repertory and everything that commercial theatres cannot always afford to try."[12] New York, Hartford, Detroit, and Cincinnati had large numbers of unemployed actors. So did Boston, a tryout town where plays and musicals were prepared, tested, and revised prior to opening in New York.[13] As a result, Massachusetts would become one of twenty-one states chosen as FTP sites.[14]

The Racial Units: An American Paradox

One of the most striking features of the FTP was its division into Italian, Yiddish, Anglo-Jewish, German, and French Units. These were grouped with the "Negro Theatre Project" into a category called "the racial units." Today they might be called ethno-linguistic, rather than racial. On its face this grouping looks very much like Jim Crow segregation, which leading black organizations would normally have denounced and vehemently opposed, but the circumstances were unique. It should be remembered that W. E. B. Du Bois, who in an early stage of his intellectual evolution had been an integrationist, founded the Krigwa Players as an expressly all-black group. Opting to add Negro Units in addition to those created for other "racial" groups (including Italian, Yiddish, and "English"), and requiring integrated audiences for all performances, the Federal Theatre took a step that held "the potential to take on the country's deep-seated racism."[15]

Ultimately, Flanagan praised "our three racial groups in Boston—Yiddish, Italian, and Negro, [who] are playing a repertory from their respective literatures to thousands of people weekly."[16] Toward the end of the project Flanagan described it as Boston's most talented and active, with two shows in particular contributing strongly to the Boston FTP's turnaround after some initial difficulties. Apparently, the Negro Unit had become Boston's most successful.[17]

The Boston Negro Unit revived black theatre on a larger scale than its leaders had thought possible. With one stroke of Flanagan's pen, black actors, technicians, and a host of other theatre professionals began to receive salaries for the work they loved, going from the unemployed rolls to a living wage of twenty-five dollars a week. Flanagan and her team, learning that Ralf Coleman had been conspicuous on Boston's theatre scene for many years as an actor and director, appointed him straightaway to head the Negro Unit in Boston: he was the only African American director in the FTP and would remain so until late 1936, when at last a black director replaced a white one at the helm of the famous Harlem unit. Another black Bostonian who saw his fortunes changed by the FTP was James Henderson, who led his own performing group and was appointed as an administrator at the FTP's central office on Boylston Street. Henderson was told that only professionals were eligible for hiring but, he said, he did not have the heart to turn away all the amateurs.[18]

Despite their uniqueness, very little has been published on Coleman and the Boston Negro Unit. The history of the Massachusetts FTP has not been chronicled for reasons that include the difficulty of accessing primary source materials. In 1939, after Congress defunded the FTP, a vast trove of hastily collected documents was sent to an airplane hangar outside Baltimore. There the collection remained in obscurity until Lorraine Brown, an English professor at George Mason University, rediscovered them and negotiated a transfer to her institution. The thirty-four years the valuable trove had spent in storage, uncatalogued and uncurated, worked to the detriment of researchers and theatre historians, but through Brown's efforts the documents were ultimately saved and distributed among the Library of Congress, the National Archives, and George Mason University.[19] Scholar Rena Fraden successfully mined them for crucial information and quotations from production notes written by Ralf Coleman for her authoritative book *Blueprints for a Black Theatre,* published in 1994.[20] Even so, today's researchers are still hard pressed to locate, consult, and study the poorly catalogued records.

Before Federal One was organized, the Federal Emergency Relief Administration (FERA or ERA), an agency established by Congress on May 22, 1933, was in charge of aid operations. The agency's mandate was to provide immediate relief in the form of gainful employment for millions who had fallen on hard times.[21] Although it is best remembered for engineering and construction projects like the Tennessee Valley Authority, FERA also funneled aid to state authorities to provide food, clothing, small allowances, and jobs to the unemployed.

Most relevant here is that eligibility for relief was extended to artists, writers, and professional theatre people, over half of whom were unemployed. Four hundred and fifty of FERA's first hires were incorporated into small performing units established in cities across the country, and 13,162 actors, musicians, carpenters, electricians, and other stage technicians found employment. The FERA performing units played spot bookings, staging variety and vaudeville shows at Civilian Conservation Corps sites, community churches, and schools.[22]

In a dramatic turnabout, during the lean years of the New Deal, this new program brought hopeful prospects. The theatre units' productions ranged from *The Taming of the Shrew* to *The Trouble I've Seen,* about the struggles of relief families and the operations of rural rehabilitation projects. After two years FERA became part of the Works Progress Administration (WPA), and between 1935 and 1943, the WPA became the largest employer in the country, providing almost 8 million jobs. According to one author, "The old centers of power were being rudely knocked about [and] new opportunities opened for those able and ready to respond to them."[23]

The first black Bostonian production to be funded—and the first anywhere in America written, staged, and acted by FERA workers—was *Genesis*, a play given on August 30, 1934, by the FERA Civic Theatre of Boston and Chorus, officially known as "Company C." The cast included nine black actors and fifteen black singers from the FERA Chorus.[24] H. Jack Bates, who had gotten his start with Maud Cuney Hare and the Allied Arts Players, cowrote the play with Charles Flato (1908–84), a little known figure described by the *Boston Herald* as "the only member of the company who was not black." *Juba*, a three-act comedy written by Warren Coleman, a Boston FERA worker at the time, was performed on March 27, 1935, at the English High School, then located on Montgomery Street, Boston. Complementing the performance was a program of southern melodies and dances, and music performed by the Boston ERA Civic Chorus.[25] Bates was also part of the *Genesis* cast, as were Allied Arts Players Lou Oneal (or Louoneal) Mason, Granville Stewart, Cornelius Crosson, and Eleanor Trent Wallace.[26] The press advertised *Genesis* as a reimagination of the biblical story transformed into a folk play—with no racial theme and no concrete political agenda—significant because it was staged by an all-black cast at a time when the American public had very little exposure to black artistry.[27]

Genesis attracted much attention when it came close to being banned. Flato had planned a play in the nude—"not a single fig leaf [was] available in Boston," wrote the critic from the *Boston Herald* with rank sarcasm. Fearing that stage nudity could cost him his federal funding, Flato hastily dressed the actors "in draperies" and covered the ushers in what the *Globe* described as "primeval ooze."[28] Had he not done so the Boston Watch and Ward Society, whose mission was to detect breaches of conventional morality, would have stopped the production.[29] Before vanishing into obscurity, Flato directed a black cast, members of the Boston Players, founded by Ralf Coleman in 1929, in *Juba*, a three-act comedy written by Warren Coleman.[30] It is ironic that Flato, known for his apolitical productions, would later be revealed as a career spy for the Soviet government.[31]

Ralf Coleman also enjoyed FERA sponsorship of *Macbeth*, which he staged with a group he called the Negro Shakespeare Troupe, in September 1935, at the Town Hall of Salem, Massachusetts; it had another performance on October 18, 1935, in Roxbury. Lisa N. Simmons, a granddaughter of Coleman's stage manager, Lorenzo Quarles, has suggested that the Harlem Unit's *Voodoo Macbeth*, "the most well-known black Shakespeare play in American history, might need to be contextualized . . . by the possibility that Welles was following a black director's precedent. Coleman's silent ghost of a production might even push Welles' 'Macbeth' from its stool."[32]

Although the Boston *Macbeth* is minor in comparison to the legendary New York extravaganza, it was significant because it preceded the famed *Voodoo Macbeth* in Harlem. Simmons points out that the chronology invites speculation that Welles was "partially inspired by this 1935 version in Boston," which was presented some six months earlier. That point having been made, the differences of scale must also be recognized: whereas Welles's *Voodoo Macbeth* ran for many months at Harlem's Lafayette Theatre, Coleman's *Macbeth* had merely two performances. But Simmons's larger point remains: Coleman produced *Macbeth* in its original version because he strongly believed in presenting the talent and range of his black actors. His production was an early example of nontraditional casting, that is, assigning black actors to roles in plays not previously intended for black people. The Shakespeare performance in black demonstrated that African Americans, like European Americans, are rightful heirs to the Western tradition. Simmons underlines Coleman's insistence that black actors should be eligible for any role, including those traditionally reserved for whites.

Stevedore: A Radical Departure

Coleman had not yet assumed his position as the head of Boston's Negro Unit when he decided to produce *Stevedore*, a play that had caused great excitement at its New York premiere in April 1934. It was received so enthusiastically at the Civic Repertory Theatre that members of the audience rushed the stage to embrace the actors. Brooks Atkinson, the *New York Times* theatre critic, hailed the production as a "a swift and exciting drama of a race riot seasoned with class propaganda and presenting the American Federation of Labor as the Negro's best friend."[33] Even Alain Locke, the philosophical architect of the New Negro Renaissance, known for his disdain for "propaganda" plays, added his voice to the chorus of approval, proclaiming that a "synthesis of race and class" had created "a new type of problem drama." Two of the most powerful issues of the contemporary scene had met in *Stevedore*, Locke proclaimed.[34] In Boston, *Stevedore* would prove equally successful, even if theatregoers did not rush the stage like the less-inhibited New Yorkers.

A display ad in the Boston *Transcript* billed the play as "Stevedore, the New York and London Hit" when announcing its Boston opening at the Repertory Theatre.[35] It acquired the nickname "the race riot play" because it depicted the mobilization of embattled black dockworkers in New Orleans to defend a black labor organizer. The trouble starts when black workers are frustrated in their efforts to join the all-white union, and one union member threatens to defect rather than allow blacks into the local branch. At the same time, Lonnie Thompson, the organizer of the black workers, dares to accost a white supervisor who cheats black workers of their pay.

The police hire a team of thugs to pursue Thompson, and as tensions heighten, Thompson is forced to flee. The stevedores, backed by the black community, rush to his defense and build a barricade. Unexpectedly (if improbably), some white organizers defect to join forces with the black stevedores. Thompson dies in a hail of bullets, a martyr to the cause but also a powerful symbol of the workers' struggle for justice. The depiction of militancy on stage was a major feature of the 1930s, which saw the birth of social consciousness films and agit-prop theatre, and its prevalence fed the suspicion of legislators that communist activism was at work.

Coleman, who was close to the uphill struggle of black workers barred from joining unions and himself a member of a union, received backing for his production from the New Repertory Players, a group whose politics were similar to those of the left-leaning (Civic) Theatre Union in New York. Having staged a number of major dramas of black life by Ridgley Torrence, Paul Green, and others who had reinvigorated American theatre of the 1920s and 1930s, Coleman was primed for a new challenge.

It was Coleman's first radical play, undertaken at great risk to his career, but it was not to be his last. How he came to turn his attention from relatively apolitical black-themed folk plays to radical drama is something of a mystery. Thus far his political activities had been limited to voting for the Democratic Party ticket (while his wife Luella voted Republican), but over the previous four years Coleman had supported the black cause by

Scene from *Stevedore*, Federal Theatre Project, Boston Negro Unit. Courtesy Mason/Quarles Collection.

staging benefit performances for the Women's Service Club and the Urban League.[36] Now, however, Coleman was engaging with politically charged theatre, which would become a hallmark of the Federal Theatre Project.

Coleman contracted with FERA employees, who were free to moonlight after hours as long as they rehearsed on their own time and agreed to have their earnings deducted from their pay. But *Stevedore* came close to being banned, despite Coleman's compliance with federal regulations. Boston's infamous Watch and Ward Society, which worked hand in glove with the city censor and the local police, got involved. In 1929, the society had famously banned Eugene O'Neill's *Interlude* on the grounds that it involved marital infidelity, but the producers foiled the censors by moving the play to Quincy, a city directly south of Boston.[37]

Forewarned by Flato's brush with censorship, Coleman preemptively erased all profane language from the script (replacing "goddamns" with "damns")—and without further ado, on Tuesday, September 18, 1935, *Stevedore* opened at the Repertory Theater without incident.[38] Two inspectors and six assistants to the city censor stood vigil in the theatre but did

Members of Boston's Negro Unit of the Federal Theatre Project. Courtesy Mason/Quarles Collection.

nothing to stop the show. The Wednesday and Thursday performances on September 18 and 19 also went smoothly. But on Friday, when Coleman and his cast were rehearsing, they learned that local authorities were pressuring FERA to cancel *Stevedore.* As Coleman recalled, "The big office [of the agency] was against the play because of its controversial nature and because we were doing it with a so-called group of Communists." The coauthors of the play were indeed Communist Party members, as was Charles Flato (although this was unknown at the time), but the cast members were likely not. Nonetheless, FERA took a preventative measure to thwart the production, dispatching eight cast members, including Ralf Coleman, to Salem, a city some eight miles north of Boston, to perform *Macbeth* at Salem City Hall. The curtain time for the performance was the same as for *Stevedore* in Boston, a move to prevent that show from going on. Inspectors were sent to Salem to ensure that the actors complied, and they knew they would lose their jobs if they did not do so.[39]

But Coleman and his producers devised a way to foil FERA censorship.[40] They placed a call to Rose McClendon, the founder of the Negro People's Theater in Harlem, asking her to send substitute actors. McClendon promised eight understudies from the original New York cast. That night two cars drove to pick them up in New York. By 8:30 the following evening the Repertory Theatre was sold out and the theatre overflowed. Meanwhile, the Salem contingent performed a rush *Macbeth* and headed back to Boston.[41]

By curtain time, however, only three New York actors had arrived (one of the cars was delayed on its way back), and Coleman's group had not arrived either. Two officials of the New Repertory Theatre stepped out in front of the curtain to announce the delay and the reasons for it, including the attempt to ban the play on moral grounds and the threats that the use of profane language would lead to arrests. A New York playwright, Albert Maltz, flew in from New York and delivered a speech in which he declared that censorship "without gloves" must be defeated if America was to avoid what was occurring in Germany: "It is an old method," he told the audience, "to censor social plays on the ground that they are immoral or profane or that the theatre where they are to be presented is a fire-trap. . . . It is a peculiar thing that the theatre always ceases to be a fire-trap as soon as the offending play is withdrawn."[42]

Lorenzo Quarles, Coleman's stage manager, could not delay the show indefinitely because of regulations stipulating that performances must end before midnight. While awaiting the missing actors the cast hastily put on *Waiting for Lefty* by Clifford Odets, a left-wing play that assailed capitalism and corrupt unions in a series of vignettes that brought the desperation of suffering Americans to center stage. It had previously been banned several times in Boston. After nine o'clock the actors had still not arrived. Quarles was about to call for volunteers from the audience to read parts, a tactic that would later be used in New York to avoid the banning of *The Cradle Will Rock* in 1937, when the actors arrived from Salem. They received a standing ovation.[43]

The first scene of *Stevedore* was already in progress, the actors from Salem already on stage, but it was restarted when the New Yorkers arrived. Police inspectors stood by and federal timekeepers wrote down the names of the cast members. Theatre historian James Haskins comments that the production was excellent, "but both cast and audience enjoyed it all the more because the FTP officials had been outsmarted."[44] William Worthy, a black Bostonian and international journalist who witnessed the incident, saw it as "a clear-cut case of Boston's notorious police censorship."[45]

Remarkably, Coleman's defiance generated wide press coverage but no repercussions for having set art and politics on a collision course.

Haskins compares Coleman to Lonnie Thompson in *Stevedore*—"strong, courageous, and determined."[46] The near banning of *Stevedore* has been forgotten, but it merits attention because it was a prelude to the censorship that would plague the FTP and effectively lead to its demise. After a staging of the play in Seattle, it became one of the works most prominently targeted for investigation by the Dies Committee (also known as the House Un-American Activities Committee, or HUAC), originally created in 1938 to investigate citizens with alleged ties to the Nazis. The blacklisting and ruination of writers, actors, and others accused of being communists had not yet begun in earnest.

The most provocative scene in *Stevedore* has black and white longshoremen uniting in a violent confrontation with the union. The labor riot seen on the stage was based on strikes taking place around the country. Labor leader A. Philip Randolph had recently rallied mass support to protest discrimination by the Pullman Company, much to the consternation of the Roosevelt administration.[47] On March 19, 1935, the Harlem Race Riot would break out. It was an expression of frustration over unemployment, discrimination, and racial injustice, further hastening the demise of the Harlem Renaissance.

Coleman's embrace of a protest play such as *Stevedore* suggests that he agreed with W. E. B. Du Bois that theatre should serve as "propaganda" in the most positive sense of the word: advocacy for racial justice. By contrast, though, Du Bois wanted to confine "real" black theatre to black-authored plays, black actors, black audiences, and black neighborhoods.[48] Coleman disagreed. He was no fan of dividing audiences by race. As a dyed-in-the-wool integrationist he focused on reaching across the color line, as had his mentor, Maud Cuney Hare.

The Boston Negro Unit Expands Its Range to Include Musicals

The record of Coleman's later productions is incomplete and even their exact sequence is unknown. However, a brief discussion of four important productions—*Brother Mose* in 1936; *Bloodstream* and *The Trial of Dr. Beck*, both of 1937; and *Jericho*, in 1938—serve to illustrate the Boston director's versatility and his ability to successfully stage both protest plays and musicals that were often lighter, amusing, and even heartwarming.[49]

The Boston Negro Unit followed up *Stevedore* with another success, *Brother Mose: A Comedy Drama of Negro Life* by Frank H. Wilson, the distinguished black actor of the Broadway stage.[50] The play debuted on November 14, 1936, at the Veterans Building in Concord, Massachusetts, less than a year after *Stevedore*.[51] A small, embattled community in rural Texas finds itself under considerable pressure to sell its land to a developer who is offering them another property in exchange. The town preacher, Moses Perkin, puts his trust in the white landowner and urges his people to accept the dubious deal. Enos Greene, the leader of an opposition movement, comes forward to protest that the property, called "the Gut," is a useless swampland and calls on the community to rebel. But Greene is revealed to be a racketeer, and the community learns to trust their preacher. The clincher is that oil has been discovered on the Gut. Historians Errol G. Hill and James V. Hatch express reservations about the play, noting that "the humble protagonist who counsels patient suffering" is a source of weakness in the play.[52] Drama critic Rena Fraden appears to fault the play for failing to challenge "the status quo" and for featuring black people who "are good and bad but mostly comic as they sing and dance."[53] But in his director's report to the FTP administration Coleman described *Brother Mose* as "a play that appeals to the average audience combining broad comedy and deep pathos." At the same time, Coleman allowed that "the theme, 'the meek shall inherit the earth' . . . is objectionable to the so-called Negro intelligentsia of Boston."[54] The plays had to pass muster with a double audience: one black and one white. Even the subtitle, "Comedy Drama of Negro Life," indicated that serious social issues would not be raised. *Brother Mose* was a far cry from *Stevedore* or even *Potter's Field* (*Roll Chariot, Roll*) in its absence of social critique. In his production notes Coleman praised the great Frank Wilson for "know[ing] his people and his public. 'Negro folk plays' are not anachronistic; rather, they are 'the greatest contribution of the Negro theatre to the American stage,'" Coleman wrote in a spirited defense that indicates his directorial decisions were strategic.[55]

Two additional Coleman productions, both staged in 1937, merit close attention: *Bloodstream*, a protest play not unlike *Stevedore*, and *The Trial of Dr. Beck*, a tense courtroom drama. *Bloodstream* was scheduled to open at the Copley Theatre on March 17, 1937. This political drama set in

Alabama was designed to hold audiences in horror-filled suspense; it was also an exposé of violent and inhumane conditions in southern prisons.[56] As in *Stevedore*, cross-racial solidarity is depicted as the solution, a potent source of hope and power for oppressed people. It was also "the first white and negro production of the Federal Theatre Project."[57] In early March, however, the National Association for the Advancement of Color People (NAACP) had to intervene in a fight to gain the use of the Copley Theatre by the black WPA actors, as the venue was refusing its use because the play would be performed by a black unit (though, in fact, half the cast members were white). The NAACP mounted a campaign against the theatre, and Julian Steele, the bold director of the Robert Gould Shaw House, led the ultimately successful drive to desegregate the theatre.[58] On March 17, *Bloodstream* opened to a packed house, and critics found much to commend in the production. The *Boston Daily Record* praised it as "a blood and thunder melodrama" (melodramas were wildly popular with Depression-era audiences).[59]

The curtain rises on the dark tunnels of a coal mine as conflict breaks out between a group of five convicts and a sadistic (white) warden. An indomitable spirit named Knox has just endured a severe beating at the hands of the warden, but he seizes the warden's gun and leads an escape. Five convicts, four black and one white, follow Knox, who stumbles upon an armed guard and kills him. This act triggers a manhunt through the underground labyrinth. A prisoner named Gypsy Kale, who has a hidden stick of dynamite, joins Knox, and the two men, one white and the other black, become "like the fingers on a hand."[60] Knox, gravely wounded, retreats into the tunnel, clearing the way for others to escape but encountering the warden in the darkened recesses of the mine.

The action-packed performance ran for ten nights. Contemporary readers of the script (like some of the critics at the time) might find its dialect wooden. One reviewer complained specifically about "one of the longest death scenes on record," but the play was a rousing success anyway. It was also full of dramatic and sociologically important possibilities, wrote the same critic.[61] The *Boston Daily Record* classified *Bloodstream* as a "Dixie Prison Play," skirting the issue of race. Another reviewer observed obliquely that the work, "carefully steering away from the dangerous shoals of prison reform propaganda," was "frankly a blood-and-thunder melodrama."[62] Melodrama was exactly what the beleaguered audiences wanted as the noose of the Depression tightened. As in *Stevedore*, the play hails cross-racial alliances as a weapon to fight oppression. The Marxist tenet that class interests run deeper than race is made manifest, but critics largely ignored the play's ideological implications.

Strong political message plays were no longer a rare event in the Federal Theatre or the commercial stage, and *Bloodstream* met with no official interference. Boston's intolerance of "moral infractions" had not abated, however. Langston Hughes, who attended a dress rehearsal at the Copley, was asked if he thought his play *Mulatto*, coauthored with Zora Neale Hurston, would come to Boston. Hughes responded, "It was barred in Philadelphia, so I don't think they would have it here."[63] (*Mulatto* includes a rape scene, so Hughes was quite correct that it would never have seen the light of day in 1930s Boston.)[64] Shows that played in Boston before heading to Broadway were subject to the worst censorship in the country.[65]

There is perhaps no better example of Ralf Coleman's success in merging art and activism than *The Trial of Dr. Beck: A Play in Three Acts* by the African American Hughes Allison (1908–74).[66] Until the FTP era, very few black-authored plays saw the footlights. Errol Hill and James Hatch describe the play as "an amazing tour de force": "Using the device of a murder mystery, Allison constructed a courtroom suspense drama in such a way that white and black audiences agreed that color in American had the power to influence courtroom justice."[67] It was first produced in 1937 in Newark by the New Jersey Negro Unit, which had made "overly cautious choices" for fear of becoming like "the naughty New York 'Communists.'" Blacks made up 9 percent of Newark's population, as compared to Boston's 3 percent, but Newark's black unit had remained dormant until it staged *Dr. Beck*. After unanimous critical praise it had a second performance in Union City, New Jersey, where it ran for four weeks. In fact, the show had such success that it became the only Federal Theatre production to move to Broadway. The Boston production of *Dr. Beck* took place at the Copley Theatre in 1939.[68]

The plot revolves around Dr. John Beck, a young physician. His medical school tuition was paid by a wealthy black woman who insisted that he marry her. Like the famous Madame C. J. Walker, Amanda Beck had acquired her wealth from a popular hair-straightening product. The Becks' marriage was for convenience only, and John is involved with an attractive and light-skinned woman. When Amanda is found dead, murdered with a surgical knife, the doctor is the obvious suspect. The remainder of the drama hinges on the question of his culpability.

Allison's play was problematic for the readers charged with play selection. Some were shocked by the intra-racial animosity based on color stratification among well-to-do-blacks showcased in the play. A rare glimpse of the behind-the-scenes politics of FTP play selection is provided by the selection committee's production notes: one reader, who was white, found "the conflict between the black and yellow [to be] highly explosive dramatic material" and wondered "how deeply the Negroes might feel on this subject or in what degree resentments might be aroused." Carlton Moss, one of the chief black consultants to the FTP in New York, agreed that it could be "a dangerous experiment" for Harlem (where, in fact, it was never staged). The committee debated whether it could be presented at all, anywhere. In the end they decided that *Dr. Beck* was "sound, well constructed, suspenseful and effective in its climactic ending." It was "a living tragedy of Negro Americana with sociological implications" that dealt "forcefully and vividly with the peculiar color prejudices found within modern American Negro Life."[69]

Dr. Beck had a motive to kill his wife: to inherit her fortune. It does not help his case that he is the author of a book that exhorts black men to marry light-skinned women in hopes of effecting a transformation of skin color among African Americans. Beck's bizarre genetic engineering scheme sways the jury against him, but the defense attorney (who is black) presents factual evidence that leads to the identification of the true killer. This summary, however, does not begin to convey the complexity of Allison's script. Coleman's production opened on June 20, 1939, at the Copley, where it ran for four weeks, the same length of time as on Broadway.

Coleman's interracial cast found favor with the critics. The Boston *Transcript* noted that "a white and Negro cast play[ed] along to the solution [of the suspenseful drama] with skill and relish, holding the stage and captivating the audience."[70] The actors were impressive, with Herbert Jackson (a real-life attorney and judge!) in the role of Dr. Beck. Frank Silvera, the future Hollywood star, played the defense attorney. The bold treatment of color stratification as a divisive force in the black community highlighted the extent to which the noxious racial codes of the white mainstream had penetrated black society. The exposure of intra-racial prejudice was "disquieting to black audiences," writes theatre critic Quita Craig, because "the black error of buying into myths of white superiority" was supposed to remain within the community.[71] Boston reviewers, however, valued the play's power to hold audience attention and its many suspenseful moments. "There's always room for a good murder trial in the theatre," wrote the *Boston Herald.* "No matter how many there have been before, the process of examination and cross-examinations, the acrimonious discussions between rival attorneys, the objections and over-rulings make for an entertaining show, even though some blood-thirsty souls would rather see a stage murder than a play about one."[72] Both white and black audiences saw that color in America had the power to influence courtroom justice.[73]

Dr. Beck was significant in that Coleman successfully staged it in a city unaccustomed to edgy plays, particularly those related to race. In the end it was deemed "an example of the black productions that were among the most spectacular given by the FTP."[74] There is no stronger example of the successful fusion of art and social consciousness than Coleman's success with this riveting courtroom drama.

August 1938 saw the debut of *Jericho: A Modern Negro Drama,* a successful and highly popular play set in a small southern town. Jericho is a minister's son who is enthralled by the excitement of nightlife at the club where he works. As the play opens, we see Jericho is on the verge of succumbing to the charms of the seductive Delilah, a "nawthern sinner," according to Jericho's father, a minister who decries the nighttime goings-on at the hall, where young men "sell their souls to Satan." In the wake of the preacher's failed attempt to physically remove Jericho from the premises confusion reigns. The club's bouncer assaults Jericho, but to the surprise of all, the preacher's son defeats the bouncer and takes off for New York with Delilah. In the big city Delilah connives with a savvy, if shady, Harlemite named Horace Williams, who has a scheme to enroll Jericho in a fight club. Quite improbably, Jericho is a great success and skyrockets to fame as a contender for the world championship.[75]

News of Jericho's triumph reaches his hometown and he becomes a local hero. But an altercation with Horace ends with the Harlem man's death, and Jericho flees to take refuge in his hometown. In a climactic scene, Jericho makes a full confession and (most improbably) is absolved. Despite the contrivance of this melodrama, audiences were enthusiastic. Coleman had wisely transformed a play that was "too countrified" by incorporating jazz and scenes from New York nightlife."[76] One reviewer gave Coleman's production high praise, writing, "Drama was catapulted to a new high at the Empire Theatre last evening as an all-Negro cast of Federal theatre players thrilled an enthusiastic audience. No play during the current season of Federal theatre productions has captured an audience more completely on its first showing than this rugged and forceful story."[77] Coleman also introduced what was at the time an advanced technique—a split stage, a technique whereby two or more scenes are performed on stage at the same time—to accelerate the action and increase the dynamism. *Jericho* provided much-needed fun and entertainment for a Depression-weary audience.

In 1938, Coleman wrote his original one-act play *Swing Song*, which deserves mention because it complements *Stevedore* and *Bloodstream* by dramatizing racial strife and implicitly denouncing violence against blacks.[78] Its interracial love story, set in the South, would have fascinated audiences at a time when most states prohibited interracial marriage and criminalized "miscegenation." A black man and white woman who are expecting a baby marry hastily and in secret to prepare for their escape to the North. But as the woman goes into labor the sound of a lynch mob reaches the house. Unable to flee, the woman dies in childbirth at the very moment that the mob breaks down the door. This ending and the play itself can be read as a protest against American racism and the tragedies it brings, not to mention the failure of Congress to pass an anti-lynching law.

Nearly four decades later E. L. Doctorow would publish the novel *Ragtime*, in which a black man and his white wife meet a tragic end, but their child survives, suggesting that American audiences were ready to imagine a more hopeful future.[79] In 1938, however, it would have been difficult to write such an optimistic ending. As a director of a Federal Theatre Unit, Coleman clearly felt empowered to take on controversial and provocative issues. Like other lynching plays, *Swing Song* can be identified as a site of struggle against white supremacist ideologies. Staging this play was a bold and defiant move for Coleman and the Negro Unit of the Massachusetts FTP.

Had it enjoyed a longer period of time to further hone its technique, the Negro Unit would most likely have gone from strength to strength. But on June 30, 1939, despite Hallie Flanagan's bold and eloquent response to interrogation on the floor of Congress, opposition mounted to the allegedly subversive FTP, culminating in the cancellation of the historic and never-repeated project. This was an enormous loss for the nation. For the fortunate participants whose lives were transformed, however, the era was golden, so much so that "the Great Depression was not depressing."[80]

This chapter has brought to the fore black Boston's unique experience with the FTP and the unprecedented, if short-lived opportunities it created for the development of African American and ethno-linguistic minority art. The historical narrative given here is meant to encourage further research, which is sorely needed, in an enlarged context. The examination of a small number of the hundreds of plays produced by the FTP raise critical questions: What can be learned from America's bold experiment with government-funded art? Given the success achieved by art financed solely by the cultural capital and funds of private citizens and supported by community institutions, how does this paradigm compare to the model of government funding and intervention? What have the struggles of recent decades with government-supported foundations like the National Endowment for the Arts taught us about the risk of censorship? What potential lies in art as a political tool in the search for social justice? What does the FTP experience say about race in America? Finally, how much or little have we advanced in the pursuit of inclusive art that adheres to the highest aesthetic and ethical standards?

AFTERWORD

A Retrospective View of the Boston Renascence, 1920–1940

The primary goal of this study has been to rediscover the cultural initiatives undertaken by leading black Bostonians during the interwar era in Boston. Delving into this lost chapter in history reveals that the artistic production of African Americans in Boston was distinctive in and of itself, but it was also a strategy deployed by blacks in their struggle for equality. Above all, they deliberately merged activism with art and ethics with aesthetics, just as their predecessors had done since the time of Phillis Wheatley. While mobilizing their resources to confront the anti-black bias that permeated society, and working to counteract the unrelentingly negative representations of their race, black organizers focused on developing the intellectual and artistic creativity of their peers, demonstrating that black intellectual potential was easily equal to that of whites. For leaders like Maud Cuney Hare, Ralf Coleman, and James Henderson, as well as for artists like Allan Crite, Lois Mailou Jones, and Roland Hayes, the conviction that cultural production could furnish irrefutable proof of African Americans' right to full acceptance was an article of faith.

Electoral politics, which in the past had enabled nonracial minorities like the Irish and the Italians to assimilate and achieve status, was a blocked avenue for African Americans, not only because they made up less than 3 percent of the city's population, but because their endeavors were met with outright institutionalized and systemic discrimination—in short, Jim Crow northern style.

It was under this set of circumstances that black Bostonians exerted their influence by the conjoining of activism with art. For two and a half centuries, from the arrival of the first Africans on New England soil in 1638 to the first all-black performance at Symphony Hall in 1920, black people had demonstrated their potential, creating poetry, oratory, novels, visual art, music, journalism, and independent scholarship. In this way they forged the image of a people endowed with courage, determination, boundless energy, and high aspirations, and projected black excellence into public discourse. At the turn of the twentieth century an apparent lull in productivity was in fact the prelude to a renascence of artistic, literary, dramatic, and musical activity during the Harlem Renaissance. The analysis of this body of work, as presented in this study, illuminates the complexity of artistic production, at once a reach for the starry sky of art and a war waged along the color line.

The upsurge of art and its renascence during the interwar era survived the onset of the Great Depression and into the era of federal funding for the arts. In the 1940s, a population shift occurred out of Boston's centralized South End and Roxbury neighborhoods and into the outlying districts of Roxbury and North Dorchester. These displacements had the effect of dispersing the community and diluting its cultural energies. Despite a dramatic increase in the black population of Boston by 5 percent, there was no appreciably new wave of cultural production.[1] Demographic growth alone did not result in an intensification of creative activities such as those witnessed during the 1920s and 1930s. But the opening in 1947 of Wally's Café in the South End—at the famed intersection of Massachusetts and Columbus Avenues—signaled the invigoration of a thriving jazz scene, and new leadership worked to revitalize the civil rights cause.[2]

With the post–World War II era would come a reconfigured sense of black identity. New leaders spearheaded the struggle for justice in such areas as employment, housing, education, and human services. Malcolm X, deeply affected by the failure of gradualist approaches to reform, embraced radical religion and politics in Boston before doing so in the spotlight of national attention. Eugene Wolcott, a musical prodigy on the violin, became Louis Farrakhan, leader of the new religion, the Nation of Islam. Martin Luther King, Jr., who preached at the Twelfth Baptist Church in Roxbury while a student at the School of Theology of Boston University, chose yet another path, that of nonviolent civil disobedience. But too many broken promises and unfulfilled hopes had stoked deep frustration, which peaked and was unleashed during the busing crisis of the 1970s.[3] Boston's black community would redefine itself henceforth by turning not to the arts but to far more direct means of engagement with social and political activism.

Nonetheless, the historic tradition of practicing the arts as a means of social change did not disappear. Recent decades have seen the establishment in Boston of new institutions devoted to culture, of which the Museum of African American History on Beacon Hill is the most salient example. The Black Theatre Collective is another of the many initiatives that have brightened the cultural horizon, just as the founding of the Roxbury International Film Festival and its successful incorporation into the Museum of Fine Arts' programming is a hallmark of renewal. Black artists now cross the color line as a matter of course. A residency program for gifted black playwrights, established at the Huntington Theatre in partnership with the Boston Center for the Arts, has been fruitful in its productions of black-authored plays. An ample allotment of resources has made it possible for a passel of plays by a noted black author to be presented to great acclaim at the Huntington.

Meanwhile, the Boston renascence, which thrived at a time when the arts were perceived as a major avenue for advancement and socially conscious expression, has left a paradoxical legacy: some of it endures but most is ephemeral. The archived copies of the *Saturday Evening Quill* magazine are a resource that allows researchers a glimpse of the lives and thoughts of talented black native sons and daughters in 1920s Boston; the canvases of Allan Rohan Crite and Lois Mailou Jones may be seen in galleries across the country; and the voices of Roland Hayes and other classically trained musicians survive on old records. But leaders like Maud Cuney Hare, Ralf Coleman, and Eugene Gordon either wrote no memoirs or left them unfinished—the stories of their lives' work are lost, a loss that diminishes the city's cultural treasure trove.

New life was breathed into local culture in 1950 with the founding of the Elma Lewis School of Fine Arts. The legendary Elma Lewis (1921–2004), a Boston-born black woman of strength and stature, ran this school to nurture the talents of black youth. She also established Langston Hughes's gospel musical *Black Nativity* as an annual and much-awaited event every December. Lewis's associate John Ross provided the music, and every role is played by a black Bostonian, including small children. Forty-six years after its inception *Black Nativity* is up in lights on the Paramount Theatre marquee and attracts white and black theatregoers by the droves. As if that were not enough, Lewis was also instrumental in the establishment of another institution, the National Center for African American Arts, located in a beautiful mansion surrounded by a sweeping lawn in Roxbury. For her part, a younger leader, Lisa N. Simmons, a descendent of black actors from the Federal Theatre in Boston, and her associates founded the Roxbury International Film Festival, which continues to bring young filmmakers and their films to the public eye. Over the past twenty years, the festival has become the largest in New England dedicated to celebrating the work of filmmakers who create films celebrating people of color.

These outsized efforts at black cultural and societal advancement, made possible by earlier generations of inspired black Bostonians, has come to fruition, making it possible for black actors to play traditionally white roles and see their own plays produced in the Athens of America. In this way, certain key objectives of the former era have been realized in our times. Talented black people, both elites and nonelites, have progressed remarkably in achieving recognition for their artistic output.

NOTES

Introduction

1. U.S. Census Bureau, QuickFacts, Boston, Massachusetts, www.census.gov/quickfacts/table/PST045215/2507000.
2. Alain Locke, ed., *The New Negro: An Interpretation* (New York: A. C. Boni, 1925), 3; George Hutchinson, *The Harlem Renaissance in Black and White* (Cambridge: Harvard University Press, 1995); William D. Piersen, *Black Yankees: The Development of an Afro-American Subculture in Eighteenth-Century New England* (Amherst: University of Massachusetts Press, 1988).
3. Anna Julia Cooper, "Angry Saxons and Negro Education," *Crisis*, May 1938, 148.
4. See Pierre Bourdieu and Jean-Claude Passeron, *Reproduction in Education, Society and Culture* (London: Sage, 1990).
5. The terms "African American" and "black" are used interchangeably, following the example of John Hope Franklin and Evelyn Higginbotham in *From Slavery to Freedom: A History of African Americans* (New York: McGraw-Hill, 2011). However, in this volume, the term "Afro-Bostonian," endorsed by historian Lois Horton, serves to remind us of fundamental transatlantic cultural connections. Throughout the early twentieth century, "Negro" and "colored" were widely used, often interchangeably (for example, in publications such as *Crisis* magazine).
6. Edmund Barry Gaither, "Allan Rohan Crite: An American Original," in *Allan Rohan Crite: Artist-Reporter of the African American Community*, ed. Julie Levin Caro (Seattle: Frye Art Museum, 2001), 22.
7. W. E. B. Du Bois, "Krigwa Players Little Negro Theater: The Story of a Little Theater Movement," *Crisis*, July 1926, 134.

1. Where Is Black Boston?

1. Meta Warrick Fuller is widely known as one of the leading female artists of

the Harlem Renaissance. She created the original plaster sculpture *Emancipation* in 1913.

2. See Alain Locke, ed., *The New Negro: An Interpretation* (New York: A. and C. Boni, 1925).
3. The classic study on (antebellum) black Boston is James O. Horton and Lois Horton, *Black Bostonians: Family Life and Community Struggle in the Antebellum North* (New York: Holmes and Meier, 1979).
4. David Delaney, *Race, Place and the Law, 1836–1948* (Austin: University of Texas Press, 1998), vii. In defining "community" I follow James Oliver Horton and Lois E. Horton: "Community" may signify "both institutions (social, political, ethnic and religious) and sentiments based on shared experience, and a common destiny that bound community members together." Horton and Horton, *In Hope of Liberty: Culture, Community and Protest among Northern Free Blacks, 1700–1860* (New York: Oxford University Press, 1997), x.
5. John Winthrop, *The Journal of John Winthrop, 1630–1649*, ed. Richard S. Dunn, James Savage, and Laetitia Yeandle (Cambridge: Harvard University Press, 1996), 246 (entry for February–March 1638). New England ship owners routinely obtained slaves from English-speaking Caribbean islands such as Barbados and Antigua. During the first half of the eighteenth century, colonists also engaged in slave expeditions to Africa. Most of the enslaved Africans were sold in the South, with small numbers reserved for sale in Boston. See Gregory O'Malley, *Final Passages: The Intercolonial Slave Trade of British America, 1619–1807* (Chapel Hill: University of North Carolina Press, 2014), 202–3, and Karen Ordahl Kupperman, *Providence Island, 1630–1641: The Other Puritan Colony* (New York: Cambridge University Press, 1995).
6. Rob Heinrich, "The *Desire* and the Beginnings of Slavery in Boston," unpublished typescript, commissioned by the National Park Service, January 8, 2014, 5. Thanks to historian Martin H. Blatt for providing this document. According to Heinrich, "Historians have determined that, in all likelihood, at least three of the slaves who arrived on the *Desire*, two women and a man, were purchased by English merchant Samuel Maverick of Noddle's Island, a trading post located in Boston Harbor" (3).
7. "If upon a just warre the lord should deliver [the Narraganset] into our hands, wee might easily haue men woemen and Children enough to exchange for Moores, which wilbe more gaynefull pilladge for vs then wee conceive, for I doe not see how wee can thrive vntill wee get into a stock of slaves sufhtient to doe all our business. . . . Our servants will still desire freedome to plat for them selves, and not stay but for verie great wages. And I suppose you know verie well How wee shall maynteyne Moores chaper than one Englishe servant." Emmanuel Downing to John Winthrop, August 1645, in *The Winthrop Papers*, ed. Stewart Mitchell, Allyn Bailey Forbes, and Malcolm Freiberg, 6 vols. (Boston: Massachusetts Historical Society, 1929–92), 5:38–39.
8. The abolition of slavery by the Massachusetts Constitution of 1780 was the

culmination of a succession of landmark petitions and lawsuits. One of the most influential suits was brought by Elizabeth Freeman ("Mum Bett") of Sheffield, Massachusetts. This municipal case set a precedent that was affirmed by the state courts in the Quock Walker case and ultimately led to abolition in Massachusetts. It is interesting to note that W. E. B. Du Bois was a great-grandson of Freeman.

9. The distinction between "slave societies" (those whose economies were supported by slave labor) and "societies with slaves" (those partially dependent on slaves) is widely cited in the literature on slavery. See Ira Berlin, *Many Thousands Gone: The First Two Centuries of Slavery in North America* (Cambridge: Harvard University Press, 1998), parts 2–3.
10. On the diversity of the unfree in the colonial world, see Jared Hardesty, *Unfreedom: Slavery and Dependence in Eighteenth-Century Boston* (New York: New York University Press, 2016).
11. Adelaide M. Cromwell, *Developing a Black Meritocracy: A History of Black Graduates of the Boston Latin School* (Boston: Boston University, 1985), 1–2.
12. William D. Piersen, *Black Yankees: The Development of an Afro-American Subculture in Eighteenth-Century New England* (Amherst: University of Massachusetts Press, 1988), 35.
13. Harvard Law School removed the Royall coat of arms from its seal in 2016.
14. See C. S. Manegold, *Ten Hills Farm: The Forgotten History of Slavery in the North* (Princeton: Princeton University Press, 2010). See also www.royallhouse.org. Census and probate records from 1727 and 1778 contain the names of sixty-three Royall House slaves.
15. Roy Finkenbine, "Belinda's Petition: Reparations for Slavery in Revolutionary Massachusetts," *William and Mary Quarterly*, 3rd ser., 64, no. 1 (January 2007): 95–104. Belinda was born in the Gold Coast (present-day Ghana).
16. Whether or not Belinda Royall ever recovered the court-ordered reparations is not known.
17. See Elise Lemire, *Black Walden: Slavery and Its Aftermath in Concord, Massachusetts* (Philadelphia: University of Pennsylvania Press, 2009).
18. Prince Hall, "A Charge, Delivered to the African Lodge, June 24, 1797, at Menotomy" (Boston, 1797), *American Historical Imprints*, ser. 1, no. 24374, 10.
19. In 1796, Lucy Terry Prince became the first woman to appear before Vermont's highest governing body, successfully arguing against a white man who made repeated attempts by violent means to appropriate her family's land. On Prince and her court appearances, see Gretchen Holbrook Gerzina, *Mr. and Mrs. Prince: How an Extraordinary Eighteenth-Century Family Moved out of Slavery and into Legend* (New York: Amistad, 2008), 183. Gerzina's research has determined that Prince did not argue before the Supreme Court, as some sources have suggested. See Gerzina, *Mr. and Mrs. Prince,* 181.

    Tradition (and some print sources) have it that Prince advocated eloquently for one of her sons to be admitted to Williams College—lecturing the trustees, although ultimately unsuccessfully, for three hours, quoting chapter and verse of the Bible. Gerzina notes that the Prince family was turned down "because of race." See Gerzina, *Mr. and Mrs. Prince*, 164.

20. "Bars Fight," in George Sheldon, *A History of Deerfield, Massachusetts, the Times When and the People by Whom It Was Settled, Unsettled, and Resettled, with a Special Study of the Indian Wars in the Connecticut Valley, with Genealogies*, 2 vols. (Deerfield, Mass.: E. A. Hall, 1895–96), 1:545–46.
21. Phillis Wheatley, *Poems on Various Subjects, Religious and Moral. By Phillis Wheatley, Negro Servant to Mr. John Wheatley* (London: A. Bell, and Boston: Cox and Berry, 1773).
22. Philip A. Jamison, "Square Dance Calling: The African American Connection," *Journal of Appalachian Studies* 9, no. 2 (Fall 2003): 388; John Adams, diary, Nov. 25, 1760, in *Diary and Autobiography of John Adams*, ed. L. H. Butterfield et al., 4 vols. (Cambridge: Harvard University Press, 1961), 1:172.
23. Mrs. Gardner (first name unknown) hired Andrew Law, an itinerant singing-master and composer, to give the still enslaved Newport Gardner music lessons. The latter composed a choral work based on scriptural verse, published in Boston the same year that he left the United States for Liberia. For a comprehensive study, see Edward E. Andrews, "The Crossings of Occramar Marycoo, or Newport Gardner," in *The Atlantic World: Individuals and People in the Atlantic World*, ed. Mark Meuwese and Jeffrey Fortin (Leiden: Brill, 2014), 101–24.
24. Andrews, "The Crossings of Occramar Marycoo," 104.
25. Mark Sammons and Valerie Cunningham, *Black Portsmouth: Three Centuries of African-American Heritage* (Durham: University of New Hampshire Press, 2004), 88.
26. Vincent Carretta, "Introduction," in *Unchained Voices: An Anthology of Black Authors in the English-Speaking World of the Eighteenth Century*, ed. Carretta (Lexington: University Press of Kentucky, 1996), 1.
27. The petition of Felix and four others reached Lieutenant Governor Thomas Hutchinson and the General Court of Massachusetts on January 6, 1773. It was the first of five appeals within a two-year period. In each one the plaintiffs sought the recognition of their constitutional rights. The enslaved men never received a response. "Felix," Slave Petition for Freedom (January 6, 1773), in Herbert Aptheker, ed., *A Documentary History of the Negro People in the United States*, vol. 1, *From Colonial Times through the Civil War* (New York: Citadel Press, 1962), 6–7.
28. Finkenbine, "Belinda's Petition." For a discussion of Belinda's petition as a proto-text of the reparations movement, see Raymond A. Winbush, *Belinda's Petition: A Concise History of Reparations for the Transatlantic Slave Trade* (Bloomington, Ind.: Xlibris, 2009).
29. June Jordan, "The Difficult Miracle of Black Poetry in America or Something Like a Sonnet for Phillis Wheatley," *Massachusetts Review* 27, no. 2 (Summer 1986): 252–62.

30. In late 1779, the year after Wheatley was freed, she published without success a proposal for a second volume of poems, with letters, in two Boston newspapers. Vincent Carretta believes that if Wheatley had remained in London after her six-week visit to that city, she "very probably would have found a publisher for her second volume." Vincent Carretta, ed., *Phillis Wheatley: Complete Writings* (New York: Penguin, 2001), xxxv. The first black poet to gain international notice in British America was Francis Williams, who wrote in Latin.
31. See Jeannine Hensley, ed., *The Works of Anne Bradstreet* (Cambridge: Harvard University Press, 1967).
32. By comparing Wheatley to Dickinson I do not mean to suggest specific thematic or stylistic parallels.
33. The ever-growing bibliography on Phillis Wheatley includes John Shields, *Phillis Wheatley and the Romantics* (Knoxville: University of Tennessee Press, 2010). In this remarkable study Shields argues that Wheatley influenced the English Romantics and that literary influences flowed not only from Europe to the Americas but in the opposite direction as well.
34. All Wheatley poems cited here appeared in her volume *Poems on Various Subjects, Religious and Moral.*
35. This etching, which graced the cover of *Poems on Various Subjects, Religious and Moral,* is attributed to Moorhead.
36. For a thorough study of Wheatley's life, see Vincent Carretta, *Phillis Wheatley: Biography of a Genius in Bondage* (Athens: University of Georgia Press, 2011).
37. *Boston News-Letter,* supplement to the *Massachusetts-Gazette,* January 7, 1773.
38. *The Prodigal Daughter; or, The Disobedient Lady Reclaim'd* (Boston: Cornhill Press and the American Antiquarian Society and NewsBank, 2004). I wish to acknowledge Jared Hardesty for providing me with a copy of this document. On Pompey Fleet, his relationship with the family he served while enslaved, and his remarkable last will and testament, see Jared Hardesty, *Unfreedom: Slavery and Dependence in Eighteenth Century Boston* (New York: New York University Press, 2016), 158n84, 159.
39. Piersen, *Black Yankees,* 100n13, 101n19.
40. Piersen, *Black Yankees,* 113.
41. Horton and Horton, *In Hope of Liberty,* 162.
42. Sari Roboff, *The North End* (Boston: Boston 200, 1975), 3–4.
43. Hull and Snowhill Streets border the district where many black mariners lived. I am grateful to Aba Cecile McHardy for alerting me to the extensive cultural implications of African participation in the international maritime trade.
44. See Edward MacDonald, *Old Copp's Hill Burial Ground; with Historical Sketches* (1879; Boston: B. Parks, 1882).
45. Beacon Hill refers to the area bounded on the north (looking toward the Charles River) by Pinckney and Cambridge Streets, and on the east and to the west by Joy and Charles Streets. The West End is the contiguous flat area by the Charles River. The two names are often conflated. See Adelaide M.

Cromwell, "The Black Presence in the West End of Boston, 1800–1864: A Demographic Map," in *Courage and Conscience: Black and White Abolitionists in Boston,* ed. Donald M. Jacobs (Bloomington: Indiana University Press for the Boston Athenæum, 1993), 155–67.

46. The black population was also dispersed in other areas of the city, such as Charlestown to the north across the Charles River, and Roxbury to the south, an area later incorporated into the city.
47. Horton and Horton, *Black Bostonians,* 1–3, 6.
48. Thomas O'Connor, *Civil War Boston: Home Front and Battlefield* (Boston: Northeastern University Press, 1997), 22.
49. On the infrastructure and the demographics of the antebellum black community, see George Levesque, *Black Boston: African American Life and Culture in Urban American, 1750–1860* (New York: Garland, 1994). An African American Heritage Trail, which commemorates the presence and passage through history of black Bostonians of Beacon Hill, was inaugurated in 1980.
50. Benjamin Quarles, *The Negro in the Making of America* (New York: Collier, 1987), 56.
51. On David Walker, see Peter Hinks, *To Awaken My Afflicted Brethren: David Walker and the Problem of Antebellum Slave Resistance* (State College: Pennsylvania State University Press, 1997).
52. *David Walker's Appeal in Four Articles; Together with a Preamble, to the Coloured Citizens of the World, but in Particular and Very Expressly, to Those of the United States of America* (New York: Hill and Wang, 1995), 1, 43.
53. Quoted in Elizabeth McHenry, *Forgotten Readers: Recovering the Lost History of African American Literary Societies* (Durham, N.C.: Duke University Press, 2002), 36, 322n23.
54. Byron Rushing (b. 1943), quoted in Yawu Miller, "Effort Launched to Memorialize Black Activist David Walker," *Bay State Banner,* September 20, 2012, http://baystatebanner.com.
55. Hinks, *To Awaken My Afflicted Brethren,* appendix E, "David Walker's Death and the History of His Family," 270–71. According to Hinks, the Boston Index of Death for 1801–48 lists consumption as the cause of Walker's death and that of his daughter as well. Historians who support the poisoning hypothesis include Herbert Aptheker and Sterling Stuckey. A memorial plaque is affixed to Walker's Beacon Hill home at 8 Belknap (now Joy) Street.
56. On the Trotter family, see chapter 2.
57. Maria W. Stewart, "On Religion and the Pure Principles of Morality, the Sure Foundation on Which We Must Build," in *Maria W. Stewart, American's First Black Woman Political Writer: Essays and Speeches,* ed. Marilyn Richardson (Bloomington: Indiana University Press, 1987), 40.
58. Maria W. Stewart, "Lecture Delivered at the Franklin Hall, Boston, September 21, 1832," in Richardson, *Maria W. Stewart,* 45.
59. Pauline E. Hopkins, "Famous Women of the Negro Race, VII: Educators

(Continued)," *Colored American Magazine* 5, no. 2 (June 1902): 130. For a rich bibliography on female participation in public life and attempts to disavow their achievements, see Hanna Wallinger, *Pauline E. Hopkins: A Literary Biography* (Athens: University of Georgia Press, 2005).

60. Stewart, "Lecture Delivered at the Franklin Hall," 46.
61. Maria W. Stewart, "Mrs. Stewart's Farewell Address to Her Friends in the City of Boston, Delivered September 21, 1833," in Richardson, *Maria W. Stewart*, 70.
62. The definitive biography of William Wells Brown is Ezra Greenspan, *William Wells Brown: An African American Life* (New York: Norton, 2014).
63. William Wells Brown, *Clotel; or, the President's Daughter: A Narrative of Slave Life in the United States*, in *Clotel and Other Writings*, ed. Ezra Greenspan (New York: Library of America, 2014), 55–214. Since *Clotel* was originally published in London, not the United States (in 1853), some claim that the distinction of "first African American novel" rightly belongs to Harriet E. Wilson's *Our Nig: Sketches from the Life of a Free Black* (1859; New York: Penguin, 2005).
64. Henry Louis Gates, Jr., and Nellie Y. McKay, eds., *The Norton Anthology of African American Literature* (New York: Norton, 1997), 247. During the 1860s, William Wells Brown issued three more versions of *Clotel* (sometimes spelled "Clotelle") and two volumes of black history.
65. William Wells Brown, *Narrative of William W. Brown, a Fugitive Slave, Written by Himself*, in *Puttin' on Ole Massa: The Slave Narratives of Henry Bibb, William Wells Brown, and Solomon Northup*, ed. Gilbert Osofsky (New York: Harper Row, 1969), 190.
66. Brown, *Narrative*, 38.
67. Brown, *Clotel*, 160.
68. Brown, *Clotel*, 156.
69. Brown, *Clotel*, 159.
70. Brown, *The Escape; or, A Leap for Freedom: A Drama in Five Acts* (1858; New York: Prologue Press, 1969). Brown wrote an early play, *Experience; or, How to Give a Northern Man a Backbone*, which was not published. On William Wells Brown as a playwright, see Errol Hill and James V. Hatch, *A History of African American Theatre* (New York: Cambridge University Press, 2003), 49–51. For a detailed description of the script of the unpublished play as it was performed by the author, see *The Liberator*, August 1, 1856.
71. Hill and Hatch, *History of African American Theatre*, 50; James Spruill, founder in Boston of the African [Theatre] Company, interview by the author, March 10, 1999.
72. William Cooper Nell is best known as the author of *The Colored Patriots of the American Revolution, with Sketches of Several Distinguished Colored Persons: To Which Is Added a Brief Survey of the Condition and Prospects of Colored Americans* (Boston: Robert F. Wallcut, 1855). A plaque affixed above the doorway of 64 Kendall Street on Beacon Hill states that Nell was born there.
73. "Philomathean" derives from the Greek *philomatheia*, "love of learning."

74. On Bannister, see Marilyn Richardson, "Taken from Life: Edward Bannister, Edmonia Lewis, and the Memorialization of the Fifty-Fourth Massachusetts Regiment," in *Hope and Glory: Essays on the Legacy of the 54th Massachusetts Regiment*, ed. Martin H. Blatt, Thomas J. Brown, and Donald Yacovone (Amherst and Boston: University of Massachusetts Press in association with Massachusetts Historical Society, 2001), 94–115. According to Richardson, Edmonia Lewis died in London on September 17, 1907. Marilyn Richardson, "Sculptor's Death Date Unearthed: Edmonia Lewis Died in London in 1907," ArtFix Daily.com, January 9, 2011.
75. William Wells Brown, *The Black Man: His Antecedents, His Genius, and His Achievements* (Boston: J. Redpath, 1863), 214–17.
76. Marilyn Richardson, "Literary Traditions of African Americans in Early New England," lecture delivered at "Black Yankees: New England's Hidden Roots," Primary Source seminar, Watertown, Mass., July 6, 1999.
77. Juanita Marie Holland, "Reaching through the Veil: African-American Artist Edward Mitchell Bannister," in *Edward Mitchell Bannister, 1828–1901*, ed. Juanita Marie Holland and Corinne Jennings (New York: Kenkeleba House and Whitney Museum of American Art at Champion, 1992), 18.
78. For a detailed biography of Edmonia Lewis's remarkable career, see Harry Henderson and Albert Henderson, *The Indomitable Spirit of Edmonia Lewis: A Narrative Biography* (Milford, Conn.: Esquiline Hill Press, 2012). On her complex racial identity, see Kirsten Pai Buick, *Child of the Fire: Mary Edmonia Lewis and the Problem of Art History's Black and Indian Subject* (Raleigh, N.C.: Duke University Press, 2010). Many of Lewis's sculptures, including *The Death of Cleopatra*, are owned by the National Museum of American Art in Washington, D.C.
79. James M. Trotter, *Music and Some Highly Musical People: Containing . . . Sketches of the Lives of Remarkable Musicians of the Colored Race. With Portraits, and an Appendix Containing Copies of Music Composed by Colored Men* (1881; New York: Pantheon, 1999). On the Trotter family, see chapter 2.
80. Maud Cuney Hare, *Negro Musicians and Their Music* (1936; New York: Da Capo, 1974).
81. Rebecca Crumpler, *A Book of Medical Discourses* (Boston: Cashman, Keating, 1883). More research into the nonfiction literary and scholarly production of Afro-Bostonians is warranted.
82. See Dickson D. Bruce, Jr., *Black American Writing from the Nadir: The Evolution of a Literary Tradition, 1877–1915* (Baton Rouge: Louisiana State University Press, 1989).
83. William Wells Brown, *My Southern Home; or, The South and Its People* (Boston: A. G. Brown, 1882).
84. On Hopkins, see Wallinger, *Pauline E. Hopkins*, and Lois Brown, *Pauline Elizabeth Hopkins: Black Daughter of the Revolution* (Chapel Hill: University of North Carolina Press, 2008).

85. Florida Ruffin Ridley, "The Negro in Boston," *Our Boston* (issued by the Women's Municipal League) 2, no. 2 (January 1927): 15–20, photocopy in the possession of the author.

86. Byron Rushing, lecture and walking tour of Roxbury, October 30, 2004.

87. Horton and Horton, *Black Bostonians,* 32.

2. The Black Bostonian Elites

The epigraph comes from an unidentified informant, quoted in Adelaide Cromwell, *The Other Brahmins: Boston's Black Upper Class, 1750–1950* (Fayetteville: University of Arkansas Press, 1994), 55.

1. David Levering Lewis, *When Harlem Was in Vogue* (1981; New York: Penguin, 1997), xxii.
2. For purposes of this discussion "elite" and "upper class" are used interchangeably with the more colloquial "upper crust" and "Old Guard."
3. E. Franklin Frazier, *The Negro in the United States* (New York: Macmillan, 1949), 304–5.
4. James O. Horton and Lois E. Horton's description of Boston's antebellum black society as "a pyramid shaped by occupation, geographic origin, education, and skin color, as well as other external socioeconomic forces," could well be applied to black society as it was in the 1920s. See James O. Horton and Lois E. Horton, *Black Bostonians: Family Life and Community Struggle in the Antebellum North* (New York: Holmes and Meier, 1979), 8–9.
5. Willard Gatewood, *Aristocrats of Color: The Black Elite, 1880–1920* (Bloomington: Indiana University Press, 1990), 16ff, 368nn44–58.
6. Horton and Horton, *Black Bostonians,* 12, 139n30, 68, 145n6. The reference in the first quotation is to William Cooper Nell, *The Colored Patriots of the American Revolution, with Sketches of Several Distinguished Colored Persons: To Which Is Added a Brief Survey of the Condition and Prospects of Colored Americans* (Boston: Robert F. Wallcut, 1855).
7. On the elaborate toast traditions in African American culture, see Bruce Jackson, ed., *Get Your Ass in the Water and Swim Like Me: Narrative Poetry from Black Oral Tradition* (New York: Routledge, 2004).
8. Horton and Horton, *Black Bostonians,* 33.
9. I use the term "modernity" in its most general sense, to refer to the practices of post-traditional societies.
10. Ray Stannard Baker, *Following the Color Line: An Account of American Negro Citizenship in the American Democracy* (New York: Doubleday, Page, 1908), 124.
11. John Daniels, *In Freedom's Birthplace: A Study of the Boston Negroes* (Boston: Houghton Mifflin, 1914), 180; Adelaide Cromwell, *The Other Brahmins: Boston's Black Upper Class, 1750–1950* (Fayetteville: University of Arkansas Press, 1994).
12. Theodore Drury, a concert tenor, and the Theodore Drury Grand Opera Company performed classic operas in New England regularly from 1900 to 1910 and sporadically into the 1930s, often recruiting white talent. Daniels,

In Freedom's Birthplace, 201. See also Rayford W. Logan and Michael R. Winston, eds., *Dictionary of American Negro Biography* (New York: Norton, 1982), 192–93.

13. Daniels, *In Freedom's Birthplace*, 201, 200.
14. On Maud Cuney Hare and the establishment of the Allied Arts Centre, see chapter 4.
15. Lewis delineates three phases of the Harlem Renaissance: the first extending from 1919 to 1923, the second from early 1924 to mid-1926, and the last from mid-1926 to the Harlem Riot of March 1935. See Lewis, *When Harlem Was in Vogue*, xxiv.
16. Daniels, *In Freedom's Birthplace*, 205n1.
17. Others belonging to this cohort included the Wilsons (Butler R. and Mary E. Wilson) and the Baldwins (Louis and Maria L. Baldwin), all of whom are mentioned in Gatewood, *Aristocrats of Color*, and the Fullers (Dr. Solomon and Meta Warrick). The total black population of Boston in 1900 was 11,591.
18. The residence is listed on the Boston Women's Heritage Trail. See *Boston Women's Heritage Trail: Four Centuries of Boston Women; A Guide to Five Walks* (Gloucester, Mass.: The Curious Traveler's Press, 1999), 38–39, and http://bwht.org/beacon-hill/.
19. Despite the renown of Josephine St. Pierre Ruffin and her husband, Judge George Lewis Ruffin (1834–86), there is no biography devoted to them. See Roger A. Schuppert, "Josephine St. Pierre Ruffin," in *American National Biography Online* (2000), www.anb.org.
20. W. E. B. Du Bois, *The Autobiography of W. E. B. Du Bois: A Soliloquy on Viewing My Life from the Last Decade of Its First Century* (1968; New York: Oxford University Press, 2007), 137.
21. Walter J. Stevens, *A Chip on My Shoulder: Autobiography of Walter J. Stevens* (Boston: Meador, 1946), 45.
22. Lewis, *When Harlem Was in Vogue*, 103–5.
23. The *Courant*, coedited by Louis E. Baldwin and Butler R. Wilson, ran from 1883 to 1899. See Daniels, *In Freedom's Birthplace*, 103. In 1901, Forbes went on to cofound the Boston *Guardian* with William Monroe Trotter.
24. Du Bois, *Autobiography*, 137.
25. Elizabeth McHenry, *Forgotten Readers: Recovering the Lost History of African-American Literary Societies* (Durham, N.C.: Duke University Press, 2002), chap. 4.
26. On the cultural pursuits and accomplishments of the Ruffin children sources are few. The details included here have been gleaned from anecdotes and scattered references.
27. Franklin A. Dorman, *Twenty Families of Color, 1742–1998* (Boston: New England Historic Genealogical Society, 1998), 154, 159. Nahar's exact birth and death dates are unknown. A celebrity in her day, she is one of the many brilliant African Americans whose stories have been substantially erased. For a remarkable photograph of Nahar, see Monroe A. Majors, *Noted Negro*

Women: Their Triumphs and Activities (Chicago: Donohue and Henneberry, 1893), 245, http://digitalcollections.nypl.org. Nahar's grandfather was John Peter Nahar of Suriname, who married into the Howard family, one of black Boston's most distinguished.

28. Florida Ruffin Ridley, "The Negro in Boston," *Our Boston* 2, no. 2 (January 1927): 19–20.
29. The Boston *Guardian*, the twentieth century's first black newspaper and the only one, until the founding in 1915 of the *Boston Chronicle* by two West Indian–born men.
30. Harvard College students did not major in a particular field during this period. Harvard University Archives, personal communication, February 7, 2014.
31. Stephen R. Fox, *The Guardian of Boston: William Monroe Trotter* (New York: Athenaeum, 1970), 18. This fine biography of Trotter remains the only one to date.
32. Geraldine Pindell's great-uncle William Pindell was one of a distinguished group of militant leaders in the fight that integrated Boston's schools in the 1850s. See Fox, *Guardians of Boston*, 22, and Julie Winch, "Geraldine Pindell Trotter," *Trotter Institute Review* 2, no. 1 (1988): 10–12, http://scholarworks.umb.edu/trotter_review.
33. Photograph of Geraldine Pindell Trotter, William Monroe Trotter / Boston *Guardian* Papers, Howard Gotlieb Archival Research Center, Boston University.
34. Du Bois, *Autobiography*, 87.
35. A commemorative plaque is affixed to the house.
36. Maude Trotter attended Wellesley College for two years before marrying Dr. Charles Steward, a Harvard-trained dentist and president of the Boston Literary and Historical Society. "Miss Trotter a Bride," *Boston Herald*, February 20, 1907. The article describes the Stewards as "prominent Bostonians, members of families well known throughout the country."
37. See William D. Piersen's classic study *Black Yankees: The Development of an Afro-American Subculture in Eighteenth-Century New England* (Amherst: University of Massachusetts Press, 1988).
38. "Miss Trotter a Bride."
39. It is unclear when the Boston Literary and Historical Society ceased to exist. Elizabeth McHenry indicates as much in her study of literary clubs *Forgotten Readers*, 184.
40. Geraldine Pindell Trotter went to work at the *Guardian* in 1903 and stayed on until her death from influenza in 1918. Fox, *Guardian of Boston*, 80.
41. Robert C. Hayden, "William Monroe Trotter: A One-Man Protester for Civil Rights," *Trotter Institute Review* 2, no. 1 (1998): 5, http://scholarworks.umb.edu/trotter_review.
42. Fox, *Guardian of Boston*, 52, 53n27.
43. Adelaide Cromwell, lecture at the Museum of African American History, Boston, April 11, 2007.

44. Evan J. Albright, "Blazing the Trail," *Amherst College Alumni Magazine*, Winter 2007, www.amherst.edu/magazine.
45. Fox, *Guardian of Boston*, 207.
46. Eugene Gordon, "The Negro Press," *American Mercury*, June 1926, 214. On Gordon, see chapter 5.
47. McHenry, *Forgotten Readers*, 173, 359n7.
48. Boston Literary and Historical Society Minutes, January 13, 1902, cited in McHenry, *Forgotten Readers*, 173n67.
49. James M. Trotter, *Music and Some Highly Musical People: Containing . . . Sketches of the Lives of Remarkable Musicians of the Colored Race. With Portraits, and an Appendix Containing Copies of Music Composed by Colored Men* (1881; New York: Pantheon, 1999).
50. Fox, *Guardian of Boston*, 18.
51. Henry Chase, "Memorable Visitors: Classic White House Encounters," *American Visions*, February–March 1995, 26–33.
52. For a full account of the Trotter-Wilson clash, see Fox, *Guardian of Boston*, 175–85.
53. *Boston Post*, June 8, 1915; *Boston Evening Globe*, October 30, 1915, cited in Fox, *Guardian of Boston*, 197.
54. For a detailed account of the *Birth of a Nation* protest of 1915, see Fox, *Guardian of Boston*, 190–98, and Dick Lehr, *The Birth of a Nation: How a Legendary Filmmaker and a Crusading Editor Reignited America's Civil War* (New York: Public Affairs, 2014).
55. Dr. Cornelius Nathaniel Garland, a London-educated surgeon, founded the Plymouth Hospital and Training School for Nurses.
56. Charles Putkammer and Ruth Worthy, "William Monroe Trotter, 1872–1934," *Journal of Negro History* 43, no. 4 (October 1958): 310. In the same article, Putkammer and Worthy point out that "he helped many a boy and girl find their first job" (307).
57. Trotter, unlike his father, wrote no books. The fragmentary trove of the Boston *Guardian* issues held in libraries and archives and on microfilm is all that remains of his writings. The Trotter Papers at the Boston Public Library include six reels on microfilm: vol. 1, no. 38, to vol. 13, no. 2 (June 1902–November 15, 1913, and January 2, 1939–April 20, 1957). The issues corresponding to the 1920s and the 1930s (until 1939) are missing. Unfortunately, the collected William Monroe Trotter / Boston *Guardian* Papers at Boston University's Howard Gotlieb Archival Research Center contain little in the way of untapped primary sources.
58. Mabe Kountze, *A History of the Early Colored Press in Massachusetts & A Second Sketch of the Boston Guardian* (unpublished typescript, July 10, 1967, Brandeis University copy), 15.
59. Putkammer and Worthy, "William Monroe Trotter," 311.
60. Cunard Street runs from 65 Cabot to 778 Columbus Avenue at Roxbury Crossing in the Roxbury neighborhood of Boston.

61. Trotter's obituary in the *New York Times* states that he died "on his sixty-fifth [*sic*] birthday by jumping from the roof of the three-story house at 41 Cunard Street, Roxbury, where he lived with Mrs. Mary Gibson and her son Wallace." "Negro Crusader for Race a Suicide: William Munroe [*sic*] Trotter, Harvard Graduate, Had Lost the Control of His Newspaper," *New York Times*, April 8, 1934. Some who knew Trotter personally, like oral historian Ulysses S. Gore—as a child he "sat on Trotter's knee"—do not accept the story that the valiant *Guardian* editor, a devout Episcopalian, took his own life. Ulysses S. Gore, interview by the author, July 27, 1998.
62. *Class Book—Wellesley, '97* (Wellesley, Mass.: Published by the Class, 1897).
63. Melvin B. Miller, "Dr. Charles G. Steward: The Last of a Breed," *Bay State Banner*, July 13, 1967.
64. Melvin Miller, Address, Eliot Church, Roxbury, Patriot's Day, April 2003, http://baystatebanner.com.
65. See www.umb.edu/trotter/about.
66. Malcolm Little, later Malcolm X, was raised by parents who were members of Marcus Garvey's Universal Negro Improvement Association.
67. Louis Farrakhan was born Louis Eugene Wolcott (often misspelled as "Walcutt") in 1933 to a West Indian mother (from St. Kitts) and a father who separated from the family before Louis's birth. Black arts doyenne Elma Lewis (1921–99) knew the young Wolcott as a promising classical violinist. Lewis attributed his conversion to experiences he had in the American South, where he went with a scholarship to Winston-Salem Teacher's College. Elma Lewis, interview by the author, November 8, 1998.

3. Gender and Culture

1. See Karen J. Blair, *The Clubwoman as Feminist: True Womanhood Redefined, 1868–1914* (New York: Holmes and Meier, 1980). Blair defines the term "women's club movement" as encompassing the literary and civic clubs that proliferated between the Civil War and World War II.
2. The epigraph comes from Ruth M. Batson, personal communication, April 15, 1998. Batson was instrumental in the revitalization of Boston's Museum of African American History. She was also a tenured professor of psychiatry at the Boston University School of Medicine, where she made the medical community aware of the connection between segregation and poverty, and mental health and achievement, for people of color. Batson's papers are held at the Schlesinger Library on the History of Women in America, Harvard University, Cambridge, Mass.
3. The WSC (Women's Service Club) was also deeply involved with promoting cultural activities but primary sources on the organization are lacking.
4. All details concerning the LWCS of Boston derive from the Record Books, League of Women for Community Service, Schlesinger Library, Harvard University (minutes are handwritten and some parts are not fully legible). These

documents have not been cited previously in studies on black Boston. I wish to thank Sarah-Ann Shaw, Boston's first African American television reporter and a past president of the LWCS, for inviting me to examine the records (as well as a sheaf of minutes from the LWCS meetings and small troves of correspondence and newspaper clippings) at the LWCS headquarters at 558 Massachusetts Avenue before their transfer to the Schlesinger Library. Documents from the collection are cited hereafter as LWCS Records.

5. The city-owned William E. Carter Playground on Columbus Avenue was the first public park in Boston to be named for a black personage. Sergeant Carter fought in the Spanish-American War.
6. The minutes of the SCU are merged with the records of the LWCS.
7. Mary Evans Patterson was born in Oberlin, Ohio. At age eighteen she married Butler R. Wilson. They had five children, including two daughters, Marion Elizabeth Wilson and Lola Marie Wilson, who graduated from Radcliffe College (now Harvard University) in the classes of 1916 and 1927, respectively, and three sons. Lola Wilson Hayes, interview by the author, March 18, 1999.
8. Adelaide Cromwell, *The Other Brahmins: Boston's Black Upper Class, 1750–1950* (Fayetteville: University of Arkansas Press, 1994), 143. Cromwell categorizes the LWCS and the WSC as "charitable-social, local, and nonclique-limited" clubs. For a concise account of the LWCS's history, see Robert C. Hayden, "Boston's Black History: League of Women for Community Service," *Boston Banner*, January 5, 1978.
9. http://leagueofwomen.org. The mission statement indicates that the league "is organized exclusively for charitable, educational, literary and historic preservation purposes, relating to the history and experience of African-American women in the United States." The website also notes that "prominent abolitionists and other speakers, both White and Black, were regularly welcomed at the League's headquarters."
10. Myra McAdoo, interview by the author, November 15, 1998. McAdoo's two grandmothers, one of whom was Irish American, were founding members of the Women's Service Club at 464 Massachusetts Avenue. Myra's mother, Gladys McAdoo, and Myra herself were members as well. The WSC appears to have no web presence.
11. In 1913, W. E. B. Du Bois paid a high compliment to Fuller when he invited her to contribute sculptures to New York State's celebration of the fiftieth anniversary of the Emancipation Proclamation. For a comprehensive examination of Fuller's career see Renée Ater, *Remaking Race and History: The Sculpture of Meta Warrick Fuller* (Berkeley, CA: University of California Press, 2011).
12. The young saxophonist later thanked the SCU but for reasons unstated declined the offer.
13. Minutes, November 14, December 19, 1918, LWCS Records; E. H. Clement, "The Listening Column," Boston *Transcript*, November 21, 1918. (T. S. Eliot's

poem "The Boston Evening Transcript" portrays the readers of this conservative newspaper as conformist and essentially lifeless.)

14. Fuller pledged half of the proceeds ($75) from the exhibition to the SCU.
15. James Monroe Trotter, *Music and Some Highly Musical People: Containing . . . Sketches of the Lives of Remarkable Musicians of the Colored Race. With Portraits, and an Appendix Containing Copies of Music Composed by Colored Men* (1881; New York: Pantheon, 1999), 51.
16. Negro spirituals do not appear to have been part of the league's cultural repertoire, and it is unclear if the middle- (and upper-) class ambivalence about music created under slavery played any role.
17. The musical play *Slaves' Escape; or, The Underground Railroad* (later revised as *Peculiar Sam; or, The Underground Railroad*) by Pauline Elizabeth Hopkins was a popular success of 1879. The multitalented Hopkins continued to perform as a vocalist with the Hopkins Colored Troubadours into the 1880s. See Lois Brown, *Pauline Elizabeth Hopkins: Black Daughter of the Revolution* (Chapel Hill: University of North Carolina Press, 2008), chap. 6.
18. Minutes, March 27, 1919, LWCS, Records.
19. "Jim Europe Killed in Boston Quarrel: Drummer in 'Hell Fighters' Band Alleged to Have Slashed Leader with a Knife," *New York Times*, May 10, 1919. On Lieutenant Europe, see R. Reid Badger, "James Reese Europe and the Prehistory of Jazz Author(s)," *American Music* 7, no. 1 (Spring 1989): 48–67.
20. When the clubwomen bought the mansion, built in 1861, it had been empty for ten years and was in need of refurbishing. Currently it is listed on the National Register of Historic Places.
21. On Roland Hayes, see Marva Griffin Carter, "Roland Hayes: Expressor of the Soul in Song (1887–1977)," *Black Perspective in Music*, 5, no. 2 (Autumn 1977): 188–220.
22. On Harlem Renaissance poet Waring Cuney, see chapter 5. The first black graduate of the New England Conservatory was Rachel Washington of the class of 1876. Robert C. Hayden, *African-Americans in Boston: More Than 350 Years* (Boston: Trustees of the Public Library, 1991), 63.
23. Allan Crite, interview by the author, September 21, 1998.
24. e. e. cummings, *I: Six Nonlectures* (Cambridge: Harvard University Press, 1953), 30.
25. Of Maria Baldwin's mother nothing appears to be known aside from the fact that she came from Baltimore. The Baldwins (perhaps derived from the French surname "Baudoin") lived on Washington Street and later on Clark Street, near what became Kendall Square in Cambridge. For a substantive profile of Baldwin, see "Maria L. Baldwin," in *Encyclopedia of African-American Education*, ed. Faustine Jones-Wilson et al. (Westport, Conn.: Greenwood Press, 1996), 41–42; and the plaque at the Maria L. Baldwin School, corner of Oxford and Sacramento Streets, Cambridge.

26. By 1921 the house was known as the largest residence for single women in the world; see www.franklinsquarehousefoundation.org.
27. "Maria Louise Baldwin," in *Notable Black American Women*, ed. Jessie Carnie Smith, 3 vols. (Detroit: Gale, 1992–2003), 1:47–49.
28. Shirley Wilson Logan, *We Are Coming: The Persuasive Discourse of Nineteenth-Century Black Women* (Carbondale: Southern Illinois University Press, 1999), 132–34.
29. Fannie Barrier Williams, "The Club Movement among Colored Women of America," in *A New Negro for a New Century: An Accurate and Up-to-Date Record of the Upward Struggles of the Negro Race*, ed. Booker T. Washington, N. B. Wood, and Fannie Barrier Williams (Chicago: American Publishing House, 1900), 383, 390. Williams, a member of the Chicago Women's Club, was a news correspondent.
30. Josephine St. Pierre Ruffin, "Address to the First National Conference of Colored Women," *Women's Era*, July 1895, 13–15.
31. On the history of the Cuney family, see Douglas Hales, *A Southern Family in White and Black: The Cuneys of Texas* (College Station: Texas A&M University Press, 2003). On the Allied Arts Centre and its functions, see chapter 4.
32. See Gerda Lerner, "Early Community Work of Black Club Women," *Journal of Negro History*, 59, no. 2 (April 1974): 158–67. See also Deborah Gray White, *Too Heavy a Load: Black Women in Defense of Themselves, 1894–1994* (New York: Norton, 1999), and Anne Meis Knupfer, *Toward a Tenderer Humanity and a Nobler Womanhood: African American Women's Clubs in Turn-of-the Century Chicago* (New York: New York University Press, 1996).
33. Alain Locke, ed., *The New Negro* (1925; New York: Athenaeum, 1968), 4.
34. The strategy of using art as a tool of black advancement was also deployed by the Chicago Renaissance. See Anne Meis Knupfer, *The Chicago Black Renaissance and Women's Activism* (Urbana: University of Illinois Press, 2006), 6.
35. Martin Luther King, Jr., "I Have a Dream," speech delivered August 28, 1963, Lincoln Memorial, Washington, D.C., www.americanrhetoric.com. While studying for his doctoral degree in theology at Boston University in 1955, King preached regularly at the Twelfth Baptist Church in the city's Roxbury neighborhood.
36. Adelaide Cromwell, afterword to *The Living Is Easy: A Novel by Dorothy West* (1948; Old Westbury, N.Y.: The Feminist Press, 1982), 358.
37. See Crystal M Fleming and Lorraine E. Roses, "Black Cultural Capitalists: African-American Elites and the Organization of the Arts in Early Twentieth Century Boston," *Poetics* 35, no. 6 (2007): 368–87.
38. Ralf Coleman, speech, Black History Week Panel, Roxbury, February 1972, eighty-minute reel-to-reel audiotape, courtesy of Leona Coleman Flu.
39. On black Bostonians who participated directly in the Harlem Renaissance, see chapter 5.

40. Florida Ruffin Ridley, "The Negro in Boston," *Our Boston* 2, no. 2 (January 1927): 16. This monthly publication was issued by the Women's Municipal League.
41. LWCS, Records.
42. Robert C. Hayden, *African-Americans in Boston: More than 350 Years* (Boston: Trustees of the Public Library, 1991), 50–51. See also "Truth Award to Wilhelmina Crosson," *Bay State Banner*, October 30, 1969. Like the "Aristo Club," the Boston chapter of the Association for the Study of Negro Life and History used LWCS premises for its meetings.
43. Florida Ruffin Ridley, "Women in the News," unidentified clipping, n.d. (c. 1930), courtesy of Maude Thomas Jenkins.
44. Lois Mailou Jones graduated from the Museum School of Fine Arts in 1927 and went on to become an internationally known painter.
45. A[lpha] K[appa] A[lpha], the sorority that cosponsored the event, is the oldest Greek-letter organization established in America by African American college women.
46. Maude Thomas Jenkins, interview by the author, March 19, 2003. Jenkins's mother, Maude Thomas, was a registered nurse who took the position of "matron" at the LWCS because no hospital, public or private, would hire a black nurse. Thomas and her daughter Maude ("little Maude" or "Maudie") lived at the LWCS.
47. James Weldon Johnson, ed., *The Book of American Negro Poetry* (New York: Harcourt, Brace, 1922).
48. James Weldon Johnson, *The Autobiography of an Ex-Colored Man* (1912; New York: Penguin, 1990).
49. James Weldon Johnson to unknown, August 29, 1922, LWCS, Records.
50. Alexander Mann to Florida Ruffin Ridley, May 16, 1922, LWCS, Records. Mann was rector of Trinity Church from 1905 to 1922.
51. See Benjamin Quarles, *Black Abolitionists* (New York: Oxford University Press, 1969).
52. F.W. Coburn, "In the World of Art," *Boston Herald*, October 8, 1922, LWCS, Records.
53. Coburn also praised Tanner's *Flight into Egypt* for the "quiet lyric beauty of painting that is conceived within a narrow range of color values by an artist of much sensibility and good taste." Coburn, "In the World of Art."
54. Ridley, "Women in the News."
55. LWCS Minutes, October 24, 1918, LWCS, Records. The Tremont Temple (originally the Tremont Theatre), located at 88 Tremont Street, is an architectural landmark in Boston. The temple was the site of many an abolitionist meeting and melees caused by anti-abolitionists.
56. W. E. B. Du Bois, *Darkwater: Voices from within the Veil* (New York: Harcourt, Brace, and Howe, 1920).

57. When a number of books somehow disappeared from the bookcases the members worried that the War Service, which required a strict accounting of its loans, would demand restitution for the losses. Report by the executive secretary of the league, Record Books, January 2, 1919, LWCS, Records. Among the books lost were Maud Cuney Hare's *The Message of the Trees: An Anthology of Leaves and Branches* (Boston: Cornhill, 1918), and a set of American encyclopedias.
58. Flyer issued by the LWCS, n.d. (c. 2000), LWCS, Records.

4. Black Faces on the White Stage

1. F. W. Woolsey, "Conversation with Roland Hayes," *Black Perspective in Music* 2, no. 2 (Fall 1974): 183. Hayes's eclectic repertoire typically included "The Repose of the Holy Family" from Berlioz's oratorio *The Childhood of Christ;* "Go Down, Moses" and "By and By" (two Negro spirituals); and an aria from Mozart's *Cosí fan tutte.*
2. On Hayes, see MacKinley Helm, *Angel Mo' and Her Son, Roland Hayes* (Boston: Little, Brown, 1942); and Christopher A. Brooks and Robert Sims, *Roland Hayes: The Legacy of an American Tenor* (Bloomington: Indiana University Press, 2015). Allan Rohan Crite, interview by the author, September 10, 1998; and Allan Rohan Crite, "An Autobiographical Sketch" (unpublished typescript), Mildred Sawyer Library, Rare Books, Suffolk University Library, Boston. Jones was supported and encouraged by her parents, Caroline Dorinda Adams Jones, a beautician and milliner, and Thomas Vreeland Jones, the first African American graduate of Suffolk Law School. "Lois Mailou Jones," exhibit, Museum of Fine Arts, Boston, January 19–October 1, 2013.
3. For a discussion of the literary scene in 1920s and 1930s black Boston, see chapter 5.
4. The "little theatre" (or "art theatre") movement set out to challenge the commercial theatre. In 1912, Chicago's Little Theatre and Boston's Toy Theatre were founded. By 1925 the little theatre and its ideals had gained acceptance nationwide. Dorothy Chansky, *Composing Ourselves: The Little Theatre Movement and the American Audience* (Carbondale: Southern Illinois University Press, 2004).
5. Ralf Coleman, speech, Black History Week Panel, Roxbury, February 1972, eighty-minute reel-to-reel audiotape, courtesy of Leona Coleman Flu.
6. Kay Bourne, "Roxbury Bar Diversified with the Times, but Keeps Flame of Tradition," *Bay State Banner*, April 21, 2005.
7. The Eureka Co-Operative Bank was founded in 1910 by David E. Crawford, a delegate to the Republican National Convention in Chicago. By 1920 his holdings of apartments, stores, and commercial properties were valued at $150,000. Robert C. Hayden, *African-Americans in Boston: More Than 350 Years* (Boston: Trustees of the Public Library, 1991), 79–81.
8. Shag Taylor, an integral part of Mayor James Michael Curley's political machine, was the most powerful Democrat in the black wards of Boston from

the 1930s until the late 1950s. Hayden, *African-Americans in Boston,* 96. At the time of his death he was described as "a nationally-known Democratic Leader." "Dr. Shag Taylor Dies Following Auto Accident," *Boston Globe,* November 6, 1958.

9. Black leaders sought "better governmental representation of black interests, more and better street-lighting fixtures and paving in black neighborhoods, and finally, judicial, civil and political appointments of blacks." They also made specific demands such as the removal of electrical wires hung over the tennis courts at the William E. Carter Playground and the reopening of a branch library in one of the wards. James Jennings, "Black Politics in Boston, 1900–1950," in *From Access to Power: Black Politics in Boston,* ed. James Jennings and Mel King (Cambridge, Mass.: Schenkman, 1986), 11–22.
10. The Richard Earle Pioneer Club, which dated back to 1903, survived as a speakeasy during Prohibition. It was located near the Roxbury / South End line on an alleyway near Tremont and Northampton Streets. Its heyday as a jazz club began in the 1940s. The Boston Redevelopment Authority demolished this club. Stephanie Schorow, "Black History Month: A Spotlight on the Pioneer Club," www.unionparkpress.com.
11. George Herbert Tynes was born in 1923 to parents from Nova Scotia. He lived upstairs from William Monroe Trotter at 971A Tremont Street until age ten, when his family moved to Framingham. Biographical details from [Aba] Cecile McHardy, ed., "Sources of Strength: Oral History Project" (unpublished ms., 1987), 4, copy in possession of the author, courtesy of McHardy.
12. http://bostonjazzscene.blogspot.com. See also Stanley Dance, *The World of Swing: An Oral History of Big Band Jazz* (1974; Boston: Da Capo, 2001), 242.
13. Dorothy West, *The Living Is Easy* (1948; Old Westbury, N.Y.: The Feminist Press, 1982); Dorothy West, interview by the author, July 23, 1999.
14. Personal interviews conducted by the author are cited throughout. An additional source is Ruth Edmonds Hill and Patricia Miller King, *Guide to the Transcripts of the Black Women Oral History Project* (Westport, Conn.: Meckler, 1991).
15. Pauline Elizabeth Hopkins, who sang and acted with her family's Troubadours, is best known as the author of major serial novels. See Lois Brown, *Pauline Elizabeth Hopkins: Black Daughter of the Revolution* (Chapel Hill: University of North Carolina Press, 2008).
16. Review of July 5, 1880, performance, *Boston Herald,* quoted in Ann Allen Shockley, "Pauline Elizabeth Hopkins: A Biographical Excursion into Obscurity," *Phylon* 33, no. 1 (1972): 23.
17. See chapter 1.
18. Crite, "An Autobiographical Sketch." Crite's paintings and prints are held in permanent collections such as the Museum of Fine Arts, the Fogg Museum at Harvard University, the Boston Athenæum, the Museum of Modern Art, the Phillips Collection, the Corcoran Gallery, the Art Institute in Chicago, and many others.

19. Maud Cuney enrolled at the New England Conservatory of Music in the fall semester of 1890–91. Maryalice Perrin-Mohr, New England Conservatory archivist, personal communication, December 10, 2009. One source states erroneously that Cuney studied at Howard University.
20. Photographs of Maud Cuney Hare can be seen on a number of online sites and in Douglas Hales, *A Southern Family in White and Black: The Cuneys of Texas* (College Station: Texas A&M University Press, 2003), 121.
21. Review, *Boston Daily Globe*, January 12, 1923.
22. W. E. B. Du Bois Papers (MS 312), Series I: Correspondence, 1877–1965, Special Collections and University Archives, University of Massachusetts Amherst Libraries (hereafter Du Bois Papers).
23. For a discussion of the various stages of the Harlem Renaissance from a literary and historical point of view, see David Levering Lewis, *When Harlem Was in Vogue* (New York: Penguin, 1997), xxiv.
24. On the innovations in Russia, see Robert Leach, "Revolutionary Theatre, 1917–1930," in *A History of Russian Theatre*, ed. Robert Leach and Victor Borovsky (New York: Cambridge University Press, 1999), 302–24. The year 1924 saw the establishment in Ireland of the first state-subsidized theatre in the western world, stimulating new life in the theatre with its staging of outstanding plays by Sean O'Casey.
25. The New England Conservatory of Music was originally located in the downtown Boston Music Hall, off Tremont Street. In 1882, it moved to the St. James Hotel building in Franklin Square (the Franklin Square House) at 11 East Newton Street. In 1902, the school relocated to its permanent quarters at the southwest corner of Huntington Avenue and Gainsborough Street. Jordan Hall was added in 1903. Maryalice Perrin-Mohr, personal communication, December 10, 2009.
26. W. E. B. Du Bois, *Dusk of Dawn: An Essay toward an Autobiography of a Race Concept* (1940; New York: Schocken, 1968), 43.
27. David Levering Lewis writes that Maud was in her early twenties and began her studies in 1891. Lewis, *W. E. B. Du Bois: Biography of a Race, 1868–1919* (New York: Henry Holt, 1993), 105. According to conservatory archivists, however, she was sixteen when she matriculated in the fall of 1890, not 1891.
28. Lewis, *W. E. B. Du Bois*, 104, 605n70.
29. W. E. B. Du Bois, *The Autobiography of W. E. B. Du Bois: A Soliloquy on Viewing My Life from the Last Decade of Its First Century* (1968; New York: Oxford University Press, 2007), 85.
30. W. E. B. Du Bois, "Tribute," Boston *Guardian*, April 11, 1936. This piece is Du Bois's tribute to Maud Cuney Hare upon her death.
31. "A Row at the Hub: How the Color Line Is Drawn in Boston: The Tempest a Savannah Colored Girl Created in the New England Conservatory of Music," *Atlanta Constitution*, November 15, 1890, clipping courtesy of Maryalice Perrin-Mohr.

32. Maud Cuney Hare, *Norris Wright Cuney: A Tribune of the Black People* (1913; New York: G. K. Hall, 1995), 132.
33. Hare, *Norris Wright Cuney,* 133. When Norris Cuney was the customs agent for Texas he refused to fly the flag at half-mast to honor the death of Confederate president Jefferson Davis.
34. Hare, *Norris Wright Cuney,* 133.
35. "A Row at the Hub."
36. Du Bois, "Tribute."
37. Jamaica Plain Historical Society, "African-American Women in Jamaica Plain History," www.jphs.org.
38. Hare, *Norris Wright Cuney,* 134.
39. Among Maud Cuney's private teachers were Emil Ludwig, a pupil of Anton Rubinstein, and Edwin Klahre, a pupil of Franz Liszt. Clarence Cameron White, quoted in Josephine Harreld Love, introduction to Maud Cuney Hare, *Negro Musicians and Their Music* (1936; London: Prentice-Hall, 1996), xi.
40. Du Bois, *Autobiography,* 138–39.
41. W. E. B. Du Bois, *Darkwater: Voices from Within the Veil* (New York: Harcourt, Brace, and Howe, 1920), 9. Sociologist Caroline Bond Day classifies Du Bois as having African (5/8) and white (3/8) origins. The files on the Cuney family's racial background and that of her brother Lloyd list them as 3/16 Negro, 1/16 Indian, and 11/16 white. Caroline Bond Day, *A Study of Some Negro-White Families in the United States* (Cambridge: Peabody Museum of Harvard University, 1932), 39 and plate 50.
42. Lewis, *W. E. B. Du Bois,* 85.
43. Lewis, *W. E. B. Du Bois,* 116.
44. Thelma Thornton (Wynn), interview by the author, February 3, 1999.
45. Du Bois, "Tribute."
46. David Levering Lewis, personal communication, fall 2010. Elsewhere Lewis references Du Bois's Casanova-like exploits with other women, including novelist Jessie Fauset, who worked with him at the *Crisis.* See Lewis, *W. E. B. Du Bois,* 464.
47. The Deaf, Dumb, and Blind Institute for Colored Youth was founded in 1887 by William H. Holland (c. 1841–1907), a former slave who served in a Union Army regiment during the Civil War. Holland studied at Oberlin College for two years and returned to Texas as a school principal. Nolan Thompson, "Holland, William H.," in *Handbook of Texas Online,* www.tshaonline.org.
48. Hare, *Norris Wright Cuney,* 215.
49. Hales, *A Southern Family in White and Black,* 103–4.
50. Du Bois, "Tribute."
51. Willard Gatewood, *Aristocrats of Color: The Black Elite, 1880–1920* (Bloomington: Indiana University Press, 1990), 176.
52. Du Bois, "Tribute."
53. Maud Cuney Hare (hereafter MCH) to Du Bois, December 1907, Du Bois Papers.

54. Clarence Cameron White, quoted in Hare, *Negro Musicians and Their Music*, xxii.
55. Florida Ruffin Ridley, "Mrs. Maud Cuney Hare: A Tribute," *Boston Chronicle*, February 22, 1936. Some sources state that Cuney returned to Boston in 1906; however, she married William P. Hare in Boston in 1904. Certificate of Marriage, City of Boston, Department of Vital Statistics.
56. The Hare residence is a marked site on the Boston Women's Heritage Trail; see http://bwht.org/jamaica-plain.
57. In 1930, Hare purchased a seaside cottage (with a view of Boston Harbor) at 160 Huckins Avenue in Squantum, a section of the city of Quincy. She gave private lessons at this "studio-home."
58. MCH to Du Bois, July 18 1930, Du Bois Papers.
59. Maud Cuney Hare, *The Message of the Trees: An Anthology of Leaves and Branches* (Boston: Cornhill, 1918). Hare's anthology contains the works of American, European, Middle Eastern, and Far Eastern writers, but few black poets. William Stanley Braithwaite, the noted black Bostonian anthologist and reviewer, wrote the terse introduction.
60. Hare, *Norris Wright Cuney*, 154.
61. Elizabeth Quinlan, Jamaica Plain Historical Society, "Annual Women's History Walk through Jamaica Plain," reprinted from *Jamaica Plain Gazetteer*, August 28, 1992.
62. *Opportunity*, December 1924, 380 (with photograph of Hare).
63. Maud Cuney Hare, "As the Negro Grows Up" (review of Alain Locke, ed., *The New Negro*), *Christian Science Monitor*, January 23, 1926.
64. Du Bois solidified his literary reputation with *The Quest of the Silver Fleece: A Novel* (1911; New York: Oxford University Press, 2007), and *Darkwater: Voices from Within the Veil* (1920).
65. See Remi Omodele, "'For Us, About Us, Near Us and By Us': American Women Playwrights and the Making of NAACP–Du Bois's *Edutainment* Agenda," *Women's History Review* 11, no. 1 (Spring 2002): 49–54.
66. MCH to Du Bois, February 23, 1925, Du Bois Papers.
67. MCH to Du Bois, October 19, 1925, Du Bois Papers.
68. Maud Cuney Hare, *Antar of Araby*, in *Plays and Pageants from the Life of the Negro*, ed. Willis Richardson (1930; Jackson: University of Mississippi Press, 2007), 27–76.
69. Richardson, introduction to *Plays and Pageants from the Life of the Negro*, xlv. Violinist and composer Clarence Cameron White phrased it differently: Hare "fostered and promoted a 'Little Theatre' movement among the Negroes of Boston." Hare, *Negro Musicians and Their Music*, xii.
70. "Antar of Araby by Boston Amateurs," *Baltimore Afro-American*, December 6, 1925 (announces an upcoming performance of December 14); *Crisis*, March 1926, 244. The Fine Arts Theatre was part of the Loew's State Theatre complex adjacent to Symphony Hall.
71. The Gaiety Theatre made the decision to branch out to black audiences after

it became too expensive to compete in the vaudeville market. Jeremy Schwab, "Gaiety Theatre Draws Closer to Demolition," *Bay State Banner*, January 20, 2005.

72. Samuel A. Hay, *African American Theatre: A Historical and Critical Analysis* (New York: Cambridge University Press, 1994), 3.

73. Charles Burroughs directed *Star of Ethiopia*, the pageant by Du Bois. He was also the director of the Krigwa Players. See W. E. B. Du Bois, "Krigwa Players Little Negro Theatre: The Story of a Little Theatre Movement," *Crisis*, July 1926, 134.

74. See Benjamin Quarles, *Black Abolitionists* (New York: Oxford University Press, 1969), and *Allies for Freedom: Blacks and John Brown* (New York: Oxford University Press, 1974). His brother Henry E. Quarles, Sr., "the Dean of Black Lawyers," had one of the longest legal careers in Boston: sixty-one years in practice as an attorney. Sylvia Quarles Simmons (daughter of Lorenzo Quarles), interview by the author, April 22, 2005.

75 Mildred Davenport (1900–1990), whose Broadway credits would later include *Fast and Furious, Flying Colors*, and *Black Birds*, was the also first African American woman to perform with Arthur Fiedler and the Boston Pops. See "Guide to the Mildred Davenport Dance Programs and Dance School Materials," Special Collections and Archives, University of California–Irvine, www.oac.cdlib.org.

76. In 1925, Gordon, a journalist with the *Boston Post*, organized the Saturday Evening Quill Club, a literary conclave that published three annual issues of the *Saturday Evening Quill* magazine from 1928 to 1930 (see chapter 5).

77. Maud Cuney Hare, "Antar," *Crisis*, June 1924, 65 (part 1), and July 1924, 28 (part 2).

78. Charles Paul Freund, "Waiting for Antar: Saddam, Suicide, and Cultural Despair," *Reason*, March 2004, http://reason.com/archives.

79. Hare, *Antar of Araby*, 52.

80. Hare, *Antar of Araby*, 35, 54, 31.

81. Hare, *Antar of Araby*, 37.

82. Maud Cuney Hare, "Mabed Ibn Ouhad," *Crisis*, April 1925, 258, emphasis added.

83. Montague Ring is the pseudonym of Amanda Ira Aldridge (1866–1956), the daughter of black tragedian Ira Aldridge (1807–67). The elder Aldridge was acclaimed throughout Europe, especially for his starring role in *Othello*.

84. James Weldon Johnson, preface to *The Book of Negro Poetry* (New York: Harcourt Brace, 1922), vii.

85. A head-and-shoulders profile of Hare in costume is included with a brief notice of her joint recital with William H. Richardson on October 24, 1924 in *Opportunity*, December 1924, 380.

86. *Ethiopia at the Bar of Justice*, a pageant by Edward J. McCoo (included in Richardson, *Plays and Pageants from the Life of the Negro*), features Ethiopia and Haiti (another trope) as protagonists. Willis Richardson's introduction to the 2007 edition of

Plays and Pageants claims that *Antar* was Hare's only play. In fact, it is her only published play. The script of *Ivory, Ebony and Gold* has been lost.

87. MCH to Du Bois, June 1928, Du Bois Papers.
88. "Amateurs Present Antar of Araby," *Boston Traveler,* May 16, 1928, Harvard Theatre Collection, Houghton Library, Harvard University, Cambridge, Mass.
89. Du Bois, "Krigwa Players Little Negro Theatre."
90. Omodele, "'For Us, About Us, Near Us and By Us,'" 49. Ernestine Rose, the chief librarian at the Harlem branch library, helped to open the institution to accommodate the cultural needs of the surrounding black community.
91. MCH to Du Bois, December 5, 1926, Du Bois Papers.
92. MCH to Henry Gilbert, December 12, 1926, Henry Gilbert Papers, Irving S. Gilmore Music Library, Yale University, New Haven, Conn., emphasis added. Gilbert had a sustained interest in African American music. His *Negro Episode* was performed in New York in 1896.
93. MCH to Du Bois, January 30, 1927, Du Bois Papers.
94. Du Bois to MCH, December 14, 1926, Du Bois Papers.
95. MCH to Du Bois, January 30, 1927, Du Bois Papers.
96. By 1926 the Allied Arts Centre had become "the showcase of black artists in New England." Rena Fraden, *Blueprints for a Black Federal Theatre, 1935–1939* (New York: Cambridge University Press, 1994), 162.
97. MCH to Du Bois, January 30, 1927, Du Bois Papers.
98. Hare admitted privately, "No end of jealousy and envy have sprung up. I have been greatly surprised. Nevertheless the work is succeeding." MCH to Du Bois, May 2, 1927, Du Bois Papers. Hare was likely referring to LWCS members who envied her for establishing an institution in her own right.
99. MCH to Adelaide Smith Casely Hayford, September 25, 1927, quoted in Adelaide Cromwell, *An African Victorian Feminist: The Life and Times of Adelaide Smith Casely Hayford, 1868–1960* (London: F. Cass, 1986), 131, emphasis added. Hayford, the daughter of a half-English, half-Fante father, was born in the Gold Coast, today's Ghana. She studied at the Stuttgart Conservatory of Music. *Crisis,* June 1925, 80. Hayford's daughter, the poet Gladys Casely Hayford, published some of her poems in Harlem Renaissance magazines.
100. The studio was located in what is now Room 208 in the Gainesboro building (the street name has a different spelling from the building).
101. Coleman speech, 1972.
102. James Guilford, Jr., interview by the author, January 26, 1999.
103. Myra McAdoo, interview by the author, November 15, 1998. McAdoo, a South End housing activist and educator, and her friends, all light-skinned, made sport of testing various hotels and restaurants.
104. Du Bois, "Krigwa Players Little Negro Theatre."
105. "Emerson College Backs Art Group in Community Center: Thespians under Mrs. Maud Cuney-Hare Present Dozen Dramas in Seven Months," *Baltimore*

Afro-American, June 23, 1928, clipping courtesy of Professor Gerald R. Gill. Hare's productions included her original *Ivory, Ebony and Gold* (consisting of three vignettes: "Ivory," "From the Other Side of the South," and "Gold"), *The Festival of the Resurrection of Adonis, Plumes: A Folk Tragedy* (Georgia Douglas Johnson), *The No 'Count Boy* (Paul Green), *The Romancers, Polly Wakes Up* (playwright unidentified), and a number of plays for children.

106. Paul Green was among the first white playwrights to write groundbreaking plays of black life. *The No 'Count Boy* premiered on Broadway on May 6, 1925. Paul Green, *The No 'Count Boy*, in *Plays of Negro Life: A Source-Book of Native American Drama*, ed. Alain Locke and Montgomery Gregory (New York: Harper, 1927), 69–96.
107. Georgia Douglas Johnson, *Plumes: A Folk Tragedy*, in Locke and Gregory, eds., *Plays of Negro Life*, 287–99.
108. Other studio plays given by the Allied Players include *Back-stage*, by Allied Arts member Gertrude Schalk, and Eugene O'Neill's *The Dreamy Kid*.
109. "Table Gossip (10)," *Boston Globe*, March 9, 1930.
110. MCH to Du Bois, May 13, 1926, Du Bois Papers. Surviving letters contain no further details concerning Hare's financial dilemma.
111. Du Bois to MCH, May 18, 1926, Du Bois Papers.
112. Catharine Huntington resided at 66 Pinckney Street on Beacon Hill. Doris Abramson, personal communication, March 13, 2005.
113. MCH to Du Bois, May 2, 1927, Du Bois Papers. No script or program survives from the *Tree Fantasy* production, which Hare described as "our first public effort." This is puzzling since she had previously staged *Antar of Araby* in 1925.
114. MCH to Du Bois, May 2, 1927, Du Bois Papers. Note the word "Patronesses," an indication that some or all of the supporters for the Allied Arts Centre were female.
115. MCH to Du Bois, April 14, 1927, Du Bois Papers. Hare gives no information about this script, which has not survived.
116. MCH to Du Bois, January 10, 1928, Du Bois Papers.
117. Ralf Coleman would later be honored with the title "Dean of Black Theatre in Boston" (see chapters 6 and 7).
118. MCH to Du Bois, n.d. (between June 11 and August 5, 1928), Du Bois Papers.
119. MCH to Du Bois, n.d. (likely summer of 1928), Du Bois Papers, emphasis added.
120. See the cast photograph of *Ivory, Ebony and Gold* in Kathy A. Perkins, *Black Female Playwrights: An Anthology of Plays before 1950* (Bloomington: Indiana University Press, 1990), 71.
121. Wilbur Daniel Steele, "From the Other Side of the South," in *The Shame Dance and Other Stories* (New York: Harper, 1923), 296–324.
122. Locke and Montgomery Gregory trained black actors and producers who would later establish theatres—but not exclusively in black districts, "for that

would tend to prevent the white community from seeing their art." See Perkins, *Black Female Playwrights*, 7.

123. Clarence Cameron White wrote the score for Matheus's play *Tambour.*
124. *Baltimore Afro-American*, February 22, 1930.
125. Jacinto Benavente, *The Bonds of Interest*, in *Plays by Jacinto Benavente*, trans. John Garrett Underhill (New York: Scribner's, 1917), 112. Hare used an alternate translation entitled *Invisible Threads*, playbill, February 25, 1930, in possession of the author.
126. Avon Long obituary, *Black Perspective in Music* 12, no. 2 (Autumn 1984): 278.
127. MCH to Du Bois, February 26, 1930, Du Bois Papers.
128. *Invisible Threads*, playbill.
129. MCH to Du Bois, February 26 1930, Du Bois Papers, emphasis added.
130. William Edgar Easton, *Dessalines, a Dramatic Tale: A Single Chapter from Haiti's History* (Galveston, Tex.: J. W. Burson, 1893). An essay by Norris Wright Cuney, "A Tribute to Haïtien Heroism," is appended to the book. The Boston production was the third performance of *Dessalines*, after its debut in Chicago and a reprise in Pittsburgh. Easton was an African American Republican and a friend of Hare's father who had worked at the Galveston Customs House when Norris Wright Cuney was the collector of customs.
131. William Wells Brown, *The Black Man: His Antecedents, His Genius, and His Achievements* (Boston: J. Redpath, 1863), 111. Brown acknowledged that Dessalines was responsible for the massacre of hundreds of white men, women, and children.
132. Norris Wright Cuney, "A Tribute to Haïtien Heroism," in Easton, *Dessalines*, 126, emphasis added.
133. The headquarters of the Boston branch of Garvey's United Negro Improvement Association (UNIA) were across from St. Cyprian's Church in Lower Roxbury, but its documents were lost in a fire, erasing its history. See Violet Showers Johnson, *The Other Black Bostonians: West Indians in Boston, 1900–1950* (Bloomington: Indiana University Press, 2006). Black theatre entrepreneur Elma Lewis attributed her success to the movement: "The blessing of my life is that I am a Garveyite." Elma Lewis, interview by the author, November 8, 1998.
134. MCH to Du Bois, May 28, 1930, Du Bois Papers. The notice to which Hare refers is "Dessalines Performed by Allied Arts Players," *Boston Globe*, May 16, 1930. The article describes the event as "a creditable performance."
135. MCH to Du Bois, May 28, 1930, Du Bois Papers. Easton's *Dessalines* is a precursor of Langston Hughes's 1936 play *Emperor of Haiti (Troubled Island).*
136. *Cinda*, a play featuring a black Cinderella, was written by black Bostonian Jack Bates. Catherine Huntington coached the performance, which took place on December 9, 1930, at the Elizabeth Peabody Playhouse (or Elizabeth Peabody Theatre), an adjunct of the Elizabeth Peabody settlement house at 357 Charles Street in the West End. "Allied Arts Players Present Folk Play," *Boston Globe*, December 10, 1930.

137. MCH to Du Bois, "Christmas Night," December 25, 1930, Du Bois Papers.

5. Writing While Black

1. The late 1920s witnessed the first stirrings of a jazz scene in Boston. Eddy Deas, a drummer and vocalist, performed in and led bands in the Boston area. Beginning his career with George Tynes's band, Deas left to start the Boston Brownies Orchestra, which recorded for Victor Records. On the history of jazz in Boston, see Richard Vacca, *The Boston Jazz Chronicles: Faces, Places, and Nightlife, 1937–1962* (Boston: Troy Street, 2012). On Meta Warrick Fuller as a stage designer for black theatre in Boston and white theatre in Framingham, Massachusetts, see Kathy A. Perkins, "The Genius of Meta Warrick Fuller," *Black American Literature Forum* 24, no. 1 (Spring 1990): 65–72.
2. Gwendolyn Bennett, "The Ebony Flute," *Opportunity*, October 1926, 322.
3. On Pauline Elizabeth Hopkins and *New Era* magazine, see Hannah Wallinger, *Pauline E. Hopkins: A Biography* (Athens: University of Georgia Press, 2005), 270–77.
4. Alain Locke, "Beauty and the Provinces," in "1928: A Retrospective Review," *Opportunity*, January 1929, 10.
5. On the division of the Renaissance into three phases, see David Levering Lewis, *When Harlem Was in Vogue* (1981; New York: Penguin, 1997), xxiv.
6. On the so-called little magazines of the era, see Abby Arthur Johnson and Ronald M. Johnson, *Propaganda and Aesthetics: The Literary Politics of Afro-American Magazines in the Twentieth Century* (1979; Amherst: University of Massachusetts Press, 1991), 65–96.
7. Johnson and Johnson, *Propaganda and Aesthetics*, 89.
8. For a discussion of the Saturday Night Quill Club and its members, see Verner Mitchell and Cynthia Davis, *Literary Sisters: Dorothy West and Her Circle, A Biography of the Harlem Renaissance* (New Brunswick, N.J.: Rutgers University Press, 2012), 85–93.
9. Four *Quill* members—Gertrude Toki Schalk, Ralf Coleman, Joseph S. Mitchell, and Alvirah (sometimes spelled "Alvira") Hazzard—appeared in Maud Cuney Hare's stage productions. Schalk, Coleman, and Mitchell were also amateur playwrights.
10. Eugene Gordon, "Negro Fictionists in America," *Saturday Evening Quill*, no. 2 (1929): 16.
11. All quotations from Gordon and subsequent information concerning his early life are taken from Eugene Gordon, "Biographical Sketch," Eugene Gordon Papers, Special Collections of the Schomburg Center for Research in Black Culture, New York Public Library.
12. The Robert Charles Riots of 1900, mentioned by Gordon, came in the wake of a shooting of a white police officer by a black laborer.
13. On Edythe Mae Chapman Gordon, see Lorraine Elena Roses, introduction

to *Selected Works of Edythe Mae Gordon*, ed. Lorraine Elena Roses (New York: G. K. Hall, 1996), iii–xxx.

14. Eugene Gordon, commissioned as second lieutenant, was one of the few black soldiers to attain that rank.
15. See profile of Gordon in *Who's Who in Colored America*, 4th edn., 1933–37 (New York: Who's Who in Colored America Corporation, 1937), 215.
16. "Journalist Lauds Soviet Union. There Three Years," *New York Amsterdam News*, February 5, 1938.
17. Charles S. Johnson, ed., *Ebony and Topaz: A Collectanea* (New York: Journal of Negro Life / National Urban League, 1927), 11.
18. See John Daniels, *In Freedom's Birthplace: A Study of the Boston Negroes* (Boston: Houghton Mifflin, 1914), 357. Daniels's analysis is based on the 1900 U.S. Census.
19. Gwendolyn Bennett, "The Ebony Flute," *Opportunity*, October 1926, 322.
20. On Helene Johnson and Dorothy West, see Mitchell and Davis, *Literary Sisters*.
21. The full roster of Quill Club participants, in addition to Helene Johnson and Dorothy West, includes Ralf Coleman, Marion Conover, Waring Cuney, Alice Furlong, Edythe Mae Gordon, Eugene Gordon, Aloysius Greene, Florence Marion Harmon, William Edward Harrison, Alvirah Hazzard, Allyn Hill, Joshua H. Jones, Jr., Lois Mailou Jones, Gertrude Parthenia McBrown, George Reginald Margetson, Clifford Miller, Joseph S. Mitchell, Grace Vera Postles, Florida Ruffin Ridley, Ferdinand Roussève, Gertrude Schalk, and Roscoe Wright.
22. Eugene Gordon, "A Statement to the Reader," *Saturday Evening Quill*, no. 1 (1928), inside front cover.
23. Johnson and Johnson, *Propaganda and Aesthetics*, 92. The Johnsons are referring to the two short-lived magazines, *Fire!* and *Harlem*, founded and edited by the brilliant Wallace Thurman.
24. Gordon, "A Statement to the Reader."
25. George Reginald Margetson, "Motto," *Saturday Evening Quill*, no. 1 (1928), inside cover, emphasis added. Margetson published two volumes of Victorian-style verse. The first was *Songs of Life* (Boston: Sherman, French, 1910). The same publisher issued the first edition of James Weldon Johnson's *The Autobiography of an Ex-Coloured Man*. Margetson published another collection of his archaic poetry in *The Fledgling Bard and the Poetry Society* (Boston: Richard G. Badger, 1916). Johnson included some stanzas from *The Fledgling Bard* in *The Book of American Negro Poetry* (Boston: Sherman, French, 1922). All of Margetson's work follows a neo-Victorian paradigm. At various times in his life Margetson supported his large family by working as a car cleaner, a factory hand, and a superintendent of buildings. Rupert Margetson, son of George Margetson, interview by the author, October 16, 1998.
26. "Excerpt from Comments on the First Number of the Saturday Evening Quill," *Saturday Evening Quill*, no. 2 (1929), inside front cover.

27. References to jazz and gritty street life are found in the writings of Roscoe C. Wright and Gertrude "Toki" Schalk.
28. Edward J. O'Brien, *Prize Stories of 1928* (Garden City, N.Y.: Doubleday, 1928), 281, 289, 292.
29. "The Listener," Boston *Transcript*, June 14, 1930.
30. See Dickson D. Bruce, Jr., *Black American Writing from the Nadir: The Evolution of a Literary Tradition, 1877–1915* (Baton Rouge: Louisiana State University Press, 1989).
31. Eugene Gordon, "A Statement to the Reader," *Saturday Evening Quill*, no. 1 (1928), inside front cover.
32. *Saturday Evening Quill*, no. 1 (1928), table of contents, emphasis added.
33. *Saturday Evening Quill*, no. 3 (1930), table of contents, emphasis added.
34. "Rootbound," a short story by Eugene Gordon, was published in *Opportunity* and awarded a prize for fiction in the magazine's literary contest (September 1926, 279–83, 299). Another of Gordon's short stories, "Game," won a prize in the *Opportunity* contest the following year and was published (September 1927, 264–69).
35. Lewis, *When Harlem Was in Vogue*, xxviii.
36. For a biographical profile of Edythe Mae (Chapman) Gordon, see Roses, *Selected Works of Edythe Mae Gordon*, iii–xxx.
37. William Edward Harrison graduated from Harvard in 1932 and earned an M.A. from the university in 1934. Joshua H. Jones, Jr., the personal secretary of Mayor James Curley, was the only *Quill* member to publish a novel in the 1920s. He is one of the unjustly ignored writers of the Harlem Renaissance era.
38 For a scathing indictment of the education obtained by African Americans at mainstream (white) universities and colleges, see Carter Woodson, *Miseducation of the Negro* (Washington, D.C.: Associated Publishers, 1933).
39. The term "cultural capital" as defined by sociologist Pierre Bourdieu reflects the concept that people of differing economic backgrounds have access to distinctive kinds of cultural practices and knowledge. These exposures shape their aesthetic tastes and preferences. See Bourdieu, *Distinction: A Social Critique of the Judgment of Taste*, trans. Richard Nice (Cambridge: Harvard University Press, 1984).
40. The list of southern-born *Quill* contributors included Eugene Gordon (Florida), Joshua H. Jones, Jr. (South Carolina), Joseph S. Mitchell (Alabama), Roscoe Wright (Kentucky), and Ferdinand Roussève (Louisiana). Waring Cuney of Washington, D.C., came north to study at the New England Conservatory of Music for two semesters (fall 1926 and spring 1927).
41. I have culled the information on *Quill* members' religious affiliations from *Who's Who in Colored America* and other sources.
42. Eugene Gordon's anti-religious stance is anomalous for the *Quill*, where expressions of religious devotion are more prominent than agnosticism or

skepticism. The poems of Earl Lawson Sydnor and Grace Vera Postles, for example, convey a distinct religious reverence, as do Dorothy West's stories.

43. "Crazy Jesus," *Saturday Evening Quill*, no. 3 (1930): 60–68. W. E. B. Du Bois called this story "strong but overdone. . . . It is in need of re-working and careful shading in clarity and restraint." Du Bois, "The Browsing Reader," *Crisis*, October 1930, 341. Gordon's most impressive short story in craft, elegance, and poignancy is "Rootbound," published in *Opportunity*, September 1926, 279–83, 299.
44. Eugene Gordon "The God I Know," *Saturday Evening Quill*, no. 3 (1930): 12.
45. Eugene Gordon, "The Relativity of Morality," *Saturday Evening Quill*, no. 3 (1930): 21, 34–37. Reed Smoot, a Republican senator from Utah, was notorious for advocating censorship. *New York Times*, March 18, 1930.
46. Gordon, "The Relativity of Morality," 36.
47. Dorothy West, "An Unimportant Man," *Saturday Evening Quill*, no. 1 (1928): 21–32.
48. Eugene Gordon, "Sarcophagus," *Saturday Evening Quill*, no. 2 (1929): 36–39.
49. See Martin Bernal, *Black Athena: The Afroasiatic Roots of Classical Civilization*, 3 vols. (New Brunswick, N.J.: Rutgers University Press, 1987–2006).
50. Reisner, a distinguished archaeologist of ancient Egypt, served as curator of Egyptian Collections at the Museum of Fine Arts from 1910 to 1942.
51. Maud Cuney Hare to W. E. B. Du Bois, April 1, 1925, W. E. B. Du Bois Papers (MS 312), Series I: Correspondence, 1877–1965, Special Collections and University Archives, University of Massachusetts Amherst Libraries. See also "Harvard Unearths Ancient Ethiopia," *New York Times*, November 27, 1921.
52. Johnson and Johnson, *Propaganda and Aesthetics*, 93.
53. Anonymous review of the 1930 *Saturday Evening Quill*, "The Listener," Boston *Transcript*, June 14, 1930.
54. Lewis, *When Harlem Was in Vogue*, 84.
55. "I Am Not Proud," *Saturday Evening Quill*, no. 2 (1929): 75.
56. "Preface: Other Bostonians," *Saturday Evening Quill*, no. 1 (1928): 54–56; also in *Harlem's Glory: Black Women Writing, 1900–1950*, ed. Lorraine Elena Roses and Ruth Elizabeth Randolph (Cambridge: Harvard University Press, 1996), 125–30. The Ruffin family's papers are held at the Moorland-Spingarn Research Centre, Howard University, Washington, D.C., and the Amistad Research Center, New Orleans.
57. Ridley cofounded the Society of the Descendants of Early New England Negroes, a gesture that connotes elitism as well as race pride. See Adelaide M. Cromwell, *The Other Brahmins: Boston's Black Upper Class, 1750–1950* (Fayetteville: University of Arkansas Press, 1994), 83, 127, 128.
58. Florida Ruffin Ridley, "He Must Think It Out," *Saturday Evening Quill*, no. 1 (1928): 5–8; also in Roses and Randolph, *Harlem's Glory*, 451–59.
59. Earl Lawson Sydnor, "Mute," *Saturday Evening Quill*, no. 3 (1930): 72. Du Bois, in commenting on the best of the *Quill*'s contents, quoted the first two verses

of "Mute," a poem that he particularly admired. W. E. B. Du Bois, "The Browsing Reader," *Crisis*, October 1930, 341.

60. Gertrude Schalk, "Black Madness," *Saturday Evening Quill*, no. 1 (1928): 58–60.

61. Gertrude Schalk, "Saviour," *Saturday Evening Quill*, no. 3 (1930): 14–16. This story was one of W. E. B. Du Bois's favorites. See Du Bois, "The Third Quill," in "The Browsing Reader," *Crisis*, October 1930, 341.

62. Roscoe Wright, "Washwoman," *Saturday Evening Quill*, no. 2 (1929): 56–60.

63. Roscoe Wright, "Escape—A Story," *Saturday Evening Quill*, no. 3 (1930): 48–54.

64. Alvirah Hazzard, "Blind Alley," *Saturday Evening Quill*, no. 2 (1929): 73–74. Hazzard, a third-generation New Englander, was born in North Brookfield, Massachusetts. She graduated from Worcester State College in Worcester, Massachusetts.

65. Gertrude Schalk, "Flower of the South," *Saturday Evening Quill*, no. 3 (1930): 70–72; also in Roses and Randolph, *Harlem's Glory*, 32–37.

66. Schalk, like Gordon, used dialect as she deemed appropriate, as seen here in the old woman's speech. Dorothy West also departed from so-called standard educated English, using "nigger" in "An Unimportant Man," *Saturday Evening Quill*, no. 1 (1928): 23. The epithet "coon" appears in "Prologue to a Life," *Saturday Evening Quill*, no. 2 (1929): 5—in direct contradiction with Johnson and Johnson, who in *Propaganda and Aesthetics* claim that the *Quill*, unlike certain Harlem magazines, did not employ "dialects . . . and a variety of terms widely considered offensive, such as 'coon'" (93). In fact, the *Quill* showed no qualms about occassionally printing offensive racial epithets.

67. On January 26, 1922, the House of Representatives passed an anti-lynching bill, which the Senate blocked from coming to the floor for a vote.

68. Dorothy West, *The Living Is Easy* (Boston: Houghton and Mifflin, 1948).

69. Dorothy West, "An Unimportant Man," *Saturday Evening Quill*, no. 1 (1928): 21–32.

70. On Dorothy West's theatre experience, including her part as a supernumerary in the 1929 Theatre Guild production of *Porgy* (the play), see Mitchell and Davis, *Literary Sisters*, 8; 15.

71. Eugene Gordon, "A Word in Closing, Uncritical Criticism, *Saturday Evening Quill*, no. 1 (1928): [73].

72. See Granville Ganter, "Decadence, Sexuality, and the Bohemian Vision of Wallace Thurman," *Melus* 28, no. 2 (Summer 2003): 84–103.

73. William Edward Harrison, "The Negro's Literary Tradition," *Saturday Evening Quill*, no. 3 (1930): 5–8.

74. The first stanza of Countee Cullen's celebrated poem "Heritage" contains the lines: "What is Africa to me: / Copper sun or scarlet sea, / Jungle star or jungle track, / Strong bronzed men, or regal black / . . . Spicy grove, cinnamon tree, / What is Africa to me?" "Heritage," in Alain Locke, ed., *The New Negro* (1925; New York: Athenaeum, 1968), 250.

75. Eugene Gordon, "Negro Fictionist in America," *Saturday Evening Quill*, no. 2 (1929): 17.
76. Profile of Eugene Gordon, *Who's Who in Colored America*, 4th edn.
77. Roscoe Wright, "Is the Negro Happy?" *Saturday Evening Quill*, no. 2 (1929): 77–80.
78. Ralf Coleman's *The Girl from Back Home*, printed in the *Saturday Evening Quill*, no. 2 (1929): 25–30, explores issues such as the disorienting effects of migration from the southern countryside to the northern city.
79. Helene Johnson, "Regalia," *Saturday Evening Quill*, no. 2 (1929): 14–16.
80. See Violet Showers Johnson, *The Other Black Bostonians: West Indians in Boston, 1900–1950* (Bloomington: Indiana University Press, 2006).
81. (William) Waring Cuney (1906–76) was a cousin of Maud Cuney Hare, but they seem not to have been in contact with one another, even at the time when the young poet was studying at the New England Conservatory of Music, Hare's alma mater. This is surprising, as Hare's pride of family was great, as seen in her hagiographic biography of her father, *Norris Wright Cuney, A Tribune of the Black People* (1913; New York: G. K. Hall, 1995). The fact that Hare does not mention Waring in her work or her correspondence is all the more noticeable because in her correspondence with W. E. B. Du Bois she expresses great love for her paternal uncle Joseph Cuney, the grandfather of Waring and his twin brother, Norris Cuney.
82. Alain Locke, foreword to *The New Negro: An Interpretation* (New York: Albert and Charles Boni, 1925), ix.
83. For a succinct discussion of the vernacular in literature, see Henry Louis Gates, Jr., and Nellie Y. McKay, eds., *The Norton Anthology of African American Literature* (New York: Norton, 1997), 2–4.
84 Waring Cuney, "Jes Moochin' Along," *Saturday Evening Quill*, no. 1 (1928): 9. "Moochin'" means lazing or generally doing nothing.
85. Cuney's vernacular poems may be compared to those of Langston Hughes, whom Cuney knew personally.
86. Chiwe Gordon, the granddaughter of Eugene Gordon and June Kroll, reports that little information exists about the people who purchased her grandfather's paintings and surmises that he gave away the rest. She also states that she has two completed and one incomplete painting in her possession. Chiwe Gordon, personal communication, January 14, 2014. According to the finding aid for the Eugene Gordon Papers at the Schomburg Center for Research in Black Culture, Gordon was a painter whose work was exhibited at the Hudson Guild Gallery, the District 65 Union Hall, and the Countee Cullen Branch of the New York Public Library.
87. For an in-depth and insightful analysis of *Challenge* and *New Challenge*, see Cherene Sherrard-Johnson, *Dorothy West's Paradise: A Biography of Class and Color* (New Brunswick, N.J.: Rutgers University Press, 2014), 104–19.
88. Walter C. Daniel, "*Challenge* Magazine: An Experiment That Failed," *CLA*

Journal 19 (1976): 494; Sherrard-Johnson, *Dorothy West's Paradise,* 114. It bears mentioning that the Saturday Evening Quill Club was the only local literary group of blacks in Boston at the time.

89. It is possible that West did not invite Gordon to contribute to *Challenge* or *New Challenge* because his membership in the Communist Party made him a controversial figure. The only Quill Club members published by West in her magazine were her cousin Helene Johnson's "Widow with a Moral Obligation," *Challenge,* March 1934, 36; and Waring Cuney's "Song of a Song," *Challenge,* May 1935, 43–44, and "Let Me Sing My Song," *Challenge,* May 1935, 44.
90. Sherrard-Johnson, *Dorothy West's Paradise,* 105.
91. Sherrard-Johnson, *Dorothy West's Paradise,* 105.
92. Richard Wright, "A Blueprint for Negro Writing," *New Challenge,* 1937, 11.
93. Lorraine Elena Roses, "Interview with Dorothy West, Writer of the Harlem Renaissance," *Sage,* Spring 1985, 47–49.
94. "Dorothy West Gets Rediscovered by Jacqueline Onassis," New England Historical Genealogical Society, www.newenglandhistoricalsociety.com.
95. Dorothy West, *The Wedding* (New York: Doubleday, 1995), and *The Richer, the Poorer: Stories, Sketches, and Reminiscences* (New York: Doubleday, 1995).

6. The Boston Players

1. "Mellon Foresees Trade Revival by Spring and Year of Progress," *Boston Globe,* January 1, 1930.
2. Boston differed from other major cities in that its black population—21,000, or 2.6 percent in a total population of 781,000—was a deviation from the big-city norm of 9.4 percent. *Fifteenth Census of the United States,* vol. 3, *Population,* part I (Washington, D.C.: Governing Printing Office, 1932), 1098–1110.
3. Charles H. Trout, *Boston, the Great Depression, and the New Deal* (New York: Oxford University Press, 1977), 81. Writing on the effect of New Deal programs on Boston's political economy, Trout indicates that "Italians in the North End and East Boston, as well as the poorer Irish in South Boston and Charlestown, suffered comparable hardships."
4. Langston Hughes, *The Big Sea: An Autobiography* (1940; New York: Hill and Wang, 1993), 334.
5. Neither Hare's Allied Arts Players nor Coleman's Boston Players used a racial identifier in their title, likely to avoid the perception that they accepted racial segregation.
6. Much of the biographical information on the Coleman family, apart from print sources, is based on interviews conducted by the author with Leona Coleman, Ralf Coleman's daughter, and two Coleman granddaughters, Jocelyn Coleman Walton and Gretchen Coleman-Thomas (formerly Wortham), at Gretchen's home in Oak Bluffs (Martha's Vineyard), Massachusetts, between December 28, 1998, and May 8, 2015. Additional sources for this chapter are Ralf Coleman, speech, Black History Week Panel, February 1972, eighty-minute reel-to-reel

audiotape, courtesy of Leona Coleman Flu; a televised interview with Ralf Coleman conducted by his granddaughter Gretchen on her WCVB Boston television show *Opportunity Line,* WCVB-TV, October 9, 1975 (videotape courtesy of Coleman-Thomas); and an audiotape interview with Ralf Coleman conducted by Paula Singer on November 24, 1972, Camille Billops and James V. Hatch Archives, Stuart A. Rose Manuscript Archives and Rare Book Library, Emory University, Atlanta.

7. See Rayford Logan, *The Negro in American Life and Thought: The Nadir, 1877–1901* (New York: Dial Press, 1954).
8. Ed Cooper, in [Aba] Cecile McHardy, ed., "Sources of Strength: Oral History Project" (unpublished ms., 1987), copy in the possession of the author, courtesy of McHardy. The Boston Elevated Railway was the antecedent of Boston's current rapid-transit system, known as the Massachusetts Bay Transportation Authority (MBTA).
9. Reverend O. Paul Thompson, born c. 1886, and his second wife, Carmelite, adopted another child, Evangeline Juliet Montgomery, whom the boys regarded as their little sister. Leona Coleman, interview by the author, December 28, 1998; Evangeline J. ("Vangie") Montgomery, interview by the author, January 6, 1999.
10. Myrtle Baptist Church, located at 21 Curve Street in West Newton, Massachusetts, was founded by freed slaves in 1874. Initially they worshiped at a white church but wishing "to sit in the front of the church as well as in the rear," founded Myrtle Baptist. See "About: Our History," http://myrtlebaptist.org. Reverend O. Paul Thompson preached at nearby Mount Zion Baptist, which is no longer in existence. City of Newton Records, 1915 to 1920, Newton Free Library, Newton, Massachusetts.
11. According to Coleman, he met his future wife, Luella Tutt Barnet, in 1917 at a Harvard-Brown football game. Luella's mother, who was of Swedish descent, was disowned by her family for marrying a man who was half-black and half-Penobscot Indian. "Leona Coleman Flu, Swimming in the Rain: Highlands Childhood and a Life of the Arts," in *More Vineyard Voices: Words, Faces, and Voices of Island People,* ed. Linsey Lee (Edgartown, Mass.: Martha's Vineyard Historical Society, 2005), 6. Ralf and Luella's two children were born in 1919 (J. Riche) and 1924 (Leona).
12. Leona Coleman, interview by the author, December 28, 1998.
13. Leona Coleman, interview by the author, September 25, 2011.
14. *Boston Directory* (Boston: George Adams, 1920).
15. On the SCU, the LWCS, and their instrumentality in developing black cultural life, see chapter 3.
16. Coleman speech, 1972.
17. Coleman speech, 1972.
18. Eva Whiting White presented historically based skits and pageants (some of which she herself wrote), including an Indian War Dance with battle scenes. Trout, *Boston, the Great Depression, and the New Deal,* 19.

19. Jocelyn Coleman Walton and Gretchen Coleman-Thomas, who grew up in the Coleman household, recall their grandfather telling them that he was required to deliver his lines from offstage.
20. Coleman speech, 1972. Lola Wilson was an interpretive dancer; Mildred Davenport was a dancer who founded a music school in Boston and later appeared in Broadway shows. Myra McAdoo was the daughter of Gladys Averett, an amateur showgirl who during the 1940s entertained visiting black musicians after hours at her home and acted in several of Coleman's later productions. The Rountrees, a family known for its success in real estate, are mentioned in a Langston Hughes story, "Poor Little Black Fellow": "A rather portly brown-skinned woman, beautifully dressed, entered [the room]. '. . . From Boston, you say? My old stamping ground. Do you know the Rountrees there?'—'No'm,' Arnie said.—'Well, I used to study at the Conservatory and knew all the big shots,' the brown-skin woman went on." "Poor Little Black Fellow," in *The Ways of White Folks: Stories by Langston Hughes* (New York: Vintage Classics, 1999), 147.
21. "The Open Door, A Negro Pageant: To Be Given for Benefit of Atlanta University," *Boston Globe*, November 4, 1920. Juba, named for a city in South Sudan, is a dance of the American South also known as "the hambone" and originally as the "Pattin' Juba."
22. Profile of Ralf Coleman in *Who's Who in Colored America* (New York: Who's Who in Colored America Corporation, 1937). Henry Wadsworth Longfellow Dana, a grandson of the poet Henry Wadsworth Longfellow, taught at Columbia University in New York until he was dismissed for his advocacy of workers' rights. He retired to the family home at 105 Brattle Street, Cambridge, Mass.
23. Coleman speech, 1972.
24. Coleman speech, 1972. On Cuney Hare, see chapter 4.
25. Lola Wilson Hayes, interview by the author, March 18, 1999.
26. Ralf Coleman, interview by Singer, 1972.
27. Leona Coleman Flu, interview by the author, December 28, 1998.
28. Jocelyn Coleman Walton and Gretchen Coleman-Thomas, interview by the author, May 8, 2015.
29. Leona Coleman Flu, interviewed by the author on several occasions, indicated that the "Four Hundred" or the "Best Society" were terms that referenced "comfortable" and solid, church-going families who, like hers, were considered elites in black society.
30. Mabe Kountze, *A History of the Early Colored Press in Massachusetts & A Second Sketch of the Boston Guardian* (unpublished typescript, July 10, 1967, Brandeis University copy).
31. W. E. B. Du Bois, "Krigwa Players Little Negro Theatre: The Story of a Little Theatre Movement," *Crisis*, July 1926, 134.
32. For a discussion of "the geography of race" as it applies here, see David Delaney, *Race, Place and the Law, 1836–1948* (Austin: University of Texas Press, 1998).

33. Maud Cuney Hare to W. E. B. Du Bois, February 11, 1931, W. E. B. Du Bois Papers (Ms. 312), Series I: Correspondence, 1877–1965, Special Collections and University Archives, University of Massachusetts Amherst Libraries.
34. The black churches of Boston played a role in nurturing dramatic and musical expressions of a religious nature. These contributions merit study in their own right. At St. Cyprian's Church in Lower Roxbury, for example, the tradition of steel drum music of the West Indies continues on with "The Celestial Infernos Youth Steel Band." See www.bostonsown.com/profile_celestialinfernos.html.
35. Isabel Eaton, Annual Report, Robert Gould Shaw House, 1930, quoted in John Daniels, *In Freedom's Birthplace: A Study of the Boston Negroes* (Boston: Houghton Mifflin, 1914), 195. Other institutions catering exclusively to blacks (e.g., the Harriet Tubman House) contributed to the development of the arts scene in ways that lie beyond the scope of this study.
36. Michael Haynes, interview by the author, September 29, October 29, 2010. Haynes's two brothers are prominent in their own right: Roy Haynes (b. 1925) is a legendary jazz musician, and C. Vincent Haynes (1922–2003) was a prominent community organizer and activist, jazz aficionado, and photographer.
37. The Allied Arts Centre may have become affiliated with the Ford Hall Forum through Hare's friendship with Catharine Huntington, a Beacon Hill resident and theatre promoter. See Rena Fraden, *Blueprints for a Black Federal Theatre, 1935–1939* (New York: Cambridge University Press, 1994), 92.
38. Trout, *Boston, the Great Depression, and the New Deal*, 136–37. David K. Niles (1890–1952) served as associate director and then director of Boston's Ford Hall Forum beginning in the 1920s. He was active in Boston politics, a conciliator respected by many, and an effective WPA administrator both in Boston and Washington, D.C.
39. Ralf Coleman, interview by Singer, 1972.
40. "Boston Players Win Theatre Tournament," Baltimore *Afro-American*, February 22, 1930, photocopy courtesy of Gerald Gill.
41. Coleman speech, 1972.
42. See Glenda Frank, "Tempest in Black and White: The 1924 Premiere of Eugene O'Neill's *All God's Chillun Got Wings*," *Resources for American Literary Study* 26, no. 1 (2000): 75–89.
43. "Women's Service Club Sponsors Play Production," *Boston Globe*, November 1, 1930.
44. Ridgely Torrence, *Three Plays for a Negro Theatre* (New York: Macmillan, 1917). The trilogy opened on Broadway to unanimous critical acclaim in 1917.
45. James V. Hatch and Leo Hamalian, eds., *Lost Plays of the Harlem Renaissance, 1920–1940* (Detroit: Wayne State University Press, 1996), 13.
46. Ralph Matthews, "The Negro Theatre—A Dodo Bird," in *Negro: An Anthology Made by Nancy Cunard, 1931–1933*, ed. Nancy Cunard (London: Wishart, 1934), 194.
47. Carter Woodson, quoted in Leslie Catherine Sanders, *The Development of Black*

Theatre in America: From Shadows to Selves (Baton Rouge: Louisiana State University Press, 1988), 11.

48. "Paradox, a One Act Play of Negro Life, Acted at the Barn," *Saturday Evening Quill*, no. 3 (1930): 10–12.
49. Trout, *Boston, the Great Depression, and the New Deal*, 15.
50. Brian Marquard, "Dean K. Denniston, Sr., at 92; Overcame Racial Barriers," *Boston Globe*, April 8, 2006.
51. Lois Mailou Jones, interview by Lani Guinier, Black Women Oral History Project, 1976–81, Schlesinger Library, Radcliffe Institute for Advanced Study, Harvard University, Cambridge, Mass.
52 "Dean Denniston, Sr., Was Vineyard Minister" (obituary), *Martha's Vineyard Gazette*, April 7, 2006, https://vineyardgazette.com. In 1971, Denniston was present at Symphony Hall to hear the Chicago Symphony Orchestra and Chorus perform a composition for orchestra and chorus by his son Donald Denniston.
53. Leona Coleman Flu, interview by the author, December 28, 1998.
54. "Cynthia Belgrave, 76, Director and Actress in Landmark Plays" (obituary), *New York Times*, March 24, 1997.
55. Paul Green, *In Abraham's Bosom* (London: Allen and Unwin, 1929).
56. Ralf Coleman, interview by Gretchen Coleman Wortham, 1975.
57. Ralf Coleman, interview by Singer, 1972.
58. "Gullah" refers to the language and culture of communities of West African descent who live on the Sea Islands of South Carolina and Georgia.
59. D. Reed, *Scarlet Sister Mary*, script based on Julia Peterkin's *Scarlet Sister Mary, A Novel* (1928; Athens: University of Georgia Press, 1998). The novel became a bestseller around the same time it was banned in Boston.
60. J. Brooks Atkinson, "The Play: Colored Sister Barrymore," *New York Times*, November 26, 1930.
61. "Scarlet Sister Mary to End Run Saturday: Ethel Barrymore Will Resume Her Tour in Play in Boston Christmas Week," *New York Times*, December 9, 1930. Barrymore stated that the New York run lasted just three weeks because "my friends in New York are determined not to come see me in blackface." The anonymous critic noted that "many important members of the cast couldn't be understood" because the play was written in Gullah dialect.
62. Langston Hughes, *Scarlet Sister Barry* (1938), in Hatch and Hamalian, *Lost Plays of the Harlem Renaissance*, 335–37.
63. Margaret Hewes (her surname is sometimes incorrectly spelled as "Hughes"), the owner and manager of the Wharf Theater in Provincetown, Massachusetts, was one of the first women to produce serious dramas on Broadway. Original program, Harvard Theatre Collection, Houghton Library, Harvard University; "Margaret Hewes Dead at 87; Producer of Broadway Plays" (obituary), *New York Times*, August 21, 1985.
64. Ralf Coleman, interview by Gretchen Coleman Wortham, 1975.

65. Paul Green, *Potter's Field: A Symphonic Play of the Negro People*, in *The House of Connelly, and Other Plays: The House of Connelly, Potter's Field, and Tread the Green Grass* (London: S. French, 1931), 121–224.
66. Boston *Transcript*, March 13, 1934.
67. "Plymouth Theatre, 'Potter's Field,'" *Boston Globe*, April 17, 1934. The Plymouth Theatre was located at 131 Stuart Street near Tremont Street (it became the Gary Cinema in 1958).
68. James Henderson, speech, following Ralf Coleman speech on audiotape, Black History Week Panel, Roxbury, February 1972.
69. George Brinton Beal, "Potter's Field at Plymouth: Remarkable Play by All Colored Cast," *Boston Post*, April 17, 1934; Elinor Hughes, "Paul Green's 'Potter's Field' Has Premiere at Plymouth—A Strange, Haunting, Unusual Play," *Boston Globe*, April 17, 1934. The Harvard *Crimson* also weighed in with its own enthusiastic review: H. R. H., "Potter's Field—Plymouth," *Harvard Crimson*, April 18, 1934.
70. "Two New Plays," *Boston Globe*, April 17, 1934.
71. Beal, "'Potter's Field' at Plymouth."
72. Elinor Hughes, "Paul Green's 'Potter's Field,' a Fine Serious Experiment," *Boston Herald*, April 22, 1934.
73. *Roll Sweet Chariot* sometimes appears as *Roll, Sweet Chariot* in reviews. The original title has no comma. See *Roll Sweet Chariot: A Symphonic Play of the Negro People in Four Scenes* (New York: Samuel French, 1935), xi.
74. Richard S. Davis, "'Roll, Sweet Chariot,' a Negro Play, Sure to Stir Debate," *Milwaukee Sentinel*, September 23, 1934.
75. "Broadway Sees and Likes 'Roll Sweet Chariot,'" *Chicago Defender*, October 13, 1934; Brooks Atkinson, "Experiment in Epic Drama: Paul Green's Saga of the Negro Race—Difficulties of an Orchestrated Form," *New York Times*, October 14, 1934.
76. Edith Isaacs, *The Negro in the American Theatre* (New York: Theatre Arts, 1947), 16ff, 95. Given Isaacs's assessment, more is the pity that Dolphe Martin has fallen into nearly complete obscurity.
77. Edith Isaacs, "Roll, Sweet Chariot," *Theatre Arts*, November 1934, 813–14.
78. Coleman speech, 1972.
79. Errol Hill and James V. Hatch, *A History of African American Theatre* (New York: Cambridge University Press, 2003), 333. See also an excellent photograph of Ralf Coleman posing in front of a billboard advertisement for *Anna Lucasta*, in Richard L. Taylor, "A Shared Vineyard Vision: Harry Burleigh, Luella Coleman, and the Rise of an African American Summer Colony," *Duke's County Intelligencer* 56, no. 2 (Summer 2015): 3–17 (inside cover). The play, written by Phillip Yordan, a white man, and having nothing to do with race, was performed by the historic American Negro Theatre with resounding success.
80. Reverend Michael Haynes, interview by the author, September 29, October

29, 2010. Haynes recalled that Dr. William Frederick Fisher was also a minister who had a church "on Kenilworth near Dudley Square." His band and choir were "different from the staid churches." Haynes's brother Roy Haynes, the world famous jazz drummer, would go to hear the music at Fisher's church.

81. Haynes, interview by the author, 2010.
82. "James Henderson, Dramatist and Poet: Specialist in Theater Arts," one-page biographical summary from a playbill, courtesy of Kay Bourne. In 1937, Henderson joined the Rhodes Opera Society, "where he has since been Drama Director and Stage Manager." "James W. Henderson, 100, a Drama Director" (obituary), *Boston Herald,* October 28, 1994.
83. Haynes, interview by the author, 2010.
84. Henderson speech, 1972.
85. Henderson speech, 1972. For a photograph of James Henderson, seen with his theatre group, see Robert C. Hayden, *African-Americans in Boston: More Than 350 Years* (Boston: Trustees of the Public Library, 1991), 69.
86. Thelma Thornton, interview by Kathy A. Perkins, July 8, 1989, Philadelphia, typescript courtesy of Perkins.
87. Among those who wrote (mostly one-act) plays for the Allied Arts drama group and Coleman's Boston Players were Alvirah Hazzard and Joseph Mitchell, and Coleman himself. All were members of the Saturday Evening Quill Club as well; see chapter 5.
88. "Rites Today for Ralf Coleman, 'Dean of Boston's Black Theatre,'" *Boston Globe,* October 22, 1976.
89. Quoted in Kay Bourne, "Ralf Coleman Keynotes Black History Program," *Bay State Banner,* February 28, 1974.

7. The New Deal for Boston's Black Theatre

1. Ralf Coleman, speech, Black History Week Panel, Roxbury, February 1972, eighty-minute reel-to-reel audiotape, courtesy of Leona Coleman Flu. Testimonies from James Henderson and Vernon Blackman, theatre and musical directors, respectively, also from 1972, follow Coleman's on the same audiotape.
2. Charles H. Trout, *Boston, the Great Depression, and the New Deal* (New York: Oxford University Press, 1977), 56.
3. While the bibliography on New Deal arts funding is extensive, studies on the participation of African Americans in Federal One are few; to my knowledge, African Americans in Boston's Negro Unit of the FTP have not previously been documented. The major sources on the Federal Theatre Project include Hallie Flanagan, *Arena: The Story of the Federal Theatre* (1940; New York: Limelight Editions, 1985); Jane DeHart Mathews, *The Federal Theatre, 1935–1939: Plays, Relief, and Politics* (Princeton: Princeton University Press, 1967); John O'Connor and Lorraine Brown, eds., *Free, Adult, Uncensored: The Living History of the Federal Theatre Project* (Washington, D.C.: New Republic Books, 1978); Susan Quinn, *Furious Improvisation: How the WPA and a Cast of Thousands Made*

High Art out of Desperate Times (New York: Walker, 2008); Bonnie Nelson Schwartz, *Voices from the Federal Theatre* (Madison: University of Wisconsin Press, 2003); Katie Louchheim, ed., *The Making of the New Deal: The Insiders Speak* (Cambridge: Harvard University Press, 1983); and Glenda Gill, *No Surrender! No Retreat! African American Pioneer Performers of Twentieth-Century American Theater* (New York: Palgrave McMillan, 2000). Among the sources I found most helpful were Rena Fraden, *Blueprints for a Black Theatre, 1935–1939* (New York: Cambridge University Press, 1994), and Lauren Sklaroff, *Black Culture and the New Deal: The Quest for Civil Rights in the Roosevelt Era* (Chapel Hill: University of North Carolina Press, 2009). Abundant additional information is available on the website of the Library of Congress Federal Theatre Project Collection, http://memory.loc.gov/ammem/fedtp/fthome.html.

4. For a concise description of the Federal Theatre Project, see Lorraine Brown, "Federal Theatre: Melodrama, Social Protest, and Genius," Federal Theatre Project Collection, http://memory.loc.gov/ammem/fedtp/ftbrwn00.html.
5. Hallie Flanagan, "The Federal Theatre Project," in *An Ideal Theater: Founding Visions for a New American Art,* ed. Todd London (New York: Theatre Communications Group, 2013), 40.
6. Historians distinguish between the First New Deal (1933–34), which created FERA, and the Second New Deal (1935–38), introduced by Roosevelt to extend benefits to the vast numbers of Americans still requiring federal relief assistance. The WPA (Works Progress Administration, later Work Projects Administration) was created in 1935.
7. Hallie Flanagan, *Shifting Scenes of the Modern European Theatre* (New York: Coward-McCann, 1928). Flanagan was the founding director of the Vassar Experimental Theatre at Vassar College in Poughkeepsie, New York.
8 John Houseman, *Run-Through: A Memoir* (New York: Simon and Schuster, 1972), 174.
9. Flanagan, *Arena,* 10.
10. Brown, "Federal Theatre."
11. Willson Whitman, *Bread and Circuses: A Study of Federal Theatre* (New York: Oxford University Press, 1937), 20, 55.
12. Flanagan, "The Federal Theatre Project," 39.
13. Elliot Norton, *Broadway Down East: An Informal Account of the Plays, Players, and Playhouses of Boston from Puritan Times to the Present* (Boston: Trustees of the Public Library, 1978), 8.
14. Trout, *Boston, the Great Depression, and the New Deal,* 174.
15. Quinn, *Furious Improvisation,* 11.
16. "Racial Groups Prominent in Boston ERA Activities," Boston *Calendar,* October 6, 1935, Harvard University Theatre Collection; Flanagan, *Arena,* 224.
17. O'Connor and Brown, *Free, Adult, Uncensored,* 175–76. The two outstanding shows in which Boston's Negro Unit were involved are *Johnny Johnson* and

Bloodstream. The first was a lavishly produced antiwar Paul Green play that ran for four weeks. The protagonist, who is a pacifist, answers the draft call in the First World War only because he believes that this could be "the war to end all wars." Tragically, after he makes a forceful case to the Allied High Command he is declared insane. *Bloodstream,* a radical protest play, is discussed in this chapter.

18. Henderson speech, 1972. In addition to his administrative post James Henderson served as director for the Outer South End division of the Boston Negro Unit.
19. The digitization at the Library of Congress remains incomplete and I have found the majority of the digitized materials to be difficult to find or unsearchable. The Boston records are classified under the New England region (Connecticut, Maine, Massachusetts, New Hampshire, Rhode Island, and Vermont) on the Library of Congress website but are not yet digitized. One of the Library of Congress websites holds some useful materials: "New Deal Stage: The WPA Federal Theatre Project, 1935–1939," http://memory.loc.gov/ammem/fedtp/ftwpa.html.
20. See Fraden, *Blueprints for a Black Theatre,* 160–62.
21. FERA operated under the aegis of the Civil Works Administration from May 12, 1933, to December 31, 1935, when the WPA absorbed it. During the same legislative session that created FERA, Congress repealed Prohibition, moved to regulate Wall Street, and took steps to protect small bank depositors. See also "Guide to Federal Records: Records of the Works Progress Administration," WPA, Record Group 69, 1922–44), National Archives, Washington, D.C., www.archives.gov.
22. Quinn, *Furious Improvisation,* 53.
23. Matthew Josephson, *Infidel in the Temple: A Memoir of the 1930s* (New York: Knopf, 1967), xi.
24. "Negro Group Gives Initial E. R. A. Play," *Boston Globe,* September 1, 1934. *Genesis* was staged at the Williams Municipal Building on Shawmut Avenue at West Brookline Street. See also Trout, *Boston, the Great Depression, and the New Deal,* 190.
25. "Negro E. R. A. Civic Theatre Gives Three-Act Comedy," *Boston Globe,* March 28, 1935. Prior to cowriting and -directing *Genesis* Flato (d. 1984) directed *All God's Chillun Got Wings,* on November 1, 1930, at the Women's Service Club; he was also associated with the Wharf Players of Provincetown, Massachusetts. "Wharf Players Open Monday," *Boston Globe,* June 27, 1928. Harvard University owns a 1931 graphite drawing of "Charlie Flato" by Jack Levine, a Boston-born painter (and left-leaning artist) with the Federal Arts Program. For a description of Flato during this period, see Shawn Purcell, "Books about Bookselling: A Backward Look," *The IOBA Standard* 8, no, 4 (Fall 2007), www.ioba.org; see also the Wikipedia article "Charles Flato."
26. "Negro Group Gives Initial E. R. A. Play."
27. On the curtailment of opportunities and suppression of plays authored by

African Americans, see Doris Abramson, *Negro Playwrights in the American Theatre, 1925–1959* (New York: Columbia University Press, 1969).

28. "Negro Group Gives Initial E.R.A. Play." See also Trout, *Boston, the Great Depression, and the New Deal,* 190.
29. See Neil Miller, *Banned in Boston: The Watch and Ward Society's Crusade against Books, Burlesque, and the Social Evil* (Boston: Beacon Press, 2010).
30. *Juba* was performed on March 27, 1935, at the English High School on Montgomery Street, Boston. Complementing the performance was a program of southern melodies and dances. *Boston Globe,* March 28, 1935. No script survives for either *Genesis* or *Juba.*
31. After the death of Charles Flato it was learned that in 1935 he had joined the Communist Party and worked as a spy for the Soviet Union for much of his life.
32. Lisa N. Simmons, "Before Welles: A 1935 Boston Production," in *Weyward Macbeth: Intersections of Race and Performance,* ed. Scott Newstok and Ayanna Thompson (Basingstoke, Eng.: Palgrave Macmillan, 2010), 82.
33. Brooks Atkinson, "Rioting on the Waterfront: 'Stevedore,' Produced by the Theatre Union—Drama of Negro Race and Labor Issues," *New York Times,* April 29, 1934.
34. Alain Locke, "The Eleventh Hour of Nordicism," *Opportunity,* January 1935, 12.
35. Display ad for *Stevedore,* Boston *Transcript,* n.d., Harvard Theatre Collection.
36. Leona Coleman, interview by the author, December 28, 1998.
37. See Don B. Wilmeth, ed., *The Cambridge Guide to American Theatre* (New York: Cambridge University Press, 2007), 71.
38. "Theatre Charges E.R.A. Tries to Halt It by Calling Eight of Cast to Its Own Show," *Boston Globe,* September 21, 1935.
39. Coleman speech, 1972. See also "'Stevedore' Hits a Snag in Boston: Rush-Order Performance of 'Macbeth' for ERA Holds up Negro Strike Play," *New York Times,* September 23, 1935.
40. Coleman speech, 1972.
41. "'Stevedore' Hits a Snag in Boston."
42. "'Stevedore' Hits a Snag in Boston."
43. *The Cradle Will Rock* was a 1937 musical with a prolabor theme sponsored by the FTP. The WPA attempted to stop the play by cutting its funding. The 1999 film *Cradle Will Rock,* directed by Tim Robbins, includes a scene where the banning is foiled.
44. James Haskins, *Black Theater in America* (New York: Crowell, 1982), 104.
45. William Worthy, "South End Memories," *Boston Sunday Globe,* December 5, 1971.
46. Haskins, *Black Theater in America,* 102. Haskins states that Coleman's was the second staging of *Stevedore,* and that Seattle's was the first. But, in fact, the play opened in Seattle in 1937, two years after the Boston production.
47. A. Philip Randolph (1889–1979), the cofounder and editor of the *Messenger,*

a socialist magazine that published black writing, had once contemplated a career in professional acting. He helped organize the Shakespearean Society in Harlem and played the roles of Hamlet, Othello, and Romeo.

48. In 1972, Coleman made a point of informing his audience that the Federal Theatre was not segregated. "All players were interchangeable. A case in point: when we did *The Trial of Dr. Beck* at the Copley Theatre for four weeks, half of the cast was white, which we borrowed from the English company." Coleman speech, 1972.
49. The unflappable Flanagan assured the press that Leonard L. Gallagher, recently appointed as the state director, was preparing to produce shows at a downtown theatre. The "English" Unit was scheduled to open on September 1, 1936, with *Class of '29*, "a story of the struggle for existence of college graduates of 1929." Another play by the English unit, *Chalk Dust*, interwove a love story with an attack on the intrusion of politics into the public school system. "Actor Projects' Head Looks for Theatre Here: Mrs. Flanagan Declares Work Will Be 'American, First of All,'" unidentified clipping, August 5, 1936.
50. Frank H. Wilson, *Meek Mose: A Comedy Drama of Negro Life* (playbill), Harvard University Theatre Collection, retitled *Brother Mose* by the FTP. Wilson, a prominent New York–born black playwright and actor, launched his writing career with *Sugar Cane*, the winner in the 1925 *Opportunity* prize for drama. See Henry Louis Gates, Jr., and Evelyn Brooks Higginbotham, eds., *Harlem Renaissance Lives from the African American Biography* (New York: Oxford University Press, 2009), 541–42.
51. Coleman had presented *Brother Mose* the previous August at Mattapan State Hospital and Danvers State Hospital.
52. Errol G. Hill and James V. Hatch, *A History of African American Theatre* (New York: Cambridge University Press, 2003), 237.
53. Fraden, *Blueprints for a Black Theatre*, 161.
54. Fraden, *Blueprints for a Black Theatre*, 165.
55. Coleman, production notebook, Federal Theatre Project Collection, Library of Congress, quoted in Fraden, *Blueprints for a Black Theatre*, 161, 233n49.
56. Frederick Schlick, *Bloodstream: A Play in Three Acts* (Boston: Walter H. Baker, 1934).
57. On the WPA Negro Theatre Unit, see Mark Sammons, "Boston Blacks in the Depression and New Deal" (M.A. thesis, Tufts University, 1974), 99–102, photocopy, courtesy of Professor Gerald Gill. Sammons's thesis, which unfortunately remains unpublished, provides unique and frank coverage of the politics of culture surrounding the Negro Unit in Boston's Federal Theatre Project.
58. Sammons, "Boston Blacks in the Depression and New Deal," 19. On tactics such as petitions, boycotts, and nonviolent force used by the Urban League and other organizations to combat discrimination, see Sammons, 36. Interestingly, Ralf Coleman, both in his speeches and when interviewed, omitted mention of this struggle.

59. "Dixie Prison Play at Copley," *Boston Daily Record*, March 19, 1937. Critic Mordaunt Hall called the play "a powerful, if periodically inconsistent drama." Hall, "W.P.A. Negro Group and Others Present a Drama about Convicts in a Coal Mine," Boston *Transcript*, March 19, 1937. The *Boston Traveler* described two hours "of suspense and horror." Helen Eager, "Bloodstream Opens at Copley: Grim Melodrama Offered by the Federal Theater," March 18, 1937.
60. Perhaps this line alludes to the famously controversial statement, delivered by Booker T. Washington in his speech at the 1895 Cotton States Exposition in Atlanta, to the effect that blacks and whites should be "as separate as the fingers, yet one as the hand."
61. J. D. B., "What's Going on in the Arts," unidentified clipping, courtesy of the Quarles-Simmons family.
62. See Eager, "'Bloodstream' Opens"; and "Dixie Prison Play at Copley," Boston *Daily Record*, March 19, 1937.
63. "Hughes Talk at Ford Hall," *Boston Chronicle*, n.d., courtesy of the Quarles-Simmons family.
64. Langston Hughes's *Mulatto: A Play of the Deep South*, performed on Broadway in 1935, was not published until 1963. The rape scene, added by the producer, damaged Hughes's reputation in the black community.
65. I have used the following additional sources to construct this narrative: "Local Federal Theatre to Move into Majestic," *Boston Globe*, March 24, 1937; Federal Theatre Calendar, Boston, V. III, no 6, 11/17/35–3/21/37 (performance notices), Harvard Theatre Collection; Mordaunt Hall, "WPA Drama Makes a Hit: Silvera Sets Pace for Splendid Acting in 'Bloodstream,'" unidentified clipping, n.d., and "At the Play: WPA Negro Group and Others Present a Drama about Convicts in a Coal Mine," unidentified clipping, both courtesy of the Quarles-Simmons family; and "'Bloodstream' to Be Offered at the Copley," *Boston Globe*, March 16, 1937.
66. *The Trial of Dr. Beck* was staged in Boston in July 1937 (manuscript in the Federal Theatre Project Collection, Library of Congress). Hughes Allison was employed by the FTP's National Service Bureau. Alain Locke described him as "more mature in dramatic technique than any Negro playwright to date." Alain Locke, *Opportunity*, February 1938: 39, quoted in Bernard L. Peterson, Jr., *Early Black American Playwrights and Dramatic Writers: A Biographical Directory and Catalog of Plays, Films, and Broadcasting Scripts* (Westport, Conn.: Greenwood Press, 1990), 27–28. For an astute analysis of Allison's work, see E. Quita Craig, *Black Drama of the Federal Theatre Era: Beyond the Formal Horizons* (Amherst: University of Massachusetts Press, 1980), 24–30.
67. Hill and Hatch, *History of African American Theatre*, 330. Coleman produced another courtroom melodrama, *Dr. Phillip Lawrence*, about which little is known.
68. See Fraden, *Blueprints for a Black Theatre*, 158–59, 232n43.
69. FTP Play Reader Reports, "The Trial of Dr. Beck," May 3, May 25, June

29, 1937, Federal Theatre Project Collection, Library of Congress, quoted in Fraden, *Blueprints for a Black Theatre,* 159–64.

70. John K. Hutchens, "With a Knife: The Federal Theater Folk Present a Courtroom Drama at the Copley," Boston *Transcript,* June 21, 1939, courtesy of the Quarles-Simmons family.
71. Craig, *Black Drama of the Federal Theatre Era,* 192.
72. Elinor Hughes, "The Trial of Dr. Beck," *Boston Herald,* June 21, 1939, Harvard Theatre Collection.
73. O'Connor and Brown, *Free, Adult, Uncensored,* 22.
74. Fraden, *Blueprints for a Black Theatre,* 158–59.
75. H. L. Fishel, *Jericho,* script held in the Federal Theatre Project Collection, 1932–43, Music Division, Library of Congress.
76. See James V. Hatch and Leo Hamalian, eds., *Lost Plays of the Harlem Renaissance, 1920–1940* (Detroit: Wayne State University Press, 1996), 94.
77. "'Jericho' Scores Hit with Colored Players at Empire: Story of Negro Boxer from South Is Presented in Three Acts and Eight Scenes; Satisfactory Climax," *Salem Evening News,* March 29, 1938.
78. Ralf Coleman, *Swing Song,* typewritten script in possession of the author, courtesy of Leona Coleman Flu. No performance information is available.
79. E. L. Doctorow, *Ragtime* (New York: Random House, 1975).
80. Josephson, *Infidel in the Temple,* xi.

Afterword

1. According to the U.S. Census Boston's black population was 23,679 in 1940 and 40,457 in 1950. In 2014, the percentage of African Americans rose to 24.4 percent of the 665,884 total.
2. On Boston's jazz scene, see Richard Vacca, *The Boston Jazz Chronicles: Faces, Places, and Nightlife, 1937–1962* (Belmont, Mass.: Troy Street, 2012). On civil rights activities in the mid- to late 1900s, see Mel King, *Chain of Change: Struggles for Black Community Development* (Boston: South End Press, 1981). The fact that urban decay set in, leading to the classification of an urban black enclave as "the ghetto" as well as the rise of gang violence in those precincts, is discussed in Melvin Miller and Howard Manley, "The Original H-Block," *Bay State Banner,* February 15, 2007, http://baystatebanner.com.
3. In 1974, a federal court order mandating school desegregation triggered a wave of anti-black violence, tarnishing Boston's image as a city of freedom.

INDEX

Page numbers in **boldface** *refer to illustrations.*

LORRAINE ELENA ROSES is professor emerita of Spanish and Latin American studies at Wellesley College. She is coauthor of *Harlem Renaissance and Beyond: Literary Biographies of 100 Black Women Writers, 1900–1945* and *Harlem's Glory: Black Women Writing, 1900–1945*. She also edited and wrote the introduction to *Selected Works of Edythe Mae Gordon*. Roses graduated magna cum laude in Latin American studies from Mount Holyoke College, studied at the Universidad Autónoma de Madrid, and earned a PhD in Romance languages at Harvard University. Her book *Voices of the Storyteller: Cuba's Lino Novás Calvo* reflects her deep continuing engagement with African diasporic culture in the Caribbean. Roses was a Fellow at the Bunting Institute at Radcliffe College and subsequently at the Du Bois (now Hutchens) Center at Harvard University. In addition to her career at Wellesley College, Roses has taught at Boston University, the University of Tel-Aviv, and Mount Holyoke College. Currently she lives in Newton Highlands, Massachusetts, with her husband, Jonathan.